IMMIGRANTS, MINORITIES AND RACE RELATIONS

Victor F. Gilbert and Darshan Singh Tatla

IMMIGRANTS, MINORITIES AND RACE RELATIONS

A bibliography of theses and dissertations presented at British and Irish universities, 1900–1981

With an introductory essay by Colin Holmes

MANSELL PUBLISHING LIMITED

London and New York

First published 1984 by Mansell Publishing Limited
(a subsidiary of The H. W. Wilson Company)
6 All Saints Street, London N1 9RL, England
950 University Avenue, Bronx, New York 10452, U.S.A.

© Victor F. Gilbert and Darshan Singh Tatla, 1984
Introduction © Colin Holmes, 1984

All rights reserved. No part of this publication may be reproduced or transmitted in any form or by any means, electronic or mechanical, including photocopy, recording or any information storage or retrieval system, without permission in writing from the publishers or their appointed agents.

British Library Cataloguing in Publication Data

Gilbert, Victor F.
   Immigrants, minorities and race relations.
   1. Minorities—Bibliography   2. Dissertations, Academic—Bibliography
   I. Title   II. Tatla, Darshan Singh
   016.305'0941   Z7164.M/

   ISBN 0-7201-1691-0

Library of Congress Cataloguing in Publication Data

Gilbert, Victor Francis.
   Immigrants, minorities, and race relations.

   Includes indexes.
   1. Emigration and immigration—Bibliography. 2. Minorities—Bibliography. 3. Race relations—Bibliography. 4. Dissertations, Academic—Great Britain—Bibliography. 5. Dissertations, Academic—Ireland—Bibliography. I. Tatla, Darshan Singh. II. Title.
Z7164.I3G5   1984   [JV6061]   016.3048   83-22185
ISBN 0-7201-1691-0

Printed and bound in Great Britain, at The Pitman Press, Bath

CONTENTS

Preface   xi

Introduction: A Bibliographical and Historical Essay by Colin Holmes   xv

PART 1: GENERAL AND THEORETICAL STUDIES ON IMMIGRANTS, MINORITIES AND RACE RELATIONS

General Theoretical Studies   3

  I Race and minority relations: theoretical studies   3
      A. Race, race theories and racial attitudes (1–32)   3
      B. Intelligence and racial differences controversy (32A–37)   4
      C. Minorities and inter-group relations (38–52)   5
  II Political studies   5
      A. Minorities and nationalism (53–64)   5
      B. Minorities and Marxism/Socialism (65–69)   6
      C. Political representation in multi-ethnic societies (70–76)   6
      D. Law and politics: national and international studies (77–90)   6
  III Educational and language issues (91–100)   7
  IV Migration: international and comparative studies (101–103)   8

General Historical Studies   9

  I Ancient history (104–114)   9
  II Black history   9
      A. General studies (115–117)   9
      B. Slavery and the slave trade societies (118–145)   10
      C. Abolitionist movements and emancipation (146–184)   11
      D. Slave risings (185–186)   12
  III Jews: general and comparative studies (187–215)   13
  IV Race, minorities and literature   14
      A. General studies (216–219)   14
      B. Race and slavery in classical literature (220–224)   14
      C. Race and imperialism in literature (225–236)   14
      D. Minorities in literature   15
      American Indians and literature (237–239); Blacks and literature (240–279); Irish in literature (280–287); Jews and literature (288–313); Orientals, Orientalism and literature (313A–383); Scots in literature (384–386); Welsh in literature (387–389)

V	Christianity and other religions	22
	A. General studies (390–399)	22
	B. Christian church and Christian missions in Africa (400–474)	22
	C. Christian church and Christian missions in Asia (475–517)	26

PART 2: NATIONAL AND REGIONAL STUDIES ON IMMIGRANTS, MINORITIES AND RACE RELATIONS

Africa 31

I	General studies (518–527)	31
II	North and North-Eastern Africa (528–528A)	31
	Algeria (529); Egypt (530–537A); Ethiopia (538–541); Libya (542–544); Sudan (545–549); Tunisia (549A)	
III	West Africa (550–554)	33
	Ghana (558–564); Liberia (565–565A); Nigeria (566–569); Senegal (570–571); Sierra Leone (572–575)	
IV	East Africa (576–580)	34
	Kenya (581–594); Tanzania (595–596); Uganda (597–605)	
V	Central Africa (606–609)	36
	Malawi (610–611); Zaire (612); Zambia (613–619); Zimbabwe (620–636)	
VI	Southern Africa (637–698)	37
VII	Malagasy Republic (699)	40

Asia 41

I	Afghanistan (700–702)	41
II	Bangladesh (703–706)	41
III	Burma (707–708)	41
IV	Cambodia (709)	41
V	China	42
	General studies (710–715); Emigration (716–726)	
VI	Formosa (727)	42
VII	India	43
	General studies (728–732); Emigration (733–737); Regionalism and nationalism (738–757); Minorities (758–806)	
VIII	Indo-China (807–808)	47
IX	Indonesia (809)	47
X	Japan (810–811)	47
XI	Korea (812)	47
XII	Laos (813)	47
XIII	Malaysia	47
	General studies (814–831); Immigrants and minorities (832–839A)	
XIV	Mauritius (840)	49
XV	Pakistan (840A–840B)	49
XVI	Singapore (841–844)	49

CONTENTS vii

XVII	Sri Lanka (845–858)	49
XVIII	Thailand (858A–859)	50

Australia 51

I	General studies (860)	51
II	Australia (861–866A)	51
III	New Zealand (867–875)	51
IV	Pacific Islands and Pacific Ocean Region (876–891)	52

Caribbean 54

I	General studies (892–897)	54
II	Barbados (898–898A)	54
III	Bermuda (899)	54
IV	Cuba (900)	54
V	Desiradé (901)	55
VI	Haiti (902)	55
VII	Jamaica (902A–912)	55
VIII	Trinidad (913–923)	55

Europe 57

I	General studies (924–927)	57
II	Austria (928–931)	57
III	Cyprus (932–933)	57
IV	Czechoslovakia (934–940)	58
V	Denmark (941)	58
VI	Finland (942–943)	58
VII	France (944–955)	58
VIII	Germany (956–983)	59
IX	Great Britain	60
	A. General studies	60

Emigration (984–991); Medieval and Early Modern immigrant communities and English attitudes (992–1004); Politics, law and race relations (1004A–1027); Regional studies (1028–1043); Employment and industry (1043A–1051); Housing (1052–1057); Educational issues (1058–1160)

B. Immigrants and minorities: specific community studies 69

Comparative studies (1161–1165); Chilean community (1166); Chinese community (1167–1172); Cypriot community (1173–1177); French community (1177A–1183); German community (1184); Gypsies/Travellers (1185–1195); Irish community (1196–1209); Italian community (1209A–1210); Jewish community and anti-Semitism (1211–1237); Maltese community (1238–1239); Polish community (1240); South Asian communities (1241–1278); Turkish community (1279); Ukrainian community (1280); West Indian/African communities (1281–1304)

C. Scotland (1305–1324) 76

	D. Wales (1325–1338)	77
X	Greece (1339)	78
XI	Hungary (1340–1341)	78
XII	Ireland (1342–1374A)	78
XIII	Italy (1375–1380)	80
XIV	Malta (1381–1383)	80
XV	Netherlands (1384)	80
XVI	Norway (1385)	80
XVII	Poland (1386–1388)	81
XVIII	Portugal (1389)	81
XIX	Romania (1390)	81
XX	Spain (1391–1403)	81
XXI	Switzerland (1404–1405)	82
XXII	USSR (1406–1422)	82
XXIII	Yugoslavia (1423)	83

Latin America   84

I	General studies (1424–1425)	84
II	Argentina (1426–1431)	84
III	Belize (1432)	84
IV	Brazil (1433–1435)	84
V	Colombia (1436–1437)	85
VI	Guyana (1438–1448)	85
VII	Mexico (1449–1450)	85
VIII	Nicaragua (1451)	85
IX	Peru (1452–1457)	86
X	Venezuela (1458)	86

Middle East   87

I	General studies (1459–1461)	87
II	Bahrain (1462)	87
III	Iran (1463–1465)	87
IV	Iraq (1466–1470)	87
V	Israel, Palestine: relations between Jews and Arabs in the Middle East (1471–1518)	88
VI	Jordan (1519)	90
VII	Lebanon (1520–1524)	90
VIII	Syria (1525–1526)	90
IX	Turkey and the Ottoman Empire (1527–1532)	90
X	Yemen (1533)	91

North America   92

I	General studies (1534–1542)	92

II	Canada	92
	A. General studies (1543–1555)	92
	B. Studies of specific minority and immigrant groups	93
	Canadian Indians/Eskimos (1556–1563); English (1564–1565); French (1566–1569); Irish (1570); Jews (1571–1572); Scots (1573–1575); Sikhs (1576)	
III	United States of America	94
	A. General studies (1577–1589)	94
	B. Studies of specific minority and immigrant groups	95
	Afro-Americans (1590–1608); American Indians (1609–1616); British/English immigrants (1617–1625); Canadians (1626); Gypsies (1627); Irish (1628); Jews (1629–1630); Mexicans (1631); Puerto Ricans (1632); Scots (1633–1636); Welsh (1637)	

Addenda (1638–1716)	98
Subject index	105
Author index	138

PREFACE

The aim of this work is to provide, as comprehensively as possible, a classified list of theses and dissertations presented at British and Irish universities between 1900 and 1981 in the field of immigrant communities, ethnic minorities and race relations. A number of 1982 theses have been included whenever found but it is in no way a comprehensive coverage for 1982. The vital relevance of this subject field to a deeper understanding of the causes of social conflict in society today has stimulated this attempt to help students and scholars discover what research has already been carried out. Perhaps we had better explain some of our self-imposed ground rules for the selection of entries. We included theses on National Socialism and Fascism as movements with a racist ideological base. Literary studies interpreting minority-majority relationships in a broad perspective have also been included. However, we have not listed several studies relating to smaller or tribal communities, who may rightly regard themselves as minorities. Studies relating to Christian minorities in Europe have been excluded. Studies of *social* minorities have also been excluded. This has meant, for example, the exclusion of feminist studies. We aim to provide a separate index for this subject area later.

The category of dissertation (not full theses but special studies presented in partial fulfilment of the regulations for the award of higher degrees) has been difficult to cover comprehensively. We would be grateful for details of any such dissertations and full theses not included in this work. It is hoped that lists of additions and amendments will appear in the journal *Immigrants and Minorities*. Some of the dissertations may not have been officially deposited in main university libraries and, in consequence, copies may be difficult to locate.

ARRANGEMENT

The material is divided into two main sections: General and Theoretical Studies, arranged by subject; and National and Regional Studies, arranged geographically and further subdivided by subject where necessary. Within each subject or subdivision the arrangement is alphabetical by author. Each entry contains the following information: author, title of the thesis, degree awarded, the university [name of the constituent college in the case of London and Wales, wherever this is known], and the year in which the degree was awarded.

There is a detailed subject index as well as an author index. Reference is to item numbers.

NOTES

The following symbol should be noted:
* = dissertation, not full thesis, in partial fulfilment of the conditions for the award of a higher degree.

It is important that the user checks in the current issue of the ASLIB *Index* to note the conditions for borrowing and consultation at the deposit libraries. Another guide to consult is Borchardt, D. H. and Thawlry, J. D. *Guide to the Availability of Theses* (London, Saur, 1981). Other useful guides are Davinson, D. *Theses and Dissertations as Information Sources* (London, Bingley, 1977) and Reynolds, M. M. *A Guide to Theses and Dissertations* (Detroit, Mich., Gale, 1975).

SOURCES

Two recent publications have greatly facilitated retrospective searching: *Retrospective Index to Theses of Great Britain and Ireland, 1716–1950. Vol. 1: Social Sciences and Humanities* edited by R. R. Biboul and F. L. Kent (Oxford, Clio Press, 1975) and *History Theses, 1901–1970: Historical Research for Higher Degrees in the Universities of the United Kingdom* compiled by P. M. Jacobs (London, Institute of Historical Research, 1976). [With 1970–1980 volume in preparation.]

Since 1951 the standard checklist has been *Index to Theses Accepted for Higher Degrees by the Universities of Great Britain and Ireland* published by ASLIB. The use of this index has been hampered by the lack of a detailed subject index. Since volume 27 such a detailed index has been provided, and the appearance of *Abstracts of Theses* since volume 26 has greatly helped to define the subject area of theses. Regrettably, there is not a complete coverage of all theses by this microfiche abstract service.

Added to the ASLIB *Index* is *Historical Research for University Degrees in the United Kingdom. Part 1: Theses Completed* published annually by the Institute of Historical Research, University of London. This is very useful with its detailed subject index and more rapid and regular publication. However, it does have a failing of not always being reliable in the citation of titles.

Several bibliographies of theses covering specific subjects and regions have been published in recent years.

Asia

Bloomfield, B. C. *Theses on Asia Accepted by Universities in the United Kingdom and Ireland, 1887–1964* (London, Cass, 1967) [With annual supplements in *Bulletin of British Orientalists* for the period 1965–1969]

Case, M. H. *South Asian History, 1750–1950: a Guide to Periodicals, Dissertations and Newspapers* (Princeton, Princeton University Press, 1968) [Includes America, British, Indian and Australasian theses]

Gopal, K. *Theses on Indian Sub-Continent, 1877–1971: an Annotated Bibliography of Dissertations in Social Sciences and Humanities Accepted with the Universities of Australia, Canada, Great Britain and Ireland and United States of America*, compiled by Krishnan Gopal; edited by Dhanpat Rai (Dehli, Hindustan Publishing Co., 1977)

Gordon, L. H. D. and Shulman, F. L. *Doctoral Dissertations on China: a Bibliography of Studies in Western Languages, 1945–1970* (Seattle, University of Washington Press for the Association of Asian Studies, 1972)

Jackson, J. C. *Recent Higher Degree Theses on Social, Political and Economic Aspects of South East Asia Presented in the Universities of the United Kingdom and the Universities of Malaya and Singapore* (Hull, University of Hull, Dept. of Geography, 1966)

Sardesai, D. R. and Sardesai, B. D. *Theses and Dissertations on Southeast Asia: an International Bibliography in Social Sciences, Education and Fine Arts* (Zug, Inter Documentation, 1970) [Includes British, American and Australasian theses]

Shulman, F. J. *Japan and Korea: an Annotated Bibliography of Doctoral Dissertations in Western Languages, 1877–1969* (London, Cass, 1970)

Shulman, F. J. *Doctoral Dissertations on Japan and Korea, 1969–1979: an Annotated Bibliography of Studies in Western Languages* (Seattle, University of Washington Press, 1982)

Shulman, F. J. *Doctoral Dissertations on South Asia, 1966–1970: an Annotated Bibliography Covering North America, Europe and Australia* (Ann Arbor, Centre for South and Southeast Asian Studies, University of Michigan, 1971)

Africa

Theses on Africa Accepted by Universities in the United Kingdom and Ireland (Cambridge, Heffer for SCOLMA, 1964) [Covering the period 1920–1962]

McIlwaine, J. S. St. J. *Theses on Africa 1963–1975 Accepted by Universities in the United Kingdom and Ireland* (London, Mansell, 1978)

Middle East

Shulman, F. J. *American and British Doctoral Dissertations on Israel and Palestine in Modern Times* (Ann Arbor, Mich., Xerox University Microfilms, 1973)

Sluglett, P. *Theses on Islam, the Middle East and North-West Africa 1880–1978: Accepted by Universities in the United Kingdom and Ireland* (London, Mansell, 1983) [We regret that it was published too late to help us in our compilation]

Latin America and the Caribbean

Zubatsky, D. S. *Doctoral Dissertations in History and the Social Sciences in Latin America and the Caribbean Accepted by Universities in the United Kingdom, 1920–1972* (London, Institute of Latin American Studies, University of London, 1973)

Theses in Latin American studies at British Universities in Progress and Completed (published annually since 1966 by the Institute of Latin American Studies, University of London)

U.S.S.R.

Dossick, J. J. *Doctoral Research on Russia and the Soviet Union* (New York, New York University Press, 1960) [1900–1959]

Dossick, J. J. *Doctoral Research on Russia and the Soviet Union, 1960–1975* (New York, Garland, 1976) [Covers American, Canadian and British theses]

Education

Theses and Dissertations in the History of Education Presented at British and Irish Universities, 1900–1976, compiled by Victor F. Gilbert and Colin Holmes (Lancaster, History of Education Society, 1979)

Register of Theses on Educational Topics in Universities in Ireland, compiled by John Coolahan [*et al.*] (Galway, Officina Typographica for the Educational Studies Association of Ireland, 1980 [With annual supplements]

Research in the History of Education (Lancaster, History of Education Society) [Annual compilation of British university theses]

ACKNOWLEDGEMENTS

We wish to express our warmest appreciation of the help given to us in so many ways. In particular Vic Gilbert acknowledges the guidance and encouragement given by Colin Holmes of the Department of Economic and Social History, and Richard Carwardine of the Department of History, University of Sheffield. Darshan Singh acknowledges with thanks Mr. G. Waller, Superintendent of Manuscripts, University Library, Cambridge; Mrs. E. J. Robinson, Librarian, Theses Section, University Library, London; and the staff of Birmingham University Library for answering various queries; Dr. Clive Dewey, Dr. P. K. Bhachu, Dr. Ajit Singh and Professor Bernard Corry for encouragement and interest; Kuldip S. Hansra for enabling a visit to Punjab during this period; Surjit S. Aulakh for providing excellent working facilities in Patti; and to Surjit S. Toor for his help in London.

We are greatly appreciative of Colin Holmes for his excellent introductory survey of the development of this field of study.

We are indebted to Mrs. Eileen Nixon for bringing clarity and order out of an unpromising original manuscript by the excellence of her typing. However, we must bear full responsibility for any sins of commission and omission, and apologise for any eccentricities in the numbering of the entries. Finally we wish to dedicate this work to our respective wives and families for their patience and forebearance during the many months this work was being prepared.

INTRODUCTION
A BIBLIOGRAPHICAL
AND HISTORICAL ESSAY

Colin Holmes

There are those who believe that the art of bibliography is a form of low-grade intellectual activity. But it is an exercise that demands its own rigorous standards. In order to be successful a bibliographer must possess a sleuth-like ability to track down sources, as well as a fine sense of organization and categorization. Furthermore, there is a need to be constantly vigilant; accuracy is crucial. Even established authors can lapse into error in their footnotes and sources but similar mistakes or oversights in a specialized bibliography would cast doubt on the whole exercise.

Victor Gilbert has now amassed considerable experience in putting together bibliographic guides which have been characterized by their comprehensive range and accuracy. In an early exercise he provided a list of theses on historical themes submitted to the University of Sheffield[1], followed by a similar study for Yorkshire Universities.[2] He then proceeded to a national study that located and categorized the large number of theses written on the history of education.[3] His next piece of work, compiled soon afterwards, was a checklist of theses in social and labour history.[4] With all this experience behind him, in collaboration with Darshan Tatla he has now turned his attention to *Immigrants, Minorities and Race Relations: A Bibliography of Theses and Dissertations presented at British and Irish Universities 1900–1981*.

A number of bibliographies have already been compiled that are indispensable tools for anyone interested in immigrants and racial and ethnic minorities in British society. For example, A. Sivanandan's *Coloured Immigrants in Britain. A Select Bibliography* (London, 1969) was an early collection of material on New Commonwealth immigration. In the same year, the Community Relations Commission published *Race Relations in Britain. Selected Bibliography with Emphasis on Commonwealth Immigrants* (London, 1969), updated yearly until 1975. A further selective listing of titles appeared soon afterwards in the *British Sociological Yearbook*, volume 2, *The Politics of Race* (London, 1975), edited by Ivor Crewe, but by the 1970s there was a need for a more comprehensive collection of references which took full account of the explosion of interest in immigration and race. This came with the publication of Raj Madan's work, *Coloured Minorities in Great Britain. A Comprehensive Bibliography 1970–1977* (London, 1979), which the compiler regarded as a continuation of Sivanandan's pioneer collection. In the following year the political dimension of the debate over New Commonwealth and Pakistani immigration was given particular attention in Zig Layton-Henry's *Race and Politics in Britain. A Select Bibliography* (Aston, 1980) and the theme of recent migrant workers was reflected in *The Employment of Migrant Immigrant Labour in Britain: A Select*

Bibliography (Aston, 1980), compiled by A. M. Phizacklea. Moreover, bibliographical enquiry has been extended to the other groups. A collection of material on the Jewish community in Britain, for example, was compiled by Cecil Roth in *Magna Bibliotheca Anglo-Judaica* (London, 1937), later supplemented in two works by R. P. Lehmann, *Nova Bibliotheca Anglo-Judaica: A Bibliographical Guide to Anglo-Jewish History 1937–1960* (London, 1961) and *Anglo-Jewish Bibliography 1939–1970* (London, 1973). As for the Gypsies, the foundation stone for any future bibliographer was laid in 1909 by G. F. Black in *A Gypsy Bibliography* (Edinburgh, 1909) and the publication of a good deal of more recent material has been located by Dennis Binns in *A Gypsy Bibliography* (Manchester, 1982). Less comprehensive but still useful is the University of Liverpool publication *In Memorian Robert Andrew Scot MacFie* (Liverpool, 1976), which lists the titles in Scott MacFie's own collection.

Apart from such bibliographical works, anyone interested in keeping up with the literature needs to consult those journals that are directly concerned with immigration, minorities and related issues and which list or review publications within their respective spheres of interest. In this respect there are a number of publications of special interest. The *Proceedings of the Huguenot Society of London*, for example, offers help on the French Protestant minority. Furthermore, *Race and Class* and *New Community*, although ideological opposites, draw attention to material on recent immigration into Britain and a similar function is filled by the *Runnymede Trust Information Bulletin* and *Race Relations Abstracts*. In the case of Anglo-Jewry references to recent work can be found in *Patterns of Prejudice*, published by the Institute of Jewish Affairs, and also in the *Jewish Journal of Sociology*, which appears under the auspices of the World Jewish Congress. Until recently the *Wiener Library Bulletin* also offered a useful service to students of Jewish history. The Gypsy population receives attention in the *Journal of the Gypsy Lore Society* and references to the Irish diaspora can be found in *Irish Historical Studies*. A broader range of references, including a number on Britain, can be extracted from *Ethnic and Racial Studies* and a new journal, *Immigrants and Minorities*, has already published a wide ranging bibliographical exercise by Victor Gilbert that includes references to immigrants and minorities in Britain written between 1980 and 1982.[5]

Apart from these sources, some students of immigration and minorities will find it necessary to consult full-scale bibliographies that have been compiled on themes such as Fascism, anti-Semitism and prejudice. Philip Rees has been diligent in tracing the scattered evidence on Fascist groups in Britain,[6] Robert Singerman has provided a useful guide to the expressions of extreme ideological anti-Semitism that have appeared in the English language since the last quarter of the nineteenth century[7] and the Wiener Library, or the Institute of Contemporary History as it came to be known in 1965, has published a series of research guides based upon its own collections of source material.[8]

Until now, however, no one has attempted to draw together a list of research theses and dissertations: one is immediately struck by the large number that have been completed (shudders to think of those uncompleted) and the range of disciplines in which they have been generated.

In this essay I have concentrated on a small number of specific themes approached from the standpoint of an historian. An examination of the list of theses makes clear that many have concentrated on British society during the past one hundred years. These studies have not been produced in a vacuum, but have grown out of the historical experience of immigration and minority life in Britain. A survey of that period, particularly the years since the Second World War, will show the variety of groups that have come to Britain either as immigrants intent on breaking with their past or as refugees or sojourners initially seeking a temporary home, and will add flesh to the bibliographer's raw listing of theses. This background will provide the context that resulted in a major burst of research activity, and against it we can see the specific contribution historians have made to our understanding of immigrant and minority life. In turn, I hope to locate the gaps in our knowledge that call for further research effort. In addition to these themes that account for the bulk of this introduction, I offer three sets of additional comment. First, although a large proportion of the theses have been concerned with British society, historians in Britain have not neglected the wider world. Secondly, although the interest in this bibliography is with research carried out in higher education, important work on British society has been conducted outside the university; there is also a wealth of non-book source material for the historian of immigrants and minorities. Finally, a warning note is sounded about the intense ideological conflict that hangs heavily over this whole area of study. Here, if anywhere, there is support for the contention that one must know the historian, or the social scientist, if one is to make sense of what ultimately appears in print.

EARLY IMMIGRATION

Although there has been a noticeable concentration of academic interest on immigrants and refugees who have arrived since 1885, it would be unwise to assume that immigration did not occur before, that there were no minority groups in what is now called Britain and an absence of issues involving race. It has been aptly noticed that 'The British are clearly among the most ethnically composite of the Europeans'.[9] The Romans and the Danes were early invaders, physical relics of whose presence still survive, and it was only with the arrival of the Normans in 1066 that 'something like two millennia of invasions, with a partial lull under the Roman shield came to an end, except for sporadic incursions'.[10]

During the medieval years, as a settled society developed after the Conquest, a number of minorities played a distinctive role in English national life: the Flemings; the Jews, until their expulsion by Edward I in 1290; the Lombards; and a little later the merchants, mainly German, who made up the trading association known as the Hansa that had its headquarters at the 'Steelyard' on the Thames near Blackfriars.

In the early modern period as the British Isles increasingly took on the form of a single state, other newcomers were in evidence. Gypsies who claimed to be natives of Egypt first arrived in the fifteenth century, a small black presence made up essentially of slaves was noticeable by 1550 and there were also refugees from Spanish persecution in the Netherlands.[11]

In the seventeenth century the country benefited from the arrival of a number of European groups. Germans imported a particular expertise in mining and metal work[12] and the 'Dutch' made a notable contribution to the drainage of the Fens.[13] The same century also witnessed the re-admission of the Jews in 1656 and the arrival of another important group, the Huguenots, Protestant exiles from France who arrived in increasing numbers after the Revocation of the Edict of Nantes in 1685.[14]

In the eighteenth century as the face of Britain changed, as the industrial revolution wrought its demonic impact, foreigners came to fill gaps, particularly in commerce and finance, and thereby added to the existing cosmopolitan atmosphere of the City. At the same time, when Britain required a supply of workers to undertake heavy labouring jobs, newcomers were drawn in from the Celtic fringe, mainly in the form of Irish labour. In the years that followed, as the agrarian surplus of Ireland was expropriated by the English, the number of Irish immigrants was to increase considerably. The threat of starvation drove workers across the water to England and Scotland; for some it was a temporary move, but for others it was permanent.[15] Finally toward its close the eighteenth century witnessed the arrival of royalist émigrés from France who were escaping not from starvation but from the revolutionary fervour that gripped France after 1789 and threatened their privileges.[16]

The impact of the Revolution in France that drove these émigrés to Britain did not end with the restoration of the French monarchy, but continued to exert its influence in the following century. Liberal and nationalist plots in Europe drove a diverse crowd of refugees from such countries as Poland, Germany, Italy, Spain and France to the relative security of Britain. Entry, in fact, was easy. Between 1826, when the legislative restrictions passed during the French Revolutionary Wars were lifted, and 1905, when the Aliens Act was introduced, movement into Britain was unrestricted.[17] It is true that an Aliens Bill was enacted in 1848 and remained on the statute-book for two years, but it was never used even though 'foreign undesirables' loomed large in the official mind at the time.

RECENT IMMIGRATION

This rapid sketch may give some indication of the continual movement into Britain that took place from the earliest recorded times to the mid-nineteenth century. Although early immigration has given rise to a number of studies, the major focus of interest has been on the last one hundred years.

In the late nineteenth century the number of refugees in Britain was increased by those fleeing Czarist persecution. With them came other Russians, mainly but not exclusively Jewish, who were not themselves under direct personal threat but were tired of the general persecution and discrimination perpetrated against racial and religious minorities. In the case of the Jews, who were largely confined to the western edge of Russia in the Pale of Settlement, westward migration was also encouraged by the pressure on resources resulting from an increase in population.

Although statistics in immigration do not allow a fully accurate assessment of the volume of immigration it would seem that by the 1890s these Russian-Polish immigrants had outstripped arrivals from Germany, who had hitherto constituted the largest immigrant minority from continental Europe. Although some immigration from the Russian Empire was temporary—a number of Jews used Britain as a staging post on the way to America—in other cases it was permanent. Indeed, the present day Anglo-Jewish community has come to be dominated by the children and grandchildren of the newcomers from Czarist Russia.[18]

Immigrants from Eastern Europe had to conform after 1905 to the provisions of the Aliens Act that made entry discretionary. However, since entry was still unrestricted for those who could be regarded as victims of political or religious persecution and since most immigrants from Russia could claim that they were in one or both categories, the main impact of the Act was probably psychological rather than practical.[19]

It was the First World War that effectively ended the immigration into Britain from Russian–Poland. In the fifty or so years preceding the war, over 100,000 of the Czar's subjects had arrived here. But if this made the Russian-Poles the largest immigrant minority from continental Europe, that community was overshadowed by the presence of the Irish. Indeed, in 1911 the last census before the war showed the Irish to be the largest single immigrant group, and not because Irish immigration continued at high levels in the late nineteenth and early twentieth centuries. It was the numerical fat of the peak Irish immigration between the 1840s and 1860s, located particularly in Lancashire and London, that accounted in large measure for the size of this community.[20]

The First World War also exercised its impact on immigrants and immigration in other respects. First, it led to a tightening of the conditions under which aliens could arrive and settle in Britain, through the 1914 and 1919 aliens acts. This post-war legislation, together with such supplementary Orders in Council as those passed in 1920, 1925 and 1953, formed the basis of control over alien immigration down to 1971.[21] The Victorian tradition of free entry was made to appear like an aberration.

But if the war and the experience of the hostilities resulted in a tougher policy of control over aliens, it did not inhibit the development of a sizeable war-time community of Belgian refugees, nor did it in any way affect the unrestricted right of entry enjoyed by immigrants from the Empire. During the war the black community in Britain was effectively reconstituted. The black presence in the sixteenth century had increased gradually as returning colonial hands brought some of their retainers with them until the nineteenth century when it declined for a variety of reasons. During the First World War, however, the arrival and discharge of merchant seamen helped to renew the black community, particularly in seaports such as Cardiff.[22]

The inter-war years saw further additions to the black community in the shape of students and intellectuals who came not only to study but also to engage in political activity. Indian students were also present at this time in somewhat larger numbers. But the most dramatic arrivals of the inter-war years were those refugees escaping from the Nazi terror.

The advent of Hitler in 1933 had serious implications for particular sections of German society and with the extension of Hitlerite influence to Austria after the *Anschluss* of 1938 and the incorporation of the Sudetenland in the same year, similar implications were present with the expanded Reich. From 1933 there were those who thought it expedient to shake the dust of Germany from their feet. Consequently, they fled to any country that would have them. While others thought the storm would blow itself out, Jewish hopes were shattered by the savagery of the Crystal Night pogrom in November 1938. Down to the outbreak of war refugees continued to flee from German territory, an estimated 50,000 coming to Britain. In many respects this was an exodus of the gifted, the full implications of which were to become evident only at a later date.[23]

The outbreak of the Second World War in September 1939 placed a brake on some movement but led to the arrival of other newcomers. Down to 1941 the Germans were prepared to engage in the export of unwanted minorities, after which their grip on Europe tightened. Even before, however, those who could escape did not find it easy to secure admittance alsewhere: in the course of the war Britain admitted only 10,000 Jewish refugees,[24] and at the same time interned many who had managed to arrive before the war and welcomed colonial labour to help in the struggle against Germany. As in the First World War, black and Asian sailors were recruited for the merchant marine and performed an important task in helping to keep the sea routes open. But the recruitment of colonial labour went further: British Hondurans were imported to work in the timber industry in Scotland, along with workers from Newfoundland; other West Indians were brought in specifically to work in the ordnance factories in Lancashire; and Indians were given training in the techniques of military production, so that they could set up similar facilities on the sub-continent.[25] Along with the Irish, who were recruited under close government control because of Ireland's neutrality, these various groups exercised a notable if ultimately unquantifiable impact on the level of war-time production. What is certain is that together with the Polish, Czech, and American troops (who exercised their own special impact on race relations in Britain), and the German and Italian prisoners of war, they added to the cultural diversity of war-time Britain.[26]

IMMIGRATION SINCE WORLD WAR II

Since the 1940s the most distinctive feature in the history of immigration and race has been the arrival and settlement of black and Asian immigrants from the New Commonwealth and Pakistan. Until recently the black and Asian communities in Britain were small. It was estimated in 1951, for example, that the 'coloured' population, born in India, Pakistan, Ceylon, the West Indies, West Africa and the Far East amounted to 74,500.[27] In 1983 as a result of immigration and births in this country, including those in mixed marriages, it was calculated that the size of the New Commonwealth and Pakistani population amounted to 2.2 million, approximately half of whom were immigrants.[28]

Although some West Indians who arrived during the Second World War decided to stay, the significant starting point for West Indian immigration was 1948. This new phase was symbolized by the arrival at Tilbury of the *Empire Windrush*. A number of vessels bringing more West Indians docked soon afterwards. These early pioneers blazed a trail that was followed by many others in the 1950s, the crucial period for West Indian immigration.

Alongside this immigration from the Caribbean in the 1950s, immigrants were entering Britain from the Indian sub-continent. At first this was a male-dominated movement, but in the course of the 1960s a change became apparent: in addition to the continued arrival of new pioneer immigrants, the dependents of those who were already established in Britain began to arrive. The major period for immigration from the sub-continent was the 1960s, particularly strong in the early part of the decade when immigrants scrambled to arrive before the possibility of exclusion arose. For the first time Commonwealth subjects had to face the Commonwealth Immigrants Act of 1962.

The movement from the West Indies and the Indian sub-continent was related partly to the demand for labour in Britain. In some instances British organizations, such as London Transport and the British Hotels and Restaurants Association, actively recruited workers in the Caribbean. But the immigration was also related to conditions within the sending societies. Both the Caribbean and the Indian sub-continent had economic problems, involving pressure on resources related in part to the long years of colonial domination that also encouraged the export of population. Moreover, in the 1950s and 1960s other specific pressures began to emerge. In 1952 the passing of the McCarran-Walter Act restricted Jamaican immigration to the United States and, as a result, some of the intending emigrants switched their focus towards Britain. On the Indian sub-continent different influences were at work. Pressures on land in the Punjab that developed after Indian independence and the submerging of 250 villages in the

Mirpur district of Pakistan in order to construct a dam at Mangla were instances of specific developments that assisted emigration from this part of the world. Once movement was under way, and immigrants started arriving in Britain, the New Commonwealth and Pakistani immigration, like many others, developed a momentum of its own as images and impressions of the new life filtered back from the pioneers to the sending societies.

In the course of the thirty or so years that this immigration has taken place it has resulted in the concentration of New Commonwealth and Pakistani immigrants in certain parts of Britain. The presence of a West Indian community in Brixton, the development of a 'Little Punjab' in Southall and the growth of a Pakistani settlement in Bradford come to mind. Apart from this spatial visibility, there has also been a marked degree of occupational concentration. Even with the apparent differences between and within the West Indian, Indian and Pakistani groups, one salient characteristic has been the great concentration of the newcomers in low-paid, low-status work. The reasons are complex, but an important factor has been the extent of discrimination that the newcomers have encountered.

Although the Irish have remained the largest single immigrant group during the years for which we have evidence, the number of arrivals from the New Commonwealth and Pakistan has been relatively large when compared with, for instance, the Jewish immigration from Russian–Poland that took place between 1880 and 1914. A good deal of academic study has been devoted to an analysis of New Commonwealth and Pakistani immigration that, apart from the question of numbers, might be justified on the grounds that it led to new departures in social policy. For the first time immigration from the Commonwealth was controlled, with a progressive tightening from 1962 onwards. Furthermore, specific measures were passed to improve race relations, starting with the Race Relations Act in 1965 and followed by further Acts in 1968 and 1976. Such departures were themselves indicative of this 'awkward' immigration for Britain which also entailed considerable difficulties for the immigrants themselves.[29]

In considering the history of entry since 1945, other groups must be mentioned. Some German POWs stayed here for a time after the war and Britain was soon busily recruiting other labour in the immediate post-war years. Members of the Polish Armed Forces were allowed to stay and bring in their dependants, and they were joined by such other Eastern European groups as the Ukrainians and Latvians. They, along with a mixture of other Europeans, made up the so-called European Volunteer Workers. Italian labour was also recruited to work in the brickyards in Bedfordshire and the foundries of South Wales, although once their initial contracts had expired these workers showed a tendency to drift towards work in the service sector where there was an already well-established Italian presence.[30] This recruitment of labour was part of an attempt to use foreign resources in order to ensure that the economy recovered from the ravages of the war. It was this same demand for labour that brought the Irish to Britain in numbers not attained since the late nineteenth century. And of course, this same demand and a corresponding awareness of the opportunities that existed in Britain helped to bring in labour from the New Commonwealth. All these immigrations should be regarded in the same general context rather than as separate, compartmentalized developments.

Other immigrant groups, such as the Maltese and the Cypriots, added to the warp and weft of British life after the war, as did the continual arrival of refugees. In 1956 approximately 20,000 of them came from Hungary after the abortive rising their against

Russian domination—an episode that historians have ignored. But it was not primarily Europe that generated the movement of refugees. In the late 1960s and 1970s Indians who had settled in Kenya and Uganda found themselves at the rough end of Africanization policies. Faced with the prospect of Kenyan or Ugandan citizenship or expulsion, they chose to leave. Some went to India but others came to Britain. But the greatest interest has focused upon the refugees from Vietnam, whose flight built up after 1979. At first this group consisted largely of the ethnic Chinese minority for whom life became difficult once Vietnam was united under Communist control. The position of alien Chinese middlemen who had flourished in the South Vietnamese economy began to deteriorate, particularly when relations between Peking and Hanoi became strained. But it was not just the ethnic Chinese who left; as time went by, the boats included Vietnamese who were unable or unwilling to adapt to life under Communist rule. The traumas that the refugees underwent were given wide and poignant publicity. However, the official British response was cautious. Limited concessions, which allowed the entry of 16,000 refugees, were slow to emerge.

Apart from these well-publicized arrivals there have been other refugees who have sought a new life here. Communal disputes in Cyprus increased the size of the Cypriot community. Iranians fearful of the Shah were followed by those unable to stomach the Islamic rigours of the Ayatollahs. Other refugees, such as the Chileans who fled after the overthrow of the Allende Government, arrived from Latin America. Fugitives also came from South Africa and from such black independent states as Ghana, where each successive coup generated its own refugees. There was also a constant trickle of arrivals from Eastern Europe. But none of the alien refugees was guaranteed a permanent stay in Britain; the liberality of the Victorian age evaporated in the twentieth century. Since 1905 the Home Secretary has had the power to decide whether or not residence would be in the public interest—a vague term that has created more than its fair share of uncertainty, anxiety and suffering.[31]

In 1701, long before these recent developments, Daniel Defoe in *The True Born Englishman* had been critical of the notion that the English were a unified race of superior origin. From this brief account of arrivals, it is clear that 'Britons true' have emerged from a diverse range of groups and cultures. None of the immigrant or refugee groups maintained an exclusive endogamy; they were all influenced by what they found here, and in turn influenced it. However, to place this persistent influx of immigrants in perspective it must not be forgotten that there has also been a continual outflow of population.

EMIGRATION

The seventeenth century colonization of America and the assisted emigration of convicts to Australia that took place in the eighteenth century, as well as the overseas distribution of British traders and merchants during these years, became dwarfed by the huge scale of emigration that began to develop in the nineteenth century. By this time organizations had been set up specifically to encourage and assist this process and the government itself played a role in furthering the outward movement of people. But the majority of those who left Britain did so independently. They went 'either alone or with members of their immediate families or with friends, to face the risks and uncertainties, the dangers and strangeness of new countries without guarantees of help from anyone other than possibly friends and relatives in the places to which they were going'.[32] In what they did they were aided not only by the improvement in communications that allowed more knowledge of other societies to become available, but also by developments in transportation, particularly the growing significance of steamships that was established on Atlantic routes by the mid-1860s. Before the First World War the majority of emigrants crossed the Atlantic and went to America; it has been estimated that sixty-five per cent of those who left the United Kingdom for destinations outside Europe had that country firmly in their sights. However, from the early twentieth century Commonwealth countries began to exercise a greater attraction that has become gradually more pronounced.[33] By contrast, very few of the British went to the territories taken over during the Imperialist expansion of the late nineteenth century. In those tropical parts of the world the British presence was limited to a small number of soldiers and administrators. A severe dent in the whole process of emigration occurred as a result of the world crisis and depression of the 1930s, but in the years since the Second World War there has been a persistent movement out of Britain.

Far fewer of the theses listed in this volume have been written on this outward movement of population than on immigration. However, emigration has not been insignificant. The language used at the time of Jewish immigration between 1881 and 1914 and the more recent immigration from the New Commonwealth and Pakistan has revealed a fear of a 'flood' of newcomers entering the country. Some concern was expressed about arrivals who came as inexorably as 'the waves of the sea' and whose cumulative presence would succeed in swamping the country. However, although it has seldom been emphasized, Britain has exported far more people over the past century than she has received as immigrants. In any discussion of immigration this fact must be kept firmly in mind.[34]

WRITINGS ON BRITISH IMMIGRATION

Against this background we might now start to consider how historians have responded to these developments. By the late nineteenth century history had become established as a university discipline and William Cunningham, one of the founding fathers of economic history, turned his attention to the question of alien immigration at a time when the arrivals from Russian-Poland had become a political issue. In *Alien Immigrants to England* Cunningham offered the view that 'So many diverse tribes and stocks have contributed to the formation of the English nation that it is not easy to draw a line between the native and the foreign elements'. In his view, past immigration had exercised a significant influence over national development, but he believed the alien immigration of his own day had to be judged on its own merits. By 1897 he was fully convinced that, possibly apart from education, there was no aspect of the social and political life of the country which was 'behindhand'. He was also certain there was 'not much to gain from imitating the institutions of the Polish Jews'.[35] Even so, Cunningham believed that the country should hesitate long and hard before any change was brought about in the traditional open door policy on immigration.[36]

Cunningham's work on immigration stands in isolation, for historians were not much absorbed in the subject. There was, however, a major interest in race at the time. Most social commentators and historians made frequent use of racial categories in an attempt to explain the world. There was clear evidence, for example, of a vague Anglo-Saxonism in the work of many prominent historians, although it has been suggested that the weight and this waned in the late nineteenth century. Where it did appear its most prominent emphases were that the Germanic peoples were inherently superior to all others; that the English were mainly of Germanic origin; that the qualities which made English political and religious institutions the most free in the world were related to this Germanic inheritance; that the English better than any other Germanic people represented the traditional genius of their ancestors and therefore carried a special burden of leadership in the world community. Such theories were justifications of the present through a study of the past.[37]

In th early twentieth century, however, historians showed less interest in such Anglo-Saxonism and, for the most part, even less in the history of immigration, minorities and race relations. The activities of popes and kings, military history, the development of constitutional procedures, these were the stuff out of which history was woven for many years. One looks in vain, for example, in the standard Oxford Histories of England for any extended discussion of immigrants and racial and ethnic minorities. Indeed, R. C. K. Ensor's *England 1870–1914* fails to register any reference to the Irish in England or the Jewish immigration that gathered pace after 1870.

Very little changed in this respect for some time. We have noticed that by the end of the Second World War the black community was in the process of being rebuilt and that in the late 1940s and early 1950s immigration from the Caribbean began to increase. In these circumstances it might be expected that an interest would develop in immigration and race. But once again academic historians were slow to respond. Indeed, they were shown a clean pair of heels by Kenneth Little, an anthropologist, whose *Negroes in Britain* was published in 1948. Although his was essentially a study of the pre-war black community in Cardiff, it did carry an historical survey of black settlement in Britain. Once Little took up an academic position at the University of Edinburgh that institution, under his influence, became an important centre of the study of immigration and race relations, producing a wealth of information on black and coloured life in Britain that future historians cannot ignore.[38]

In the course of the 1950s, as the immigration from the New Commonwealth began to assume more significant proportions, a number of important developments occurred. For example, the Institute of Race Relations was founded in 1952, though it did not become independent from Chatham House and the Royal Institute of International Affairs until 1958. The first issue of its journal, *Race*, appeared in 1959 and in the following years a number of satellite bodies and publications were brought into being. The aim of those who initiated and supported such developments was to influence government policy. However, the continuing discrimination experienced by blacks and Asians in Britain, together with the introduction and progressive tightening of immigration control after 1962, cast serious doubts on such optimism. Three years after the appearance in 1969 of its 'Royal Commission', *Colour and Citizenship*, the Institute was ripped apart. The liberal influences were routed in this 1972 upheaval and in 1974 *Race* was symbolically transformed into *Race and Class*.[39]

From the time it was established, the Institute, its journal and its series of monographs provided the dominant hue to the study of immigration and race relations. But its activities and publications did not stand in total isolation. The Social Science Research Council (SSRC) set up the Research Unit on Ethnic Relations at the University of Bristol, work commencing in 1969 under the direction of Michael Banton. In 1979, however, the unit was transferred to the University of Aston where its activities have continued under John Rex. It was intended by the SSRC that the Unit would occupy itself with fundamental issues and complement the policy-oriented research conducted by the Home Office and the Institute of Race Relations. In addition to the official support for work carried on at the Research Unit and the Home Office, government funds underwrote the publication in 1971 of the journal, *New Community*. Appearing first under the auspices of the Community Relations Commission (CRC) that was established by the 1968 Race Relations Act, since 1976 *New Community* has been published by the Commission for Racial Equality that replaced CRC in 1976. Apart from such official initiatives, a number of influential people believed that following the 'revolution' at the Institute of Race Relations in 1972 there was a need for a journal offering a different perspective from *Race and Class*; in 1978 *Ethnic and Racial Studies* answered that need.

Starting in the 1950s anthropologists, sociologists and other social scientists increasingly began to engage in the study of immigration and race relations in Britain. Such activity has resulted in a vast amount of work, often written from sharply divergent idological positions. However, the contribution made by historians so far has been more modest. Journals such as *Race*, *Race and Class*, *New Community* and *Ethnic and Racial Studies* have all carried a few articles on historical aspects of immigration, minority groups and race relations, but what of work on a larger scale?

In the case of blacks, James Walvin compiled a collection of source material, *The Black Presence: a Documentary History of the Negro in England 1555–1860* (London, 1971), and followed it with a monograph, *Black and White: the Negro in English Society 1555–1945* (London, 1973). In the following year Colin Nicolson also referred to the settlement of blacks in his general survey of immigration up to the end of the Second World War.[40] Detailed historical studies, however, have been rare, and we still await the proceedings of the conference held in London in 1981 under the auspices of the University of Edinburgh and the University of London Institute of Education which addressed this issue. As the history of Britain has often been illuminated by writers born outside its boundaries, one of the best studies of black life in Britain has come from an African historian, F. O. Shyllon,[41] and another from a Canadian, Douglas Lorimer, whose *Colour, Class and the Victorians* was impressive in its research, even if some of its conclusions might be regarded as tenuous.[42]

The history of Jews in Britain has received attention from historians. For many years the Jewish Historical Society of England has engaged in the study of Anglo-Jewry; however, it was not until 1960 that the major immigration from Russian-Poland was given sophisticated treatment by the American scholar, Lloyd Gartner, in *The Jewish Immigrant in England 1870–1914*. This was followed by J. A. Garrard's *The English and Immigration 1880–1910* (London, 1971), which appeared under the auspices of the Institute of Race Relations, and a Cambridge Ph.D. thesis written by a young American scholar, Bernard Gainer, was published shortly afterwards as *The Alien Invasion* (London, 1972). From this point the history of Anglo-Jewry has continued to forge forward, in A. J. Sherman's study of refugees from the Third Reich, in essays produced by the Jewish Historical Society of England on provincial Jewry and the End End, in the study of Manchester Jewry by Bill Williams, in histories of recent anti-Semitism by Holmes and Lebzelter, in Alderman's study of the Jewish vote, in Pollins' survey of the economic history of Anglo-Jewry and, even more recently, in Buckman's study of class conflict in Leeds between 1881 and 1914.[43]

The well-established bi-monthly, *Patterns of Prejudice*, has traditionally contained a mixture of academic work and journalism. The emphasis has been upon prejudice and hatred; the occasional article in similar vein has appeared from time to time in the

Wiener Library Bulletin. The *Jewish Quarterly*, skilfully edited throughout its life by Jacob Sonntag, has also contained articles of interest. Finally, the Board of Deputies of British Jews, through its own research unit, has provided students with demographic detail and other historical material on the recent history of Anglo-Jewry.[44]

Although some attention has been devoted to Britain's black community and Anglo-Jewry, both groups have been overshadowed numerically by the Irish. It might be assumed the history of the Irish in Britain would be well-documented, but that is not the case. There are some sound investigations, such as Lynn Lee's study of the London Irish, based for the most part on the mid-Victorian years.[45] However, after the 1840s, 1850s and 1860s, when Irish immigration began a decline that was to last nearly one hundred years, the interest of historians waned. Moreover, we do not have any satisfactory general history of Irish immigration. Neither J. A. Jackson's *The Irish in Britain* (London, 1963) nor Kevin O'Connor's *The Irish in Britain* (Dublin, 1974) digs very deeply below the surface.

This absence of published information on the Irish is mirrored in the treatment of other groups. Although the late nineteenth century immigration of Jews from Russian-Poland has been relatively well-covered, other aspects of that immigration from the Czar's Empire have remained relatively obscure. The Lithuanians have received attention in articles by J. D. White, Kenneth Lunn and Murdoch Rodgers, but we still await the completion of the Ph.D. thesis by Rodgers for a more comprehensive picture.[46] Other aspects of the immigration from Russia will become evident when J. D. Slatter's edited symposium, *From the Other Shore*, appears early in 1984. However, this still leaves open the question of the Polish subjects who left the Czar's Empire. The history of the political exiles in mid-nineteenth century Britain has been dealt with by Peter Brock[47] but the history of the emigration from Poland between 1880 and 1914 has not yet been written.

Other groups have also been neglected by historians. In spite of references to German clerical labour in G. L. Anderson's work (see for example his *German Clerks in England 1870–1914. Another Aspect of the Great Depression Debate*, Salford Papers in Economics, 1979), we remain generally ill-informed about the Germans who were in Britain in the late nineteenth and early twentieth centuries. Moreover, the history of the Italian and French immigration in the late nineteenth century has hardly been treated, and the small Chinese minority has been ignored. There are no studies of the Belgian refugees who came to Britain during the First World War, fleeing as the German army drove westwards. There are few studies of the Russians who came to Britain after the 1917 Revolution and few of the refugees from the Spanish Civil War.

After the Second World War there is another range of gaps. Before the large scale immigration from the New Commonwealth got under way, Britain engaged in the recruitment of labour from Eastern Europe, made up of Polish ex-servicemen together with their dependents and the group of so-called European Volunteer Workers from Central and Eastern Europe. The Polish immigration has been discussed by Zubryczki[48] and Sheila Patterson has produced a number of up-dated studies on this particular minority.[49] But, as yet, no one has made any serious investigation of the official government papers on this immigration even though they are now available in the Public Record Office. The European Volunteer Workers (EVWs) have received even less attention. They were the subject of an early study by the civil servant J. A. Tannahill, who was given priviliged access to Ministry of Labour papers that he used as Simon Research Fellow at the University of Manchester.[50] But there has been no follow-through. Under the provisons of the 1957 Public Records Act (as amended in 1968) the files that Tannahill used are now generally available. As yet, however they have not attracted systematic study. Moreover, although there have been scattered local studies, the recent history of the former EVWs has been mostly neglected.

Finally, although there are several outline contributions to the history of blacks in Britain, as yet there is no historical account of the lives of those immigrants from the Indian sub-continent who came to Britain before the immigration of the 1950s and 1960s. Therefore, we await with great interest Kusoom Vadgama's self-financed pioneer study on those early years.

WRITINGS ON IMMIGRATION OUTSIDE BRITAIN

Not all the work done by historians in Britain on immigrants minorities and race relations has been concerned with British society. In fact, we can isolate a number of distinct contributions made to our wider understanding of these matters. Michael Biddiss has written a number of studies dealing with racism and anti-Semitism, including a study of one of 'the founding fathers', Arthur de Gobineau,[51] and there have been other contributions to the history of anti-Semitism in Europe. For example, P. G. J. Pulzer's 1960 Cambridge Ph.D. thesis on 'Anti-Semitism in Germany and Austria', entry 973 in this work, formed the basis of *The Rise of Political Anti-Semitism in Germany and Austria*, (New York, 1964). A few years later Norman Cohn succeeded better than anyone, with the evidence then at his disposal, in unravelling the arcane mysteries of *The Protocols of the Elders of Zion*.[52] Since then Bernard Wasserstein's *Britain and the Jews of Europe 1939–1945* has unearthed British responses to the Jewish fate in Europe;[53] Jonathan Frankel has published *Prophecy and Politics: Socialism, Nationalism and the Russian Jews 1862–1917* (Cambridge, 1981), an extension and refinement of his 1961 Cambridge Ph.D. thesis (entry 1409); Robert Wistrich has written on the contribution that European Jews have made to the development of socialism;[54] Stephen Wilson in *Ideology and Experience* (London, 1982), has taken a fresh look at anti-Semitism in France at the time of the Dreyfus affair; and Brian Pullan, in *The Jews of Europe and the Inquisition of Venice* (Oxford, 1983), has been concerned with the persecution of Jews in early modern Europe in a city that was on the frontier between Christianity and Judaism.

It is not uncommon for the Jewish community to receive the attention of historians, but in Britain that interest has gone beyond this particular group. Donald Kenrick and Grattan Puxon have jointly enhanced our knowledge of Europe's Gypsy population.[55] R. A. Burchell, M. A. Jones and Philip Taylor have all concerned themselves over the past few years with immigration to the United States.[56] Others, such as Michael Craton and Hugh Tinker, have written on the West Indies and the supply of slaves or indentured labour.[57] Roger Anstey has also contributed to our understanding of the slave trade and slavery in *The Atlantic Slave Trade and British Abolition 1760–1810* (London, 1975) and *Anti-Slavery, Religion and Reform* (Folkestone, 1980).

Focusing on southern Africa, P. G. L. Richardson's 1968 London Ph.D. thesis 'The Provisions of Chinese Indentured Labour for the Transvaal Goldmines 1903–8' (entry 678), has been published as *Chinese Mine Labour in the Transvaal* (London, 1982). Southern Africa has also been discussed in Paul Rich's work, and the publication of his 1980 Warwick thesis on 'The Dilemmas of South African Liberalism: White Liberals, Racial Identity and the Politics of Social Control in the Period of South African

Industrialisation, 1887–1943' (entry 677), is now understood to be imminent. Among studies of Asia, some of the most fascinating are those that have examined the relations between Europeans and Asians. V. G. Kiernan's *The Lords of Human Kind* (London, 1969) and Kenneth Ballhatchet's more recent publication, *Race, Sex and Class under the Raj* (London, 1980) are two good examples.

This appreciation of the world outside Britain has been enhanced by the work of students from overseas. The full impact of Eric William's 1938 Oxford Ph.D. thesis, 'The Economic Aspects of the Abolition of the West Indian Slave Trade and Slavery' (entry 184), became evident when it was published in 1944 under the title *Capitalism and Slavery*. In this form it succeeded in generating a major debate on the motives for the abolition of the British slave trade in 1807. Moreover, the genesis of Orlando Patterson's well-known book, *The Sociology of Slavery* (London, 1967) was also laid in his doctoral work in this country, at the London School of Economics (entry 135). Finally, one can also detect the origins of Belinda Bozzoli's work on *The Political Nature of a Ruling Class. Capital and Ideology in South Africa 1890–1933* (London, 1981) in her doctoral dissertation, 'The Roots of Hegemony: Ideologies, Interests and the Legitimation of South African Capitalism, 1890–1940', presented to the University of Sussex in 1975 (entry 640).

OTHER WRITINGS

In discussing the writing that has been generated on immigration, minorities and race relations we have so far concentrated on work produced by academics, whether in the form of books or theses. But historians would be unwise to neglect the contribution made by people who have not been in an academic post. For instance, Jerry White's work on *The Rothschild Buildings* (London, 1980) was soon recognized as an important addition to the history of the East End during the years that immigration was taking place from the Russian Empire, and Paul Foot's *Immigration and Race in British Politics* (Harmondsworth, 1965) quickly established itself as a lively study of the political aspects of immigration from the 1880s down to the 1960s.

Biographies and reminiscences written by members of immigrant and minority groups have also provided much useful information. Gandhi's *An Autobiography or the Story of my Experiments with Truth* (Ahmedabad, 1927), touched upon his student days in Britain; the impressions of Irish working-class life in D. Macamlaigh's, *An Irish Navvy. The Diary of an Exile* (London, 1964); the recollections of Pepito Leoni, the Italian restaurateur, *I Shall Die on the Carpet* (London, 1966); the reactions of a West Indian immigrant in Donald Hinds' *Journey to an Illusion* (London, 1966); Joe Jacobs' *Out of the Ghetto* (London, 1978), with its discussion of East End Communist Party politics; and the experiences of Martha Lang, a refugee from Nazism, which appeared in *The Austrian Cockney* (London, 1980), are just a small sample from a much larger collection. Anyone interested in locating this type of material should consult the list of autobiographical writings compiled by John Burnett, David Vincent and David Mayall, scheduled for publication in 1984.[58]

Furthermore, historians of immigration, minority groups and race relations cannot afford to ignore official publications. Various reports on emigration and immigration were prepared in the late nineteenth century, and the arrival of the Russian-Poles led to the 1903 *Royal Commission on Alien Immigration*, that has remained a fundamental source.[59] The more recent immigration from the New Commonwealth and Pakistan has also resulted in a fair crop of official publications. We mentioned earlier that the

INTRODUCTION xxix

Community Relations Commission and the Commission for Racial Equality have been involved in the publication of academic research; along with the Race Relations Board that preceded them, they have published their own official reports. Official comment has also come from parliamentary committees.[60] The Home Office has not only engaged in its own research into race relations, but has produced surveys on racial disadvantage, ethnic crime, public disorder and the Vietnamese refugees.[61] Finally, there are such official enquiries as the Scarman Report, produced in response to the disturbances in Brixton, Toxteth, and elsewhere in the spring of 1981.[62]

NON-BOOK SOURCES

At the risk of adding to the weight of sources, the study of immigrants, minorities and race relations can be enriched by searching for non-book sources. In the early days of the British cinema Cecil Hepworth provided his audience with flickering images of *The Aliens' Invasion*[63] and the siege of Sidney Street was captured by newsreel cameras.[64] In the inter-war years Paul Robeson was much in demand for such films as *The Proud Valley* (1935) and to improve black-white relations during the war, *An African in London* was produced by the Ministry of Information in 1943. The feature film *Sapphire* attracted considerable interest on its release in 1959 in the wake of the Notting Hill and Nottingham riots and more recently, we have seen the completion of films such as *Pressure*, *Babylon* and *Burning an Illusion*.[65] Such images reflected the times in which they were produced and now constitute source material that historians should not ignore. In television a number of investigative programmes on New Commonwealth immigration appeared in the 1950s, the Open University has made its own programmes for a course on 'Ethnic Minorities and Community Relations' and an independently produced ten-part programme on immigration is currently being made for Independent Television's Channel 4.

We also need to look elsewhere for information. Postcards, cartoons and advertisements provide a fruitful source of visual evidence. For those with a keen eye there is also an architecture of immigration in the shape of workshops, houses, churches, synagogues and mosques, as well as the scattering of blue plaques on the walls of London. There is, moreover, a wide range of creative literature that we should consider, particularly the work of popular novelists whose writings have often introduced stereotypes of aliens and newcomers.[66] Furthermore, the past few years have seen the publication of a growing body of literature written by members of immigrant and minority communities. All these avenues need to be explored.[67] In addition, for those who prefer to talk and listen we now have a fund of oral evidence that needs to be considered.[68] Finally, the impact of newcomers on food, clothing and music extend the range of evidence the historian can profitably use.[69]

CONCLUSION

One final stress needs to be made in concluding this introduction. Bibliographies such as that offered here are value free; they are intended to be comprehensive and the entries are offered without comment. But anyone who works in the area of immigration, minorities and race relations is aware of the differing interpretations that prevail over key issues; the dispute that ripped apart the Institute of Race Relations in 1972 was just one result. On fundamental issues – the definition of race, racist, and racism, the significance of ethnicity, the influence of the external environment on race relations, and the interrelationship of race and class – serious fissures have emerged among those dealing with contemporary issues that seem almost irreconcilable. Moreover, when they have turned to history as a guide with which to support their arguments they have sometimes adopted an 'inductivist' approach, assessing their evidence in terms of its compatibility with the present.[70] As such, this part of their work has been totally un-historical. This is not the place to develop these arguments but any historian venturing into this area needs to be constantly vigilant. On that cautionary note we can now turn to the bibliography, which innocuously masks such differences.

NOTES

1. C. Holmes and V. F. Gilbert, *Sheffield University Theses, Dissertations and Special Studies in Economic and Social History, 1920–1974* (Sheffield, 1974).
2. V. F. Gilbert and C. Holmes, *Theses and Dissertations in Economic and Social History in Yorkshire Universities, 1920–1974* (Sheffield, 1975).
3. V. F. Gilbert and C. Holmes, *Theses and Dissertations in the History of Education presented at British and Irish Universities between 1970 and 1976* (Lancaster, 1979).
4. V. F. Gilbert, *Labour and Social History Theses: American, British and Irish University Theses and Dissertations in the Field of British and Irish Labour History presented between 1900 and 1978* (London, 1982).
5. V. F. Gilbert, 'Current Bibliography of Immigrants and Minorities: Monographs, Periodical Articles and Theses, Parts 1, 2 and 3', *Immigrants and Minorities*, vol. 1, nos 1, 2, 3 (1982).
6. P. Rees, *Fascism in Britain* (Hassocks, 1979).
7. R. Singerman, *Antisemitic Propaganda. An Annotated Bibliography and Research Guide* (New York, 1982).
8. See, for example, *Prejudice* (London, 1971), and especially Helen Kehr and Janet Langmaid, *The Nazi Era 1919–1945, a Select Bibliography of Published Works from the Early Roots to 1980* (London, 1982).
9. J. Geipel, *The Europeans. An Ethnohistorical Survey* (London, 1969), pp. 163–4.
10. V. G. Kiernan, 'Britons Old and New', in C. Holmes (ed.), *Immigrants and Minorities in British Society* (London, 1978), p. 25.
11. Kiernan, in Holmes, *Immigrants*, p. 23ff, provides a useful summary of ancient, medieval and early modern developments.
12. H. Kellenbenz, 'German Immigrants to England' in Holmes, *Immigrants*, pp. 63–80, carries a survey of German immigrants down to the nineteenth century.
13. N. Goose, 'The "Dutch" in Colchester: The Economic Influence of an Immigrant Community in the Sixteenth and Seventeenth Centuries', *Immigrants and Minorities*, vol. 1 no. 3 (1982), pp. 261–80, is a recent study of Dutch influence.
14. The impact of the Huguenot invasion was long-felt. Samuel Smiles, *The Huguenots* (London, various editions), attests to the great Victorian interest in this particular minority. There were frequent references to the Huguenots in the debate over Jewish immigration. Pro-immigrant circles drew parallels between the Huguenots and the Jews.
15. J. A. Jackson, *The Irish in Britain* (London, 1963), is a general survey of the Irish influx.
16. E. M. Wilkinson, 'French Emigrés in England, 1789–1802. Their Reception and Impact on English Life', unpublished B.Litt. thesis, University of Oxford, 1952.

17. B. Porter, *The Refugee Question in Mid-Victorian Politics* (Cambridge, 1979), is a good study of these refugees.
18. The pioneering study of this immigration is L. Gartner, *The Jewish Immigrant in England 1870–1914* (London 1960 and 1973).
19. Porter, *The Refugee Question*, discusses these issues.
20. C. Holmes, 'The Promised Land? Immigration into Britain 1870–1980', in D. A. Coleman (ed.), *Demography of Immigrants and Minority Groups in the United Kingdom* (London, 1982), pp. 7–8, assembles the statistical evidence on Irish immigration.
21. Vaughan Bevan is at present making a detailed survey of legislation on immigration.
22. K. Little, *Negroes in Britain* (London, 1948).
23. A. J. Sherman, *Island Refuge. Britain and Refugees from the Third Reich 1933–1939* (London, 1973).
24. B. Wasserstein, *Britain and the Jews of Europe, 1939–1945* (London, 1979), p. 82.
25. A. Richmond, *Colour Prejudice in Britain: A Study of West Indian Workers in Liverpool 1941–1951* (London, 1954), remains the fullest study of colonial labour in Britain during the war.
26. There is no adequate study of the Irish in Britain between 1939 and 1945. The most comprehensive study of any of the foreign forces in Britain is G. Smith, 'Black American Soldiers in Britain 1942–1945', unpublished Ph.D. thesis (2 vols.), University of Keele, 1982. On the German POWs see M. Kochan, *Prisoners of England* (London, 1980).
27. This 1951 figure was extracted from evidence in the census returns of that year and was given in E. J. B. Rose (ed.) *Colour and Citizenship* (London, 1968), p. 97.
28. O.P.C.S. Monitor PP 1, 83/2. O.P.C.S. (Office of Population and Census Surveys) monitors provide a continual up-dating on the size of the population of New Commonwealth and Pakistani ethnic origin.
29. It would be invidious to select a small number of titles from the multitude that have discussed the immigration from the New Commonwealth and Pakistan. It might be pointed out, however, that most of the studies have been conducted at a local or restricted level of investigation. No one has yet attempted to draw together the salient features of the immigration in the form of a general historical survey from the end of the Second World War to the present.
30. J. Zubrzycki, *Polish Immigrants in Britain* (The Hague, 1956), and J. A. Tannahill, *European Volunteer Workers in Britain* (Manchester, 1958), are basic sources on Polish and EVW groups. On the Italians, see R. King, 'Italian Migration to Great Britain', *Geography*, vol. 62 (1977), pp. 176–86.
31. Although some episodes, such as the arrival of the Ugandan Asians in 1972, have generated interest, in general the arrival of these refugees would repay further attention.
32. C. Erikson (ed.), *Emigration from Europe* (London, 1976), p. 9.
33. B. Thomas (ed.), *Economics of International Migration* (London, 1958), pp. 65–6.
34. R. K. Kelsall, *Population* (4th ed. London, 1979).
35. W. Cunningham, *Alien Immigration to England* (London, 1897), p. 3.
36. Cunningham, *Alien Immigration*, pp. 266–67.
37. H. A. MacDougall, *Racial Myth in English History* (Montreal, 1982), is a recent study that discusses such matters. See also C. Bolt, *Victorian Attitudes to Race* (London, 1971). S. Gilley, 'English attitudes to the Irish in England', in Holmes, *Immigrants* pp. 81–110, injects a cautionary note into the discussion of Victorian attitudes that has often been missing. See also M. D. Biddiss, 'Myths of the Blood', *Patterns of Prejudice*, vol. IX (September-October, 1975), pp. 11–18, and his introduction to his edited book, *Images of Race* (Leicester, 1979), pp. 11–35. For one particular case study, there is C. J. W. Parker, 'The Failure of Liberal Racialism: The Racial Ideas of E. A. Freeman', *Historical Journal*, vol. 24 (1981), pp. 825–46.

38. K. Little, 'Research Report No. 2: Department of Social Anthropology, The University of Edinburgh', *The Sociological Review*, n.s. vol. 8 (1960), pp. 255–66, discussed 'the Edinburgh school' and lists its major contributions.
39. C. Mullard, 'Race, Power and Resistance. A study of the Institute of Race Relations, 1952–1972', unpublished Ph.D. thesis, University of Durham, 1980, discusses these developments.
40. C. Nicolson, *Strangers to England. Immigration to England 1100–1945* (London, 1914).
41. F. O. Shyllon, *Black Slaves in Britain* (London, 1974).
42. D. Lorimer, *Colour, Class and the Victorians*, English Attitudes to the Negro in the Mid-Nineteenth Century (Leicester, 1978).
43. Sherman, *Island Refuge*, Jewish Historical Society of England, *Provincial Jewry in Victorian Britain* (London, 1975); A. Newman (ed.), *The Jewish East End 1840–1939* (London, 1981); B. Williams, *The Making of Manchester Jewry 1740–1875* (Manchester, 1976); C. Holmes, *Anti-Semitism in British Society 1876–1939* (London, 1979); G. Lebzelter, *Political Antisemitism in England 1918–1939* (London, 1979); G. Alderman, *The Jewish Community in British Politics* (Oxford, 1983); H. Pollins, *Economic History of Jews in England* (London, 1983).
44. Dr. Barry Kosmin has been particularly energetic in the work he has carried out at the Board.
45. L. H. Lees, *Exiles of Erin: Irish Immigrants in Victorian London* (Manchester, 1979).
46. J. D. White, 'Scottish Lithuanians and the Russian Revolution', *Journal of Baltic Studies*, vol. 6, no. 1 (1975), pp. 1–8; K. J. Lunn, 'Reactions to Lithuanians and Polish Immigrants in the Lanarkshire Coalfield 1880–1914', in K. Lunn (ed.), *Hosts, Immigrants and Minorities, Historical Reponses to Newcomers in British Society 1870–1914* (Folkestone, 1980) pp. 308–42; M. Rodgers, 'The Lanarkshire Lithuanians' in B. Kay, *Odyssey. Voices from Scotland's Past* (Edinburgh, 1980), pp. 18–25, and 'The Anglo-Russian Military Convention and the Lithuanian Immigrant Community in Lanarkshire, Scotland', *Immigrants and Minorities*, vol. 1, no. 1 (March, 1982), pp. 60–88.
47. See, for example, 'Joseph Cowen and the Polish Exiles', *Slavonic and East European Review*, vol. 32 (1954), pp. 52–69; 'Polish Democrats and English Radicals 1832–62', *Journal of Modern History*, vol. 25 (1953), pp. 139–56; 'The Polish Revolutionary Commune in London', *Slavonic and East European Review*, vol. 35 (1956), pp. 116–28.
48. See above note 30.
49. See S. Patterson, 'The Poles: An Exile Community in Britain', in J. L. Watson (ed.), *Between Two Cultures* (Oxford, 1977), pp. 214–41.
50. See above note 30.
51. M. D. Biddiss, *Father of Racist Ideology. The Social and Political Thought of Count Gobineau* (London, 1970); see also his edited book, *Joseph Arthur Gobineau. Selected Writings* (London, 1970).
52. N. Cohn, *Warrant for Genocide* (London, 1967).
53. Wasserstein, *Britain and the Jews of Europe*.
54. R. Wistrich, *Socialism and the Jews. The Dilemmas of Assimilation in Germany and Austria-Hungary* (London, 1982).
55. D. Kenrick and G. Puxon, *The Destiny of Europe's Gypsies* (London, 1972).
56. R. A. Burchell, *The San Fransisco Irish 1848–1880* (Manchester, 1979); M. A. Jones, *American Immigration* (Chicago, 1966) and *Destination America* (London, 1976); P. A. M. Taylor, *The Distant Magnet. European Emigration to the USA* (London, 1971).
57. M. Craton, *Sinews of Empire. A Short History of British Slavery* (London, 1974); M. Craton, et al., *Slavery, Abolition and Emancipation* (London, 1976); H. R. Tinker, *A New System of Slavery. The Export of Indian Labour Overseas 1830–1920* (London, 1974). Tinker's *Race, Conflict and the*

International Order (London, 1977) is a useful primer on race in world affairs since the end of the Second World War.
58. J. Burnett, D. Vincent, D. Mayall (eds.), *The Autobiography of the Working Class. An Annotated Bibliography, 1790–1900* (Hassocks, forthcoming 1984).
59. See House of Commons, *Select Committee on Emigration and Immigration* (Foreigners) Report, Proceedings and Minutes of Evidence. British Parliamentary Papers, XI (1888) and X (1889); *Royal Commission on Alien Immigration*, British Parliamentary Papers, IX (1903).
60. See, for example, First Report from the *Select Committee on Race Relations and Immigration* (1977–8), 303–1, and Fifth Report from the Home Affairs Committee, Session 1980–81, *Racial Disadvantage*, vol. 1, Report and Proceedings, (1981), HC 424–1.
61. S. Field, *et al.*, *Ethnic Minorities in Britain. A Study of Trends in their Position since 1961*, Home Office Research Study no. 68 (London, 1981); M. Tuck and P. Southgate, *Ethnic Minorities, Crime and Policing. A Survey of West Indian and White Experience*, Home Office Research Study no. 70 (London, 1981); P. Southgate and S. Field, *Public Disorder. A Review of Research and a Study in One Inner City Area*, Home Office Research Study no. 72 (London, 1982); P. R. Jones, *Vietnamese Refugees*, Home Office Research and Planning Unit Paper, 13 (London, 1982).
62. *The Brixton Disorders, 10–12 April 1981*, Report of an Inquiry by the Rt. Hon. the Lord Scarman, OBE (1981) Cmnd. 8427.
63. See R. Low and R. Manvell, *History of the British Film 1896–1906* (London, 1973), pp. 58–9.
64. There is a copy in the Tower Hamlets Library, Bancroft Road, E.1.
65. All the films mentioned here except *An African in London* were among those shown at the National Film Theatre, London, in July 1983, during the season on blacks in British Cinema. Peter Noble's *The Negro in Film* (London, 1948), could form the basis for a more up-to-date study; p. 127 carries a reference to *An African in London*.
66. For a specific example see G. M. Mitchell, 'John Buchan's Fiction: A Hierarchy of Race', *Patterns of Prejudice*, vol. VII (November-December, 1973), pp. 24–30. For other comment see H. Pollins, 'Coloured People in Post-War English Literature', *Race*, vol. 1 (May, 1960), pp. 3–13 and 'East London in Post-War Fiction', *East London Papers*, vol. 4 (April, 1961), pp. 15–24.
67. See the article by Salman Rushdie in *The Times*, 3 July 1982. Rushdie's work is one example of the contribution that newcomers have made to recent English literature.
68. Some indication of the richness that oral history can provide is evident in White, 'Scottish Lithuanians', and Kay, 'Lanarkshire Lithuanians'. See also Kay's *Odyssey. The Second Collection* (Edinburgh, 1982). *Oral History*, vol. 8, no. 1 'Oral History and Black History' and other issues (e.g. vol. 7, no. 1 (Spring, 1979) and vol. 7, no. 2, (Autumn, 1979)) contain useful testimony. Attention might also be drawn to certain radio programmes such as 'Haven of Refuge', a series of broadcasts on refugees that began on BBC Radio 4, 28 September 1982, and Bill Fishman's investigation of Brick Lane in the East End of London that went out on BBC Radio 4, 20 September 1983. The Open University course, 'Ethnic Minorities and Community Relations', was taught partly through audio-cassettes. Finally, there is a good collection of material grouped under the heading 'Britain and the Refugee Crisis 1933–1947' at the Imperial War Museum, London.
69. For immigrants and food see the comments in C. Driver, *The British at Table* (London, 1983).
70. M. Banton, *Race Relations* (London, 1967), p. 20. See also his article 'The Idiom of Race: A Critique of Presentism', *Research in Race and Ethnic Relations*, vol. 2 (1980), pp. 21–42, and his 'Race, Prejudice and Education: Changing Approaches', in Minority Rights Group, *Teaching about Prejudice*, Report no. 59 (London, 1983), pp. 4–7.

PART 1

GENERAL AND THEORETICAL STUDIES ON IMMIGRANTS, MINORITIES AND RACE RELATIONS

GENERAL THEORETICAL STUDIES

I. RACE AND MINORITY RELATIONS: THEORETICAL STUDIES

A. RACE, RACE THEORIES AND RACIAL ATTITUDES

1. ADINARAYANSIH, S.P. The psychology of colour prejudice.
M.A., London, 1939.

2. BAGLEY, C.R. A study of some social, psychological and cultural aspects of prejudiced attitudes.
D.Phil., Sussex, 1977.

3. BARBU, Z. The psychology of Nazism, Communism and Democracy.
Ph.D., Glasgow, 1954.

4. BARKER, A.J. British attitudes towards the Negro in the seventeenth and eighteenth centuries.
Ph.D., King's College, London, 1972.

5. BEECHEY, V. Ideology of racism.
D.Phil., Oxford, 1978.

6. BHOWNAGARY, A. A psychological study of Eastern concepts of self.
M.A., Sussex, 1977.

6A. BIRD, J.R. Racial discrimination in occupational situations.
M.A., Newcastle upon Tyne, 1977.

7. BUTLER, A.F. Social Darwinism in American thought with special reference to eugenics and eugenic doctrines, 1880-1918.
M.A., Warwick, 1979.

8. CAIRNS, H.A.C. Race and cultural attitudes of the British precursors of imperialism in Central Africa 1840-1890.
D.Phil., Oxford, 1963.

9. CARTER, R.S. An examination of some sociological and Marxist theories of fascism.
M.Soc.Sc., Birmingham, 1978.

10. CHAPMAN, W.R. Ethnology in the museum: A.H.L.F. Pitt-Rivers (1827-1920) and institutional foundations of British anthropology.
D.Phil., Oxford, 1982.

11. DEARBORN, N.W. Eighteenth century Scottish views of primitive society.
M.Litt., Edinburgh, 1967.

12. DURANT, J.R. The meaning of evolution: post-Darwinism debates on the significance for man of the theory of evolution, 1858-1908.
Ph.D., Cambridge, 1978.

13. GABRIEL, J.G. Concepts of race and racism: an analysis of classical and contemporary theories of race.
Ph.D., Liverpool, 1976.

14. GHOSH, R.N. The colonisation and colonies in English thought, 1766-1874.
Ph.D., Birmingham, 1963.

15. GRAUMAN, R.A. Methods of studying the cultural assimilation of immigrants.
M.Sc., London, School of Economics and Political Science, 1952.

Part 1: General and Theoretical Studies

16. HOSKIN, A.J. Racialism and popular consciousness.
M.A., Birmingham, 1974.

17. JACOBS, S. Some social and personality variables of racial prejudice.
Ph.D., Edinburgh, 1970.

18. JONES, G.J. Darwinism and social thought: a study of the relationship between science and development of sociological thinking in Britain 1860-1914.
Ph.D., London School of Economics and Political Science, 1978.

19. LYON, M.H. An enquiry into the origins of British racism.
Ph.D., Aberdeen, 1980.

20. LYONS, A.P. The question of race in anthropology from the time of Johann Friedrich Blumenbach to that of Franz Boas, with particular reference to the period 1830-1890 (approx.).
D.Phil., Oxford, 1975.

21. McINTYRE, S.S. Social and cultural basis of prejudice.
Ph.D., Edinburgh, 1950.

22. MACKENZIE, A.J. British Marxists and the empire: anti-imperialist theory and practice.
Ph.D., Birkbeck College, London, 1979.

23. MARSH, T.N. English voyages to America 1496-1603 and the idea of primitive society.
B.Litt., Oxford, 1956.

24. MUNN, G.H. Thought on race as part of the ideology of English imperialism 1894-1904.
B.Litt., Oxford, 1976.

25. PITT-RIVERS, G.L.F. The clash of race and clash of culture.
B.Sc., Oxford, 1926.

26. POULTER, C.E. The proper study of mankind: anthropology in its social context in England in the 1860s.
Ph.D., Cambridge, 1982.

27. REEVES, F.W. British racial discourse: a study of political discourse about race and race-related matters at parliamentary and borough council levels.
Ph.D., Aston, 1981.

28. STANLEY, N.S. Race relations as administrative sociology.
M.Soc.Sc., Birmingham, 1974.

29. VAIDYA, Y.C. A comparison of emotional maturity in an Eastern and a Western culture.
Ph.D., Bedford College, London, 1955.

30. WEBSTER, Y.O. Race relations: a theoretical displacement.
Ph.D., Warwick, 1976.

31. WOOD, G.A. Theories of primitive mentality in social anthropology.
Ph.D., Birkbeck College, London, 1980.

32. WORBOYS, M. Science and British colonial imperialism, 1895-1940.
D.Phil., Sussex, 1980.

B. INTELLIGENCE AND RACIAL DIFFERENCES CONTROVERSY

32A. BERGER, M. A study of the Eysenck-Furneaux approach to the analysis of performance in intelligence tests.
Ph.D., Institute of Psychiatry, London, 1976.

33. CASEY, T. Ideology and scientific theory: an analysis of the debate on race and intelligence.
M.Sc., Manchester, 1974.

34. LAWRENCE, E.M. An investigation into the relation between intelligence and inheritance.
Ph.D., London School of Economics and Political Science, 1930.

34A. McGOVERN, P.G. A test of A.R. Jensen's two-level hierarchical theory of mental abilities.
M.Sc., Trinity College, Dublin, 1980.

35. PENNY, H.H. An analysis of the current views of intelligence.
Ph.D., Institute of Education, London, 1935.

36. TURNER, W. Jensen's theory of intelligence and its relation to special school recommendations.
M.Sc., Manchester, 1978.

37. WILSON, J.A. A survey, historical and critical, of intelligence tests.
M.Ed., Leeds, 1923.

C. MINORITIES AND INTER-GROUP RELATIONS

38. BILLIG, M.G. Social categorization and inter-group relations.
Ph.D., Bristol, 1972.

39. BREAKWELL, G.M. The mechanisms of social identity in inter-group behaviour.
Ph.D., Bristol, 1977.

40. CADDICK, B.F. Status legitimacy and the social identity concept in inter-group relations.
Ph.D., Bristol, 1978.

41. CHEAL, D.J. Religion and political participation: a study of religious and political groups as alternative foci of commitment.
Ph.D., University College, London, 1945.

42. GRIFFIN, C.E. Intergroup discrimination and social identity: the role of normative influence.
Ph.D., Birmingham, 1979.

43. HAINES, J.T. The self-concept in minority groups.
M.A.*, Lancaster, 1973.

44. HEISLER, H. Class and class competition in the plural society.
Ph.D., Wales (Cardiff), 1971.

45. LAISHLEY, J. Ethnic stereotyping: a study of the influence of group norms in stereotyping of ethnic and occupational groups.
M.Phil., Sussex, 1976.

46. MASSOUD-MOGHADDAM, F. Social categorisation and intergroup behaviour.
Ph.D., Surrey, 1979.

47. MILNER, D.L. Ethnic identity and preference in minority-group children.
Ph.D., Bristol, 1971.

48. PHILO, N.J. Social categorisation in accentuation of intergroup similarity.
Ph.D., Bristol, 1980.

49. ROSS, G.F. Multi group membership, social mobility and intergroup relations: investigation of group boundaries and boundary crossings.
Ph.D., Bristol, 1980.

50. SKINNER, M.R. The effects of group identity and interaction on the expression of attitudes.
Ph.D., Nottingham, 1977.

51. SYKES, M.St.C.D. Achievement, motivation and ethnic group mobility: the relationship reconsidered.
M.A., Manchester, 1974.

52. TURNER, J.C. Social categorisation and social comparison in intergroup relations.
Ph.D., Bristol, 1975.

II. POLITICAL STUDIES

A. MINORITIES AND NATIONALISM

53. CATER, J.J. The sentiment of nationality.
Ph.D., Edinburgh, 1924.

54. GOLDMAN, S.M. Beyond discrimination: the culturally heterogenous society as a problem in political theory.
D.Phil., Oxford, 1978.

55. JOSEPH, B. Nationality, its meaning, development and problems.
Ph.D., London, 1928.

56. KENNETT, W.A. Nationalism and internationalism in English liberal thought from J.S. Mill to L.T. Hobhouse.
M.Sc., London School of Economics and Political Science, 1966.

57. MACARTNEY, W.J.A. Nationalism and democracy.
B.Litt., Glasgow, 1966.

58. MAGÓ, M.S. Nationalism as a secular religion: the evolution of Jules Michelet's historical thought, 1840-1846.
Ph.D., Cambridge, 1976.

59. MAHMOUD, Z.N. Self-determination.
Ph.D., King's College, London, 1947.

60. MAINWARING, D.J. Some problems with theories of nationalism as applied to national minorities in contemporary Europe.
M.A., Sussex, 1976.

Part 1: General and Theoretical Studies

61. SAUNDERS, D. Patterns of political instability: a cross national analysis.
Ph.D., Essex, 1978.

62. SCOTT, D.W. A political sociology of minorities.
Ph.D., Bristol, 1972.

63. SMITH, A.D.S. Nationalism and modernisation: a critical review of theories and typologies of nationalist movements.
Ph.D., London, External, 1970.

64. YOUNG, W.L. Minority groups and military service: case studies in world perspective.
Ph.D., Cambridge, 1979.
(Case studies of Belgium, Canada, Great Britain and U.S.A.)

B. MINORITIES AND MARXISM/SOCIALISM

65. BAILEY, A.M. On the specificity of the Asiatic mode of production: the genealogy of a concept.
M.Phil., University College, London, 1975.

66. BASHEAR, S. The Arab East in Communist theory and political practice 1918-1928.
PhD., Birkbeck College, London, 1976.

67. EGGER, V.T.C.E.F. Nationalist currents in nineteenth century socialist doctrines.
Ph.D., London School of Economics and Political Science, 1949.

68. NAJENSON, J.L. Borochovism: an early Marxist theory of the National Question.
Ph.D., Cambridge, 1981.

69. WARLICK, J.R.Jr. The East in Marxist thought, 1848-1924.
M.Litt., Oxford, 1979.

C. POLITICAL REPRESENTATION IN MULTI-ETHNIC SOCIETIES

70. BEAGLEHOLE, J.H. The minorities in South Asia and public policy with special reference to India, mainly since 1919.
Ph.D., London School of Economics and Political Science, 1965.

71. BLUNT, M.E. Problems of political representation in multi-racial societies with special reference to British East Africa.
PhD., London School of Economics and Political Science, 1966.

72. KAUFMAN, S.D. Communalism and constitution-making in East and West Africa.
M.A., Manchester, 1968.

73. LINCOLN, I.S. Regionalism and the pursuit of national interest in South-East Asia.
M.Phil., London School of Economics and Political Science, 1975.

74. ROSBERG, C.G. A study of communal representation in constitutional systems of the British Commonwealth with special reference to Ceylon, Kenya and Fiji.
D.Phil., Oxford, 1955.

75. SPACKMAN, A. A study of representation in multi-racial communities with special reference to Ceylon and Trinidad from 1946 to 1961.
B.Litt., Oxford, 1964.

76. WATTS, R.L. Recent experiments in federalism in Commonwealth countries: a comparative analysis.
D.Phil., Oxford, 1963.

D. LAW AND POLITICS: NATIONAL AND INTERNATIONAL STUDIES

77. ABOAGYE-DA-COSTA, A.A. The control of aliens.
LL.M., Manchester, 1961.

78. BARBER, P. The League of Nations and national minorities.
M.A., Wales, 1924.

79. CASPER, E.R. The refugee and international law.
LL.M., University College, London, 1948.

80. CHAKRAVARTI, R. Human rights and the United Nations.
B.Litt., Oxford, 1956.

81. COCKRAM, G-M.G.E. The legal aspects of intra-commonwealth migration.
Ph.D., London, External, 1963.

81A. EZEJIOFOR, G.O. The protection of human rights under international law and under the law of certain Commonwealth countries.
Ph.D., London School of Economics and Political Science, 1963.

82. GEY VAN PITTINS, E.F.W. Nationality within the British Commonwealth of Nations.
Ph.D., London, 1928.

83. INENEJI, N.B.C. Legal protection of minorities and the balance of power.
Ph.D., University College, London, 1977.

84. ISSALYS, P.F. Ethnic pluralism and public law in selected Commonwealth countries.
Ph.D., London School of Economics and Political Science, 1972.

85. KANGWANA, J.B.B. The law and practice of immigration control in the United Kingdom and Kenya.
LL.M., Edinburgh, 1977.

86. KATZNELSON, I. The politics of race under the impact of migration: the United States (1900-1930) and the United Kingdom (1948-1968).
Ph.D., Cambridge, 1969.

87. KEMPER, K.D. The police response: a comparative study of the ways in which police in British and American cities have coped with problems of community and race relations.
Ph.D., Cambridge, 1972.

88. MISRA, B. Legal position of aliens in the Commonwealth.
Ph.D., University College, London, 1966.

89. WEIS, P. Nationality in public international law.
Ph.D., London School of Economics and Political Science, 1955.

90. YATES, J.S. The right of aliens to compensation for the expropriation of private property.
M.Litt., Cambridge, 1956.

III. EDUCATIONAL AND LANGUAGE ISSUES

91. ARUMUGAM, V. Comparative study of language policies and problems in Ceylon and India since independence.
M.Phil., Institute of Education, London, 1973.

92. CALLAWAY, H.L. Social anthropology and education: a critical review of major theoretical approach to education in non-literate societies.
B.Litt., Oxford, 1977.

93. CHANDY, V. A cross-cultural study of bilingualism in the Hebrides, Nigeria and Pakistan.
M.Ed., Aberdeen, 1971.

93A. GLENDENNING, F.J. The evolution of history teaching in British and French schools in the nineteenth and twentieth centuries with special reference to attitudes to race and colonial history in history textbooks.
Ph.D., Kent, 1975.

93B. HICKS, D.W. Textbook imperialism: a study of ethnocentric bias in text books, with particular reference to geography.
Ph.D., Lancaster, 1980.

94. HOUGHTON, V.P. Cultural differences in some perceptual responses among school children.
Ph.D., Nottingham, 1971.

95. HOY, C.H. Education and minority groups in the United Kingdom and Canada: a comparative study of policies and objectives.
Ph.D., London School of Economics and Political Science, 1978.

96. JEFFCOATE, R.L. Education for a multi-racial society.
M.A.*. Lancaster, 1972.

97. LAU WAI, H. Attitudes towards family, race, teaching and self among Malayan and English students.
Ph.D., Birmingham, 1964.

98. STONE, M.A. Black culture, self-concept and schooling.
Ph.D., Surrey, 1979.

99. VILDOMEC, V. Multilingualism and education.
M.A., London Institute of Education, 1958.

100. YOUNG, L.Y. A comparative study of the evaluative meaning of colour: implications for identity and the development of self esteem in young black children.
M.Phil., Surrey, 1978.
(Britain, U.S.A. and Jamaica)

IV. MIGRATION: INTERNATIONAL AND COMPARATIVE STUDIES

101. GISH, O. International medical migration: Britain and Ireland.
M.Phil., Sussex, 1970.

102. PLENDER, R.O. Trans-national migration from an international perspective.
Ph.D., Southampton, 1971.

103. ROSTOWSKI, R. A study of the economics of international migration, 1820-1914.
Ph.D., Edinburgh, 1943.

GENERAL HISTORICAL STUDIES

I. ANCIENT HISTORY

104. BAKIR, A.M. Slavery in Pharaonic Egypt.
D.Phil., Oxford, 1946.

105. BARROW, R.H. Slavery in the first two centuries of the Roman Empire.
B.Litt., Oxford, 1926.

106. DUFF, A.M. Freedmen in the early Roman Empire.
B.Litt., Oxford, 1926.

107. HARRIS, H. The Greek, the barbarian and the slave.
M.Litt., Cambridge, 1929.

108. HARRIS, J. Race relations in the first two centuries of the Roman Empire, based on Pliny and Juvenal.
M.A., Nottingham, 1969.

109. HISCOCK, P.R. Some problem connected with the influence of the freedmen upon the civil service under Claudius.
M.A., Reading, 1947.

110. LINGARD, A.W. The ethnic connection and status of civilians of non-British origin in the Roman province of Britain.
M.A., Sheffield, 1954.

111. RAPAPORT, I. Slavery in ancient Mesopotamia and its bearing on the Old Testament.
M.A., King's College, London, 1939.

112. THOMAS, E.M. The slave's peculium in Rome and the protection afforded to it by Roman law before the year 180 A.D.
M.A., Wales, 1927.

113. WEAVER, P.R.C. Familia Caesaris: a social study of the slaves and freedmen of the Roman imperial administration.
Ph.D., Cambridge, 1965.

114. WILSON, A.J.N. Immigration and settlement in the province of Dalmatia from the first Roman contacts to the death of Commodus.
D.Phil., Oxford, 1949.

II. BLACK HISTORY

A. GENERAL STUDIES

115. LYNCH, H.R. Edward W Blyden, 1832-1912 and pan-Negro Nationalism.
Ph.D., School of Oriental and African Studies, London, 1964.

116. MILLER, P.D. Marcus Garvey, Garveyism and Britain, 1887-1940.
M.Litt., Edinburgh, 1975.

117. O'TOOLE, J.J. Watts and Woodstock: family and politics among American Negroes and Cape Coloured.
D.Phil., Oxford, 1971.

B. SLAVERY AND THE SLAVE TRADE AND SLAVE SOCIETIES

118. AKERS, J.N. Slavery and sectionalism: some aspects of church and society among Presbyterians in the American South, 1789-1861.
Ph.D., Edinburgh, 1973.

119. ATKINSON, M. The English slave trade, 1698-1739.
M.A., Exeter, 1974.

120. BECKLES, H.M. White labour in black slave plantation society and economy: a case study of indentured labour in the seventeenth century.
Ph.D., Hull, 1981.

121. BUSH, B.M. Slave women in British West Indian slave society, 1650 to 1832.
M.Phil., Sheffield, 1979.

122. DANCEY, R.M. Shipping in the Jamaica slave trade, 1686-1807.
M.A., Exeter, 1971.

123. FRENCH, C.J. The role of London in the Atlantic slave trade, 1680-1776.
M.A., Exeter, 1970.

124. GOVEIA, E.V. Slave society in the British Leeward Islands, 1780-1800.
Ph.D., University College, London, 1952.

125. HIGMAN, B.W.C. The population geography of slavery in the British Caribbean, 1807-1834.
Ph.D., Liverpool, 1976.

126. HOBBS, P. The slave trade to the British West Indies, 1784-1808.
M.A., Exeter, 1971.

127. JONES, M.K. The slave trade at Mauritius, 1811-1829.
B.Litt., Oxford, 1936.

128. LAMB, D.P. The English Atlantic slave trade in its final phase from the early 1770s to 1807.
M.A., Exeter, 1974.

129. MAHER, J. Ireland and U.S. slavery.
M.A., National University of Ireland, 1929.

130. MERRITT, J.E. The Liverpool slave trade, 1789-1791: an analytical study of the returns to the Committee of Enquiry into the Slave Trade 1788, 1790, 1791 with special reference to the profitability of the slave trade and the nature of the triangular trade.
M.A., Nottingham, 1959.

131. MILNE, A.T. The slave trade and Anglo-American relations, 1807-1862.
M.A. University College, London, 1930.

132. MORGAN, P.D. The development of slave culture in eighteenth century plantation America.
Ph.D., University College, London, 1978.

133. MURRAY, D.R. Britain, Spain and slave trade to Cuba, 1807-1845.
Ph.D., Cambridge, 1967.

134. OROGE, E.A. The institution of slavery in Yorubaland, with particular reference to the nineteenth century.
Ph.D., Birmingham, 1971.

135. PATTERSON, H.O.L. The sociology of slavery: a study of the origins, development and structure of negro slave society in Jamaica.
Ph.D., London School of Economics and Political Science, 1965.

136. REES, D.G. The role of Bristol in the Atlantic slave trade, 1710-1769.
M.A., Exeter, 1970.

137. RICHARDS, A.M. The connection of Bristol with the African slave trade.
M.A., Bristol, 1923.

138. RICHARDS, W.A. The Birmingham gun manufactory of Farmer and Galton and the slave trade in the eighteenth century.
M.A., Birmingham, 1973.

139. RICHARDSON, P.D. The Bristol slave trade in the eighteenth century.
M.A., Manchester, 1969.

140. SMITH, C.A. An analysis of direct and violent methods of control of plantation field slaves in the ante-bellum South.
M.A., Warwick, 1980.

141. SMITH, J.E. The history of slavery in Bermuda.
M.A., Wales (Bangor), 1972.

142. STEINER, F.B. A comparative study of the forms of slavery.
D.Phil., Oxford, 1949.

143. TADMAN, M. Speculators and slaves in the Old South: a study of the American domestic slave trade, 1820-1860.
Ph.D., Hull, 1978.

144. TENKORANG, S. British slave trading activities on the Gold and Slave Coasts in the eighteenth century and their effects on African society.
M.A., School of Oriental and African Studies, London, 1964.

145. WAITE, P. The English and English-colonial trade in slaves to Virginia 1698-1769.
M.A., Exeter, 1973.

C. ABOLITIONIST MOVEMENTS AND EMANCIPATION

146. ALLEN, G. The resistance of the planters of America to the movement for the abolition of slavery.
M.A., Durham, 1952.

147. ASIEGBU, J.U.J. Liberated Africans and British policies, 1840-1920.
Ph.D., Cambridge, 1966.

148. ASPINWALL, B. William Smith, M.P., 1756-1835, and his importance in the movements for parliamentary reform, religious toleration and the abolition of the slave trade.
M.A., Manchester, 1962.

149. BETHELL, L.M. Great Britain and the abolition of the Brazilian slave trade, 1830-1852.
Ph.D., University College, London, 1963.

150. BILLINGTON, L. Some connections between British and American reform movements, 1830-1860, with special reference to the anti-slavery movement.
M.Litt., Brisol, 1966.

151. BINGHAM, R.L. The anti-slavery movement in the West of Scotland in the nineteenth century.
M.Litt., Glasgow, 1973.

Black history   11

152. BIRTWHISTLE, T.M. The development of abolitionism, 1807-1823.
M.A., Birkbeck College, London, 1948.

153. CATHERALL, G.A. The Baptist Missionary Society and Jamaican emancipation 1814-1845.
M.A., Liverpool, 1965.

154. CAWTE, L.H. Great Britain and the suppression of the Cuban slave trade, 1817-1865.
M.A., King's College, London, 1934.

155. COUSINS, W.M. The emancipation of the slave in Jamaica and its results.
Ph.D., London, 1928.

156. DIXON, P.F. The politics of emancipation: the movement for the abolition of slavery in the British sugar colonies, 1807-1833.
D.Phi., Oxford, 1972.

157. GARTON, I.M. The abolition and emancipation movements in England.
M.A., Leeds, 1919.

158. GLYN-JONES, E.M. Britain and the end of slavery in East Africa.
B.Litt., Oxford, 1957.

159. HARGEY, T.M. The suppression of slavery in the Sudan, 1898-1939.
D.Phil., Oxford, 1982.

160. HERRINGTON, E.I. British measures for the suppression of the slave trade from the West Coast of Africa 1807-1833.
M.A., London, 1923.

161. HOWELL, R.C. The role of the Royal Navy in British slave trade suppression policy off the East Coast of Africa, 1860-1890.
Ph.D., King's College, London, 1978.

162. HUMM, P. Religion and the freeing of black America.
M.Phil., Sussex, 1971.

163. HUNT, E.M. The north of England agitation for the abolition of the slave trade, 1780-1800.
M.A., Manchester, 1959.

Part 1: General and Theoretical Studies

164. MACKENZIE, K. Great Britain and the abolition of the slave trade by the other powers (1812-1822) with special reference to the efforts of Castlereagh.
B.Litt., Oxford, 1953.

165. MACLEAN, J.R. The effect of the slave emancipation in British Guiana and Trinidad.
B.Litt., Oxford, 1931.

166. MIERS, S. Great Britain and the Brussels Anti-Slave Trade Act of 1890.
Ph.D., Bedford College, London, 1969.

167. OWEN, G.E. Welsh anti-slavery sentiments, 1795-1865: a survey of public opinion.
M.A., Wales (Aberystwyth), 1965.

168. PILGRIM, E.I. Anti-slavery sentiment in Great Britain, 1841-1854: its nature and its decline with special reference to its influence upon British policy towards the former slave colonies.
Ph.D., Cambridge, 1953.

169. REES, A.M. The campaign for the abolition of the British slave trade and its place in British politics, 1783-1807.
B.Litt., Oxford, 1952.

170. REID, J.M. The origins of English attitudes towards the black African, 1554-1807, with particular reference to the anti-slave movement.
M.A., Hull, 1976.

171. REIS, J.B.G. The abolition of slavery and its aftermath in Pernambuco, 1880-1920.
D.Phil., Oxford, 1975.

172. RIACH, D.C. Ireland and the campaign against American slavery 1830-1860.
Ph.D., Edinburgh, 1976.

173. RICE, C.D. The Scottish factor in the fight against American slavery 1830-1870.
Ph.D., Edinburgh, 1969.

174. SHORT, K.R.M. A study in political nonconformity: the Baptists, 1827-1845, with particular reference to slavery.
D.Phil., Oxford, 1972.

175. SMALLPAGE, E. Great Britain and the abolition of the slave trade, 1807-17.
M.A., Liverpool, 1922.

176. STANGE, D.C. British Unitarians and the crisis of American slavery, 1833-65.
D.Phil., Oxford, 1981.

177. STUART, F.C. A critical edition of the correspondence of Sir Thomas Fowell Buxton, Bart. with an account of his career to 1823.
M.A., Queen Mary College, London, 1957.

178. SYDER, S.N. The abolition of the slave trade and its effects on the commerce of Liverpool, 1770-1835.
M.A., Liverpool, 1955.

179. TAYLOR, G.C. Some American reformers and their influence on reform movements in Great Britain from 1830 to 1860.
Ph.D., Edinburgh, 1960.
(Includes material on American abolitionists.)

180. TOYE, E.C. Abolitionist societies, 1787-1838.
M.A., King's College, London, 1936.

181. TURLEY, D.M. Relations between British and American abolitionists from British emancipation to the American Civil War.
Ph.D., Cambridge, 1970.

182. WASTELL, R.E.P. History of slave compensation 1833-1845.
M.A., King's College, London, 1933.

183. WHALLEY, W. Slavery and its abolition particularly with regard to England's efforts for its extinction to the year 1846 and with special reference to the West Indies.
M.A., Manchester, 1926.

184. WILLIAMS, E.E. The economic aspects of the abolition of the West Indian slave trade and slavery.
D.Phil., Oxford, 1938.

D. SLAVE RISINGS

185. FOX, P.C. An examination and comparison of the revolts led by Nat Turner and John Chilembwe.
M.Sc., Bristol, 1974.

186. SYNOTT, A.J. Slave revolts in the Caribbean.
Ph.D., London, External, 1976.

III. JEWS: GENERAL AND COMPARATIVE STUDIES

187. BROTZ, H.M. An analysis of social stratification in Jewish society.
Ph.D., London School of Economics and Political Science, 1952.

188. CARLEBACH, J. Karl Marx and the critique of Judaism.
D.Phil., Sussex, 1974.

189. COHEN, A. The Jewish economic religious and social life in medieval Europe as illustrated by the Responsa of Rabbi Meir ben Baruch of Rothenberg (1215-1293).
Ph.D., Wales, 1941.

190. COSGRAVE, I.K. Three homilies against the Jews by Jacob of Serug edited with introduction, translation and notes.
Ph.D., London, External, 1941.

191. CROMER, G.N. A comparison of Jewish and non-Jewish family life with special reference to intergenerational relations.
Ph.D., Nottingham, 1973.

192. DAJANI, A.M. The polemics of the Quran against Jews and Christians.
Ph.D., Edinburgh, 1953.

193. DE LANGE, N.R.M. Origen and the Jews: aspects of Jewish-Christian relations in third century Palestine.
D.Phil., Oxford, 1970.

194. FISHMAN, I. The history of Jewish education in Central Europe from the beginning of the seventeenth century to 1782 (the edict of toleration issued by Joseph II of Austria).
Ph.D., London, External, 1941.

195. FORTH, C.E. Jewish identity and identification in Great Britain and North America with special reference to family and kinship.
B.Litt., Oxford, 1974.

196. GRANEEK, J.J. Anti-semitism in the Greco-Roman Diaspora (323 B.C.-325 A.D.).
M.A., Birmingham, 1938.

197. GWARZO, H.I. The life and teachings of al-Maghili with particular reference to the Saharan Jewish community.
Ph.D., London, External, 1973.

198. HAYMAN, A.P. An unpublished Christian-Jewish disputation attributed to Sergius the Stylite; edited from a Syrian manuscript in the British Museum (BM add. 17199) with translation and commentary.
Ph.D., Durham, 1969.

199. JACOBS, L. The business life of the Jews in Babylon from the third to the sixth century.
Ph.D., London, External, 1952.

200. JACOMBS, M.E. The Jewish community in Rome from its foundation until A.D.313.
M.A., Birmingham, 1915.

201. JAKOBOVITS, I. Jewish medical ethics: a comparative and historical study of the Jewish religious attitude to medicine and its practice with special reference to the sixteenth century.
Ph.D., London, External, 1955.

202. JOSEPH, B. Responsa of Rabbi Benjamin (Ze'eb) ben Matisyahu: a contribution to the history of Jews in Southern Europe at the end of the fifteenth and the beginning of the sixteenth centuries.
Ph.D., University College, London, 1942.

203. LEVENE, M. Jewish diplomacy at war and peace: a study of Lucien Wolf, 1914-19.
D.Phil., Oxford, 1981.

204. MEYERS, S.R. The ideas of nationhood, authority and law in ancient Jewish thought.
Ph.D., London School of Economics and Political Science, 1975.

205. PARKES, J.W. The religious element in anti-Semitism up to the time of Charlemagne in the West and Leo the Isaurian in the East.
D.Phil., Oxford, 1934.

206. PERLMAN, M. Moslem polemics against Jews and Judaism.
Ph.D., School of Oriental and African Studies, London, 1941.

207. RAJAK, T. Josephus: Jewish history and the Greek world.
D.Phil., Oxford, 1975.

14   Part 1: General and Theoretical Studies

208. ROBSON, P.C. A study of Ephraem Syrus' hymns against Julian the Apostate and against the Jews.
B.Litt., Oxford, 1969.

209. SHACHAR, I. Studies in the emergence and dissemination of the modern Jewish stereotype in Western Europe.
Ph.D., Warburg Institute, London, 1967.

210. SMALLWOOD, E.M. The relation between the Jews and the Roman Government from 66 B.C. to the foundation of the Christian Empire.
Ph.D., Cambridge, 1951.

211. STEINBERG, M.B.B. The emergence of contemporary Jewish educational systems: a comparative study with special reference to Israel and the U.S.A.
Ph.D., Institute of Education, London, 1968.

212. STRIZOWER, S. The social structure of an Indian-Jewish community.
Ph.D., London, External, 1967.

213. TOBIAS, A. The development of the Rabbinate in Central Europe during the years 1348-1648.
Ph.D., Jew's College, London, 1945.

214. WEISBROD, L. Ideological formation and change: the case of Zionism.
Ph.D., London School of Economics and Political Science, 1979.

215. WHITNEY, J.C. Jew and Gentile: the attitude of Jew to Gentile 586 B.C.-67 B.C.
M.A., Leeds, 1948.

IV.   RACE, MINORITIES AND LITERATURE

A.   GENERAL STUDIES

216. BROOKSHAW, D.R. Race and colour in Brazilian literature, 1850-present day.
Ph.D., University College, London, 1980.

216A. GOONETILLEKE, D.C.R.A. Between cultures: 'underdeveloped' countries in British fiction.
Ph.D., Lancaster, 1971.

217. MARSHMENT, M.A. Ideology and fictional form: a study of the treatment of the ideology of racism in contemporary British popular fiction.
Ph.D., Birmingham, 1957.

218. RAHMAN, K. Race relations in English fiction between 1919 and 1939.
Ph.D., Birmingham, 1963.

218A. RICHARDS, D. Literature and anthropology: the relationship of literature to anthropological data and theory with special reference to the works of Sir Walter Scott, W.B. Yeats and Wole Soyinka.
Ph.D., Cambridge, 1982.

219. WADDINGTON, C.S. The one and the many: some twentieth century Jewish and Negro writers and their place in American literary tradition.
M.Phil., Leeds, 1978.

B.   RACE AND SLAVERY IN CLASSICAL LITERATURE

220. ASTLEY, F.J.D. The black races of Africa in the classics.
Ph.D., London (University of Gold Coast), 1954.

221. BEESE, F.K. The slave in ancient comedy.
M.A., Wales, 1939.

222. CUSHION, K.G. The nature, originality and social significance of the slave characters of Plautus and Terence.
M.A., Queen's University, Belfast, 1964.

223. JENNINGS, P.M. Some aspects of Greek slavery as seen through the pages of Aristophanes, Lysias and Euripides.
M.A., Birmingham, 1956.

224. WILLIAMS, W.G. The slaves of Greek comedy compared with those of Plautus and Terence.
M.A., London, 1911.

C.   RACE AND IMPERIALISM IN LITERATURE

225. BAY-PETERSEN, O. Some views of imperialism in English literature since the end of the nineteenth century.
M.Litt., Cambridge, 1976.

226. BOWEN, C. Discourses on colonialism: a study of the works of Aimé Césaire.
Ph.D., Lancaster, 1978.

227. CONYBEARE, C. The role of empire in English letters after Kipling.
M.Phil., King's College, London, 1969.

228. DUNAE, P.A. British juvenile literature in an age of empire 1880-1914.
Ph.D., Manchester, 1975.

229. FORDOM, M.J. The rise of Fascism and the Second World War: its treatment in books for children published in Britain from the late 1930s to 1976.
M.A., Strathclyde, 1979.

230. GASSER, B.F. A study of the response of English poets to the South African War of 1899-1902.
D.Phil., Oxford, 1979.

231. JARRETT, M.E. The influence of imperialism on prose fiction, 1890-1914.
D.Phil., Oxford, 1973.

232. MAUND, J.C. Imperialism: a study of critical attitudes in the writings of E.M. Forster, George Orwell and Joseph Conrad.
M.A., Wales (Aberystwyth), 1972.

232A. MURRELL, P.S.J. The imperial idea in children's literature, 1841-1902.
Ph.D., Wales (Swansea), 1975.

233. PATTISON, S.D. The relationship of the work of Ezra Pound to the tradition of Vitalist and Fascist thought.
D.Phil., Oxford, 1980.

234. RASKIN, J.S. The mythology of imperialism: a study of Joseph Conrad and Rudyard Kipling.
Ph.D., Manchester, 1967.

235. SANDISON, A.G. The imperial idea in English fiction: a study in the literary expression of the idea, with special reference to the works of Kipling, Conrad and Buchan.
Ph.D., Cambridge, 1964.

236. SHAH, S.A. The empire in the writings of Kipling, Forster and Orwell.
Ph.D., Edinburgh, 1968.

D. MINORITIES IN LITERATURE

a) American Indians and Literature

237. COULTHARD, G.R. The literary treatment of the Indian in the literature of the River Plate countries.
Ph.D., London (University of the West Indies), 1952.

238. FRANCIS, I.K. A critical study of James Fenimore Cooper's Indian novels.
Ph.D., Exeter, 1977.

239. GOLD, P.J. The literature of the 'indigenista' movement in the Andean Republics since 1889.
B.Litt., Oxford, 1971.

b) Blacks and Literature

240. AGOVI, J.K.E. Theme and technique in the novel of social change with particular reference to British and West African novelists.
M.Litt., Stirling, 1972.

241. AHMAD, N. The quest for identity in the West Indian novel, with special reference to John Hearne, V.S. Naipaul, George Lamming, Dennis Williams, Roger Mais.
B.Litt., Oxford, 1974.

242. ANDREWS, W.D.E. American black activist drama of the 1960s.
Ph.D., Queen's University, Belfast, 1976.

243. ARAB, S.A. The novel as chronicle of decolonization of Africa.
D.Phil., Sussex, 1979.

244. AR-RASHEED, M.H. A typology of the African novel: celebration to alienation.
Ph.D., Lancaster, 1978.

245. BRAITHWAITE, R.H.E. The negro in English literature, 1765-1941.
M.A., King's College, London, 1957.

246. BROUGHTON, G. A critical study of the development of V.S. Naipaul as a novelist as reflected in his four West Indian novels.
M.Phil.*, Institute of Education, London, 1967.

Part 1: General and theoretical studies

247. CLARK, T.D. Political commitment in the works of Richard Wright.
M.A., Wales (Bangor), 1977.

248. COOPER, B.L. A survey of modern black African fiction with reference to independent African and South African works.
M.A., Birmingham, 1976.

249. DAVID, R. South African prose fiction of the past two decades (with special reference to Nadine Gordimer, Dan Jacobson and Alan Paton).
M.A., Liverpool, 1967.

250. GAKWANDI, A. The African novel in English and the politics of independence.
M.Litt., Edinburgh, 1972.

251. GATES, H.L. The history and theory of Afro-American criticism, 1773-1831: the arts, aesthetic theory and the nature of the African.
Ph.D., Cambridge, 1978.

252. GRANT, J.W. The literature of exile: a comparative study of writers from the West Indies and South Africa.
Ph.D., Essex, 1980.

253. GRATIER, M.N. Social consciousness in the West African novel in French medium.
M.Phil., Birkbeck College, London, 1975.

254. HOGG, E.J.L. Urbanisation and the negro novelist in the United States 1900-1960.
M.Litt., Edinburgh, 1975.

255. HUMPHRIES, M.O.W. The image of North Africa and the search for a terrestrial paradise: the Algerian journeys and the works of André Gide.
M.A., Birmingham, 1979.

256. JENKINS, M.E. The role of the negro in the modern American novel with special reference to William Faulkner.
M.A., Wales (UWIST), 1977.

257. JONES, E.D. African figures in Elizabethan and Jacobean drama.
Ph.D., Durham, 1962.

258. KILLAM, G.D. The presentation of Africa between the Sahara and the Union of South Africa in novels written in English 1860-1939.
Ph.D., University College, London, 1965.

259. LOBEL, R.F. Fiction and society in South Africa.
M.A., Leicester, 1975.

260. MACDONALD, B.F. The colonial experience in the Nigerian and Trinidadian novel.
Ph.D., Leeds, 1975.

261. McLAREN, R.M. Theatre and cultural struggle in South Africa: aspects of theatre on the Witwatersrand between 1958 and 1976.
Ph.D., Leeds, 1980.

262. MOLLOY, S.D. Black American literature in times of crisis: a study in literary and personal styles between 1840 and 1970.
D.Phil., York, 1978.

263. MONAGHAN, D.M. The socio-political implication of Faulkner's treatment of his negro characters.
M.Phil., Leeds, 1968.

264. MTUBANI, V.C.D. Slavery and the slave trade in English poetry to 1833.
Ph.D., Exeter, 1980.

265. MURPHY, T. The novels of Chinua Achebe with special reference to the theme of the conflict of European and Southern Nigerian cultures from the late nineteenth century onwards.
M.Litt., Newcastle, 1967.

266. NIVEN, A.N.R. A study of the relationship between the individual and his community as depicted in selected English language novels from Asia, Africa and the West Indies.
Ph.D., Leeds, 1972.

267. NJOROGE, S.N. The influence of traditional and Western religion on the culture and political thinking of Ngugi Wa Thiongo and Okot P'Bitek.
M.Phil., Leeds, 1978.

268. NWOGA, D.I. West African literature in English.
Ph.D., London, External, 1965.

269. OGODE, E.S. Africa between the deserts i.e. Sahara and Kalahari in English literature between 1660 and 1807.
Ph.D., King's College, London, 1971.

270. OKO, A. The individual and the community in modern Nigerian drama: a changing relationship.
Ph.D., Essex, 1977.

271. OWUSU, M.O. The impact of Greek tragedy on four West African dramatists: Ola Rotimi, John P. Clark, Efua Sutherland and Wole Soyinka.
M.Litt., Bristol, 1974.

272. RABKIN, D. 'Drum' magazine (1951-1961) and the work of black South African writers associated with it.
Ph.D., Leeds, 1975.

273. RAMACHARAN-HENRIQUES, I. The development of Black American fiction from 1920-1965.
M.A., Hull, 1975.

274. RAMSARAN, J.A. The West Indian in English literature mainly during the sixteenth and seventeenth centuries.
M.A., King's College, London, 1952.

275. RITTER, S.A.H. The propagandist craft of Langston Hughes.
M.A., Kent, 1977.

276. ROBERTS, M.J. The role of the negro in Faulkner's novels.
M.Litt., Bristol, 1968.

277. SARVAN, C.P. Aspects of freedom in Southern Africa fiction: a study of the works of Olive Schreiner, Sarah Millin, Doris Lessing and Nadine Gordimer.
Ph.D., London, External, 1979.

278. SPURLING, D.J. The influence of Christianity on African sensibility as reflected in selected novels of Nigeria and Cameroon.
M.Phil., Leeds, 1977.

279. TALA, K.I. The African political novel in English 1856-1973.
M.Phil., Leeds, 1978.

c) Irish in Literature

280. BERROW, J.H. A study of the background, treatment and presentation of Irish character in British plays from the late nineteenth century to the present day (the stage Irish man from 1800-1910).
M.A., Wales (Swansea), 1967.

281. BROWN, R.M.C.S. Yeat's early approach to nationalism.
M.Litt., Trinity College, Dublin, 1971.

282. DEVILLY, P.B. The spirit of eighteenth century Ireland as reflected in its literature (in the English language).
M.A., National University of Ireland, 1937.

283. DONALDSON, A.R. The influence of Irish nationalism upon the early development of W.B. Yeats.
M.A., Queen Mary College, London, 1954.

284. LASS, R.H. The Irish Ireland myth: a study of the Irish idea of nationality, its native and European roots and its bearing on the work of W.B. Yeats.
Ph.D., Cambridge, 1970.

285. LLOYD, D.C. The writings of James Clarence Mangan: a case study in nationalism and literature.
Ph.D., Cambridge, 1982.

286. PYLE, H.A. James Stephens: the Irish temperament in English literature.
M.Litt., Cambridge, 1961.

287. WALL, T. Academic writings of Irish exiles in the seventeenth century.
Ph.D., National University of Ireland, 1943.

d) Jews and Literature

288. AL-RAHEB, H. The Zionist character in novels written in English.
Ph.D., Exeter, 1974.

289. ARESTY, A.E. The Jew in the Victorian novel: some reflections on the relation between prejudice and art.
M.Phil., Sussex, 1977.

290. BAKER, W. The Jewish element of George Eliot's Daniel Deronda: a study of George Eliot's interest in and knowledge of Judaism.
M.Phil., Royal Holloway College, London, 1970.

291. CUSHING, P.H. American-Jewish urban fiction.
M.Phil., York, 1977.

Part 1: General and Theoretical Studies

292. DURING, S.C. *Daniel Deronda* and psychology: a contextual study.
Ph.D., Cambridge, 1982.

293. EDELSTEIN, C.S. Le juif au theatre en France.
M.A., Leeds, 1922.

294. JABBI, B.B. The coherence of *Daniel Deronda*.
M.A., Sussex, 1971.

295. KENRICK, D.S. The portrayal of the Jew in Scandinavian fiction and drama, 1700-1940.
M.A., London, External, 1966.

296. KILLEEN, J.E.M. Type and anti-type: a study of the figure of the Jew in popular literature of the first half of the nineteenth century.
M.A., Kent, 1973.

297. KLEIN, L.C. The portrait of the contemporary Jew in English and German fiction and drama from 1830 to 1860.
M.A., London, External, 1963.

298. KLEIN, L.C. The portrait of the contemporary Jew in English and German fiction and drama 1830-1933.
Ph.D., University College, London, 1968.

299. KOUTAISSOFF, E. A study of the chapters concerning the history of the Jews in Voltaire's *Introduction à l'essai sur les moeurs et l'esprit des Nations*.
B.Litt., Oxford, 1939.

300. No entry

301. MICHAEL, J.H. The Jews in the city of Rome during the first centuries B.C. and A.D. including a study of the references to them in Greek and Latin writers.
M.A., Wales, 1913.

302. MILLER, M.J. The Jew as myth in recent Jewish American fiction with special reference to the novels of Saul Bellow.
Ph.D., Keele, 1974.

303. NEWMAN, J.A. Time and history in the novels of Saul Bellow.
Ph.D., Cambridge, 1982.

304. OPPENHEIMER, A. Franz Kafka's relation to Judaism.
D.Phil., Oxford, 1977.

305. PATTERSON, D. A study of the literary qualities of the Hebrew novels (1868-1888) written in Eastern Europe and of the social background of Jewish life reflected therein.
Ph.D., Manchester, 1962.

306. PURDIE, E. The story of *Judith* in German and English literature.
M.A., London, 1916.

307. ROSEL, A. The Dreyfus affair in the literature of its time.
M.Phil., Brunel, 1977.

308. ROSS, P. Emile Zola and the church with special reference to the Dreyfus affair and its aftermath.
Ph.D., Leicester, 1977.

309. SMITH, F. The peasantry, Orthodox clergy, dissenters, and Jews as seen by Leskov.
M.A., School of Slavonic and East European Studies, London, 1948.

310. STOTT, G.St.J. A consideration of the roles assigned to Jewish characters in nineteenth century English fiction.
M.Phil., Southampton, 1973.

311. WINEHOUSE, B.I. The literary career of Israel Zangwill from its beginnings until 1898.
Ph.D., Westfield College, London, 1970.

312. WOOLF, M.P. A complex fate: Jewish American experience in the fiction of Leslie Fiedler, Edward Wallent, Chaim Potok and Jerome Charyn.
Ph.D., Hull, 1981.

313. ZUCKER, D.J. The Rabbis: a Jewish study in Anglo-American fiction and sociology.
Ph.D., Birmingham, 1978.

e) Orientals, Orientalism and Literature

313A. ABDEL AZIZ AHMED, L.N. The works of Edward William Lane and ideas of the Near East in England, 1800-1850: the transformation of an image.
Ph.D., Cambridge, 1971.

314. ABDEL-HAMID, M.S. A study of Warburton's The Crescent and the Cross in relation to the literary interest in the Near East shown by English romantic writers in the eighteenth and early nineteenth centuries.
M.A., Bristol, 1948.

315. ABDEL-HAMID, M.S. Oriental Satanism in English literature with special reference to the Romantic movement.
Ph.D., King's College, London, 1959.

316. ABDULLAH, A.M.C. The Arabian Nights in English literature up to 1900.
Ph.D., Cambridge, 1963.

317. AHMAD, M. Oriental influences in English poetry of the Romantic period.
Ph.D., Birmingham, 1960.

318. AHMAD, M.J. Persian poetry and the English reader from eighteenth to twentieth century.
M.Litt., Newcastle, 1972.

319. AMBASTHA, K.P. Traces of oriental mysticism in the poetry of the English Romantic revival.
Ph.D., Edinburgh, 1956.

320. ASLAM, M. The translation of Indian classics by Sir William Jones and his group, and the early writing of English savants on Indian literature, philosophy, theosophy and arts and their influence on English poetry of the Romantic period.
Ph.D., University College, London, 1960.

321. BARR, P.M. The writings on Japan and the Japanese of English and American visitors 1852-1910.
M.A., University College, London, 1964.

322. BOKHARI, Z.A. A study of Anglo-India in fiction.
Ph.D., Cambridge, 1965.

323. BROUGHTON, E.S. Orientalism in English poetry.
M.A., London, 1919.

324. CADWALLER, B. 'The temptation of the East': the sense of crisis in French writers of the twenties as reflected in the opposition between Europe and the East with special reference to the writings of André Malraux.
D.Phil., Sussex, 1976.

325. CHAU, H.J.S.Y. The Chinese element in the work of Ezra Pound with special reference to his translation of Cathay.
M.Litt., Bristol, 1970.

326. CH'IEN, C.S. China in the English literature of the eighteenth century.
B.Litt., Oxford, 1937.

327. DAMIANI, A.E.F. British travel attitudes to the Near East in the eighteenth century and nineteenth century.
Ph.D., Edinburgh, 1977.

328. DANIEL, N.A. The concept of Islam in Latin writers of the Middle Ages from the beginning of the twelfth century to the middle of the fourteenth century.
Ph.D., Edinburgh, 1957.

329. DAS, G.K. E.M. Forster as interpreter of India.
Ph.D., Cambridge, 1970.

330. DAVIES, J.A. The poetry of darkness: Alun Lewis's Indian experience.
M.A., Wales (Aberystwyth), 1970.

331. DOMB, R. The historical portrayal of the Arab as presented in Hebrew literature.
Ph.D., University College, London, 1978.

332. DREW, N.J. India and the imagination in English literature with special reference to the Romantic period.
Ph.D., Cambridge, 1982.

333. EL-CHANRAWI, A.S.W. Some Eastern and esoteric aspects in the work of W.B. Yeats.
Ph.D., Exeter, 1977.

334. EL-MOWAFY, M.I. Arabia in English literature 1650-1750.
Ph.D., Wales (Swansea), 1962.

335. FARAG, F.F. Oriental mysticism in W.B. Yeats.
Ph.D., Edinburgh, 1960.

336. FARAG, N.R. Al-Musqtataf 1876-1900: a study of influence of Victorian thought on modern Arabic thought.
Ph.D., Oxford, 1969.

Part 1: General and Theoretical Studies

337. FENELEY, J.E. The One and the Many: a study of some mystical movements in Europe in the twelfth-thirteenth century with special reference to Islamism and Hindu mysticism.
D.Phil., Oxford, 1974.

338. FISHER, M.J. The Eastern element in Lamartine.
Ph.D., King's College, London, 1942.

339. HAMDY MAHMOUD, A.el.H. The Western attitude towards Islam before and after the first Crusade.
Ph.D., Liverpool, 1953.

340. HAMEED, A. The influence of Arab life, language and culture in the writings of Charles Montagu Doughty.
M.A., Manchester, 1972.

341. HASSAN, R. A study of the life and works of Sir William Jones, 1746-94.
M.Litt., Durham, 1966.

342. HAWARI, R. The Arabian background of Tennyson, Thomson and Meredith.
B.Litt., Oxford, 1963.

343. HAWARI, R. A study of the 'exotic' East in the works of Thackeray, with special reference to the cult of the oriental in eighteenth and nineteenth century England.
Ph.D., Birkbeck College, London, 1967.

344. HEARN, S.A. E.M. Forster's 'access to two worlds'.
M.Phil., Southampton, 1976.

345. HUSAIN, S.S. Rudyard Kipling and India.
Ph.D., Nottingham, 1952.

346. HUSAIN, S.S.A. The impact of Indian languages on Rudyard Kipling's prose style.
Ph.D., School of Oriental and African Studies, London, 1978.

347. HUSSAIN, I. The oriental elements in English poetry (1784-1859).
Ph.D., Edinburgh, 1934.

348. ISHAK, F.M. The philosophical bearing of Eastern and Western mysticism on the poetry of T.S. Eliot.
Ph.D., Liverpool, 1962.

349. JAVADI-TABRIZI, H. The idea of Persia and Persian literature influence in English literature with special reference to the nineteenth century.
Ph.D., Cambridge, 1965.

350. JOHANPUR, F. Oriental influences on the work of Ralph Waldo Emerson.
M.A., Hull, 1965.

351. KHAN, I.M. A critical edition of th Persian correspondence of Col. Sir John Murray.
Ph.D., London, 1925.

352. LE GASSICK, T.J. Studies in contemporary Arab nationalist literature.
Ph.D., School of Oriental and African Studies, London, 1960.

353. LEWIS, A.D. Oriental influence in English literature from 1800 to 1850.
M.A., Wales, 1954.

354. LINDORES, E.A. The Oriental tale in English prose fiction from 1740-1839.
M.A., Manchester, 1924.

355. MA'AT, Y.S. Sir Richard Burton: a study of his literary works relating to th Arab world and Islam.
Ph.D., St Andrews, 1978.

356. MAHMOUD, F.M. The oriental tale in England in the early nineteenth century (1786-1824).
Ph.D., Westfield College, London, 1958.

357. MANZALAOUI, M.A. Some English translations of Arabic imaginative literature (1704-1838); a study of their portrayal of the Arab world, with an estimate of their influence on nineteenth century English literature.
B.Litt., Oxford, 1947.

358. MARTIN, T.J. The Arabic translation of Theodosius's Sphaerica.
Ph.D., St Andrews, 1975.

359. MATTAR, O.M.S. Themes in early tale of Joseph Conrad and their presentation to Arab students at the university.
M.Phil., Institute of Education, London, 1975.

360. METLITZKY, D. Prolegomena for a study of Arabic influence on the literatur and thought of the English middle ages.
M.A., University College, London, 1938.

361. MITTER, P. European attitudes to Indian art from the middle of the thirteenth to the end of the nineteenth century.
Ph.D., School of Oriental and African Studies, London, 1970.

362. No entry.

363. MUKHERJEE, S. Sir William Jones and the beginning of Indology.
Ph.D., School of Oriental and African Studies, London, 1963.

364. PARRY, B. The image of India: some literary expressions of the British experience in India.
M.A., Birmingham, 1966.

365. PITMAN, R. India's contribution to imaginative English literature.
M.A., Birmingham, 1920.

366. PLOWRIGHT, P.S. The influence of oriental theatrical techniques on the theory and practice of Western drama.
Ph.D., Royal Holloway College, London, 1976.

367. RAY, S. Anglo-Indian poetry.
Ph.D., London, 1929.

368. ROSENTHAL, P.S. Sir Hamilton Gibb: a critical historiography.
B.Phil., Oxford, 1977.

369. SAHAJPAL, T.R. Oriental influence in the poetry of P.B. Shelley.
M.A., Queen's University, Belfast, 1965.

370. SAIGH, J.S. Eastern influence in Chaucer with special reference to the Arabs.
Ph.D., King's College, London, 1946.

371. SALEH, T.A. The foreign milieu in E.M. Forster's works.
M.A., Exeter, 1965.

372. SHABOUL, A.M.H. Al-Mas'Udi with special reference to his treatment of non-Muslim history and religion.
Ph.D., Royal Holloway College, London, 1972.

373. SINGH, K.K. Kipling's India.
Ph.D., Royal Holloway College, London, 1966.

374. SINGH, N.N.P. The life and writings of Sir John William Kaye (1814-1876).
Ph.D., School of Oriental and African Studies, London, 1977.

375. SURATGAR, K. Traces of Persian influence upon English literature during the fifteenth and sixteenth centuries.
Ph.D., University College, London, 1939.

376. SWANSON, K.B. The development of British Indology 1765-1820.
Ph.D., Edinburgh, 1979.

377. TALOOKDAR, B.K. A survey of Anglo-Indian poetry.
Ph.D., Trinity College, Dublin, 1935.

378. TASEER, M.D. India and the Near East in English literature.
Ph.D., Cambridge, 1936.

379. ULLAH, F.S.K. Orientalism in the Romantics.
Ph.D., Edinburgh, 1953.

380. VARMA, S.P. True and false orientalism with special reference to Hinduism and India in the English poetry of the nineteenth century.
Ph.D., London, 1926.

381. YAGHMOUR, F.H. Some oriental elements in Restoration comedy.
Ph.D., Sheffield, 1977.

382. YU, S-P. China as treated by English and French writers in the first half of the eighteenth century.
B.Litt., Oxford, 1932.

383. ZAMICK, M. Dr. Edmund Castell 1606-1685: studies of some aspects of Eastern learning in seventeenth century Britain.
Ph.D., St Andrews, 1934.

f) Scots in Literature

384. BARNES, D.F.L. Some attitudes to Scotland in Scottish fiction, 1815-1830.
M.Litt., Edinburgh, 1979.

385. GALLOWAY, J. Reaction in literature of the relation between Scotland and England in the seventeenth and eighteenth centuries: an attempt at tracing England's literary discovery of Scotland.
Ph.D., Edinburgh, 1930.

Part 1: General and Theoretical Studies

386. SCOTT, M.J. James Thomson, Anglo-Scot: a reconsideration of his works in relation to the Scottish background.
Ph.D., Edinburgh, 1979.

g) Welsh in Literature

387. HUGHES, W.J. Wales and Welsh in English literature from the beginning of the sixteenth to the beginning of the nineteenth century.
M.A., Wales, 1919.

388. PIERCE JONES, B. The Welsh character and his development in English drama, 1590-1642.
M.A., Manchester, 1949.

389. ROBERTS, J.K. Attitudes in English literature towards Wales and the Welsh, mainly 1830-1914.
M.A., Manchester, 1967.

V. CHRISTIANITY AND OTHER RELIGIONS

A. GENERAL STUDIES

390. DEWICK, E.C. The Christian attitude to other religions.
D.D., Cambridge, 1950.

391. DOW, D.A. Domestic response and reaction to the foreign missionary enterprises of the principal Scottish Presbyterian Churches, 1873-1929.
Ph.D., Edinburgh, 1977.

392. GOODLOE, R.W. Missionaries as transmitters of Western civilisation in nineteenth century Africa.
Ph.D., St Andrew's, 1956.

393. NDYABAHIKA, J. Protestant evaluation of African religion, 1875-1925.
M.Th., Aberdeen, 1979.

394. NORRIS, J.A. An examination of the attitudes of Ernest Troebsch and Hendrick Kraemer to the non-Christian religions.
Ph.D., Bristol, 1978.

395. POTTER, S.C. The social origins and recruitment of English Protestant Missionaries in the nineteenth century.
Ph.D., London School of Economics and Political Science, 1975.

396. RYALL, D.A. The organisation of missionary societies and the recruitment of missionaries in Britain, and the role of missionaries in the diffusion of British culture in Jamaica during the period 1834-1865.
Ph.D., Bedford College, London, 1960.

397. STANLEY, B. Home support for overseas missions in early Victorian England c.1838-1873.
Ph.D., Cambridge, 1979.

398. TEMPEST-MOGG, B.D. The organisational and ideological response of the World Council of Churches to changing conditions in selected underdeveloped countries with comparative reference to the International Council of Christian Churches.
M.Litt., Oxford, 1979.

399. WILLIAMS, C.P. The recruitment and training of overseas missionaries in England between 1850 and 1900.
M.Litt., Bristol, 1977.

B. CHRISTIAN CHURCH AND CHRISTIAN MISSIONS IN AFRICA

400. ADEGEOLA, E.A.A. IFA and Christianity among the Yoruba: a study in Symbiosis and in the development of Yoruba Christology 1890-1940.
Ph.D., Bristol, 1977.

401. AGBETI, J.K. The history of the training of African Christian ministers in Ghana 1842-1965.
Ph.D., King's College, London, 1970.

402. AJAYI, J.F.A. Christian missions and the making of Nigeria 1841-1891.
Ph.D., King's College, London, 1958.

403. AJAYI, W.O. A history of the Yoruba mission 1843-1880.
M.A., Bristol, 1959.

404. AJAYI, W.O. A history of the Niger and Northern Nigeria Missions 1857-1914.
Ph.D., Bristol, 1963.

405. AKUFFO, F.W.B. The indigenisation of Christianity: a study in Ghanaian Pentecostalism.
Ph.D., Oxford, 1975.

Christianity and other religions

406. ASSIMENG, J.M. A sociological analysis of the impact and consequences of some Christian sects in selected African countries.
D.Phil., Oxford, 1968.

407. AYANDELE, E.A. The political and social implications of missionary enterprises in the evolution of modern Nigeria, 1875-1914.
Ph.D., King's College, London, 1966.

408. BHEBE, M.B. Christian missions in Matabeleland 1859-1923.
Ph.D., King's College, London, 1972.

409. BLANCHET-COHEN, T. The corporate structure of the Catholic Church in Lesotho 1930-56.
M.Phil., University College, London, 1976.

410. BLUNDEN, M.A. The Anglican clergy and the politics of Southern Africa, 1889-1909.
D.Phil., Oxford, 1980.

410A. BROCK, S.M. James Stewart and Lovedale: a reappraisal of missionary attitudes and African response in the Eastern Cape, South Africa, 1870-1905.
Ph.D., Edinburgh, 1976.

411. BRYSON, D.B. The Taita of South Kenya and the Church Missionary Society, 1833-1914.
M.Litt., Oxford, 1981.

412. BUCKLEY, E.M. The history of the mission work of the British Methodist Church in Rhodesia from the 1890's to the 1940's with particular reference to the role of African ministers and evangelists and development in education and women's work.
Ph.D., London, External, 1977

413. BUNKER, S.K. The attitude of the Church to the race problem in central South Africa during the nineteenth century viewed in the light of New Testament principles.
B.Litt., Oxford, 1933.

414. CLENDENNEN, G.W. Charles Livingstone: a biographical study with emphasis on his accomplishments on the Zambezi Expedition, 1858-1863.
Ph.D., Edinburgh, 1978.

415. CLINTON, D.K. The London Missionary Society in South Africa during the years 1798-1836.
B.Litt., Oxford, 1935.

416. COOKE, C.M. The Roman Catholic Mission in Calabar 1903-1960.
Ph.D., School of Oriental and African Studies, London, 1977.

417. COOPER, A.J. The missionary work of John William Colenso, Bishop of Natal: an analysis of the years 1853 to 1862.
M.A., Exeter, 1979.

417A. COPE, T.H. The African Inland Mission in Kenya: aspects of its history (1895-1945).
M.Phil., CNAA, 1979.

418. CRAGG, D.G.L. The relations of the Amampondo and the colonial authorities 1830-1886, with special reference to the role of the Wesleyan missionaries.
D.Phil., Oxford, 1959.

419. CRAMPTON, E.P.T. The growth of Christian communities in Northern Nigeria.
B.D., Trinity College, Dublin, 1970.

420. CREHAN, C.A.F. Khoi, Boer and missionary: an anthropological study of the role of missionaries on the Cape frontier 1799-1850.
M.A., Manchester, 1978.

421. CROSS, J.S.W. The Watch Tower Movement in South Central Africa, 1908-45.
D.Phil., Oxford, 1974.

422. CRUMMEY, D.E. European religious missions in Ethiopia, 1830-68.
Ph.D., School of Oriental and African Studies, London, 1967.

423. DACHS, A.J. Missionary imperialism in Bechuanaland, 1813-1896.
Ph.D., Cambridge, 1968.

424. DALY, C.B. The life of the Christians in North Africa in the time of Tertullian.
M.A., Queen's University, Belfast, 1938.

424A. DELLAQIACOMA, R. The missionary order of the Verona Fathers in Uganda: a sociological analysis of organizational change from 1940-1980.
M.A., Birmingham, 1981.

425. DOYLE, F.J. The Irish contribution to the Catholic Church in South Africa 1820-1900.
M.A., National University of Ireland, 1964.

Part 1: General and Theoretical Studies

426. FELDMAN, D.M. Christians and politics: the origin of the Kikuyu Central Association in Northern Muranga 1890-1930.
Ph.D., Cambridge, 1979.

426A. FIELDING, R.J. Social change among the Ila-speaking peoples of Northern Rhodesia, with particular reference to their relations with the Primitive Methodist Mission.
M.A.(Econ), Manchester, 1965.

427. FREND, W.H.C. The social and economic background of Christianity in North Africa down to 430, with special reference to the Donatist Schism.
D.Phil., Oxford, 1940.

428. GEORGE, J.G. European Protestant mission education and government policy in Southern Nigeria from 1880-1940.
M.A., Kent, 1973.

429. GITHIGE, R.M. The mission-state relationship in Kenya, 1888-1938.
Ph.D., Aberdeen, 1982.

430. GITTINS, A.J. Mende and missionary: belief, perception and enterprise in Sierra Leone.
Ph.D., Edinburgh, 1977.

431. GOODALL, N. Principles and characteristics of missionary policy during the last fifty years, as illustrated by the history of the London Missionary Society.
D.Phil., Oxford, 1950.

432. HARCUS, A.R. The Churches and the Church: a study of the nature of the Church in pre-Nicaean Councils with special reference to the Churches in North Africa.
M.Phil., London, External, 1978.

433. HOGAN, E.M. The Society of African Missions in Ireland (1877-1916).
M.A., National University of Ireland (Cork), 1973.

434. HURT, N.K. Wesleyan missions on the Eastern Frontier of Cape Colony 1820-1840 with special reference to the Kaffir war of 1834-1835.
M.A., King's College, London, 1958.

435. INYANG, P.E.B. The provision of education in Nigeria with reference to the work of the Church Missionary Society, Catholic Mission and the Methodist Missionary Society.
M.A., Institute of Education, London, 1958.

436. KIERAN, J.A.P. The Holy Ghost Fathers in East Africa 1863-1914.
Ph.D., London, 1966.

436A. KLINE, C.G. British Protestant missionary societies during the early stages of British administration in Uganda, 1895-1907.
B.Litt., Oxford, 1976.

436B. LINDEN, I. The White Father's Mission in Rwanda, 1900-1932.
Ph.D., School of Oriental and African Studies, London, 1976.

437. LOIELLO, J.P. Samuel Ajayi Crowther, the Church Missionary Society and the Niger Mission, 1857-1901.
Ph.D., School of Oriental and African Studies, London, 1979.

438. McCRACKEN, K.J. Livingstonia Mission and the evolution of Malawi 1875-1939.
Ph.D., Cambridge, 1967.

439. MASHINGAIDZE, E.K. Christian missions in Mashonaland, Southern Rhodesia 1890-1930.
D.Phil., York, 1974.

440. MIKRE-SELLASSIE, G.A. Church and missions in Ethiopia in relation to the Italian War and occupation and the Second World War.
Ph.D., Aberdeen, 1976.

441. MUBITANA, K. Christian missions and the Toka-Leya of Southern Zambia.
Ph.D., Edinburgh, 1978.

442. MULLEN, J. Church and state in the development of Uwanda, Tanzania 1894-1975.
Ph.D., Edinburgh, 1978.

443. NKETSIA, K. The effect of Christian missionary activities on some Akan social institutions from the Portuguese settlement on the 'Mine Coast' in 1482 to 1916.
D.Phil., Oxford, 1959.

444. NOLAN, F.B. Christianity in Unyamwezi, 1878-1928.
Ph.D., Cambridge, 1977.

445. NORTHCOTT, W.C. Life and expansion work of Robert Moffat, with particular reference to the expansion of missions and the white settlement, north of the Orange River 1817-1870.
Ph.D., School of Oriental and African Studies, London, 1961.

446. ODAMTTEN, S.K. The role of missions in the political economic and social development of Ghana, c.1820-c.1880.
M.A., Birmingham, 1963.

446A. O'DONOGHUE, R. The contribution of the Irish Christian Brothers to secondary education in Zambia, 1967-1980.
M.Ed., National University of Ireland (Maynooth), 1982.

447. OKEKE, D.C. Policy and practice of the Church Missionary Society in Igboland 1857-1929.
Ph.D., Aberdeen, 1977.

448. OLIVER, R.A. The missionary factor in East Africa.
Ph.D., Cambridge, 1952.

449. OMULOKOLI, W.A.O. The historical development of the Anglican Church among Abaluyia, 1905-1955.
Ph.D., Aberdeen, 1981.

450. ONYEIDU, S.O. The African lay agents of the Church Missionary Society in West Africa, 1810-1850.
M.Litt., Aberdeen, 1978.

450A. OSHUN, C.O. Christ Apostolic Church of Nigeria: a suggested pentecostal consideration of its historical, organisational and theological developments, 1918-1965.
Ph.D., Exeter, 1981.

451. OWOH, A.C. C.M.S. Missions, Muslim societies and European trade in Northern Nigeria, 1857-1900.
M.Th., Aberdeen, 1971.

452. OZIGBOH, R.A. A Christian mission in the era of colonialism: a study of the Catholic Missionary enterprise in S.E. Nigeria, 1885-1939.
Ph.D., Birmingham, 1981.

Christianity and other religions

453. PAGE, C.A. Black American in white South Africa: Church and State reaction to the African Methodist Episcopal Church in Cape Colony and Transvaal 1896-1910.
Ph.D., Edinburgh, 1978.

454. PEADEN, W.R. Christian missions in Mashonaland, 1890-1927.
Ph.D., Bristol, 1974.

455. PEETZ, E.A. Friends' Mission work in Madagascar up to 1927 and its doctrinal implications.
B.Litt., Oxford, 1961.

455A. PREMPEH, S. The Basel and Bremen Missions and their successors in the Gold Coast and Togoland, 1914-1926: a study in Protestant missions and the First World War.
Ph.D., Aberdeen, 1977.

456. REA, W.F. The missions as an economic factor on the Zambesi 1580-1759.
Ph.D., London (University College of Rhodesia), 1975.

457. REYNOLDS, K.M. The beginnings of missionary enterprise in South Africa 1795-1812.
M.A., London, 1927.

458. ROSS, A.C. The origins and development of the Church of Scotland mission, Blantyre, Nyasaland.
Ph.D., Edinburgh, 1968.

459. ROTBERG, R.I. Christian missions in Northern Rhodesia 1882-1924 (with special reference to the history of the London Missionary Society, the Primitive Methodist Missionary Society, the South African General Mission, the Plymouth Brethren and the Universities Mission to Central Africa).
D.Phil., Oxford, 1961.

460. RUSSELL, H.O. The missionary outreach of the West Indian Churches to West Africa in the nineteenth century with particular reference to the Baptists.
D.Phil., Oxford, 1973.

461. SHROPSHIRE, D.W.T. The religious institutions and beliefs of the Southern Bantu and their bearing on the problems of the Christian missionary.
D.Phil., Oxford, 1937.

Part 1: General and Theoretical Studies

462. SLADE, R.M. English-speaking missions in the Congo Independent State 1878-1908.
Ph.D., Royal Holloway College, London, 1957.

462A. STEVEN, F.M.I. The contribution of the Church to community formation, with special reference to Ankole District, Uganda.
M.Ed., Manchester, 1976.

463. STIBBS, T.P.C. The work of missionary societies in Kenya 1918-1939.
B.Litt., Oxford, 1972.

464. STUART, R.G. Christianity and the Chewa: the Anglican case 1885-1950.
Ph.D., School of Oriental and African Studies, London, 1975.

465. TASIE, G.O. Christianity in the Niger Delta, 1864-1918.
Ph.D., Aberdeen, 1969.

466. THOMAS, J.Y. The role of the medical missionary in British East Africa, 1874-1904.
D.Phil., Oxford, 1982.

466A. THOMPSON, T.J. Fraser and the Ngoni: a study of the growth of Christianity among the Ngoni of Northern Malawi, 1878-1933, with special reference to the work of Donald Fraser.
Ph.D., Edinburgh, 1980.

467. THORNTON, M. The work of the Catholic Church in British tropical Africa: a study in cooperation.
Ph.D., London, External, 1933.

468. WALIGGO, J.M. The Catholic Church in the Buddu Province of Buganda, 1879-1925.
Ph.D., Cambridge, 1976.

469. WARD, K. The development of Protestant Christianity in Kenya 1910-1940.
Ph.D., Cambridge, 1976.

470. WEBSTER, J.B. The African churches of Yorubaland 1888-1922.
Ph.D., School of Oriental and African Studies, London, 1963.

471. WEEKES, D.J. The growth of Christianity in the kingdom of Nkore (An'kole) in Western Uganda before 1912.
M.Th., Aberdeen, 1979.

472. WELCH, A.W. Colonial Stepchildren: Catholic and Methodist Missionaries in the Ivory Coast 1895-1939.
Ph.D., Birmingham, 1980.

473. WILSON, P. Christian linguists in the Senegambia area 1800-1832.
M.Th., Aberdeen, 1978.

474. ZVOBGO, C.J.E. The Wesleyan Methodist missions in Southern Rhodesia 1891-1945.
Ph.D., Edinburgh, 1975.

C. CHRISTIAN CHURCH AND CHRISTIAN MISSIONS IN ASIA

475. AHMED SHAH, S.Z. The missionary activities of the C.M.S. and the C.E.Z.M.S. in Kashmir during the second half of the nineteenth century.
M.A., Institute of Education, London, 1958.

476. AL-TAMEENI, A.M.K. The Arabian mission: a case study of Christian missionary work in the Arabian Gulf region.
Ph.D., Durham, 1978.

477. ALI, M.M. The Bengali reaction to Christian missionary activities 1833-1857.
Ph.D., School of Oriental and African Studies, London, 1963.

478. BLANCHET, W.L. The development of Christianity in Vietnam by the French Vicars Apostolic under the Chua Trinh Can, 1682-1709.
Ph.D., School of Oriental and African Studies, London, 1976.

479. CHANDRAN, J.R. A comparison of the pagan apologetic of Celsus against Christianity as countered in Origen's Contra Celsum and the neo-Hindu attitude to Christianity as represented in the works of Vivekananda, and an estimate of the value of Origen's reply for Christian apologetics against neo-Hinduism.
B.Litt., Oxford, 1949.

480. CHAUDHURI, T. Some aspects of English Protestant missionary activities in Bengal 1857-1885.
B.Litt., Oxford, 1968.

Christianity and other religions

481. CHOONG, C.P. Issues in the Hindu-Christian debate during the nineteenth century Bengal renaissance, with special reference to St Paul's teaching on the religions of the nations.
Ph.D., Aberdeen, 1976.

482. COPLANS, B.A.R. Methodism and Sinhalese Buddhism: the Wesleyan Methodist encounter with Buddhism in Ceylon 1814-1868 with special reference to the work of Robert Spence Hardy.
Ph.D., Leeds, 1980.

483. DAVIDSON, A.K. The development and influence of the British missionary movement's attitudes towards India, 1786-1883.
Ph.D., Aberdeen, 1973.

484. DAVIS, W.B.S. A study of missionary policy and methods in Bengal from 1793 to 1905.
Ph.D., Edinburgh, 1942.

485. DE SILVA, K.M. Some aspects of the development of social policy in Ceylon 1840-1855 with special reference to the influence of missionary organisations.
Ph.D., School of Oriental and African Studies, London, 1961.

486. DE SILVA, P.W. The first contribution of the Wesleyan Methodist missionaries to Southern India.
M.Phil., Institute of Education, London, 1968.

487. DRURY, C.M. Christian missions and foreign relations in China: an historical study.
Ph.D., Edinburgh, 1932.

488. FERNANDO, C.N.V. A study of the history of Christianity in Ceylon in the British period from 1796 to 1903 with special reference to the Protestant missions.
B.Litt., Oxford, 1942.

489. FORRESTER, D.B. Caste and Christianity: a study of the development and influence of attitudes and policies concerning caste held by Protestant Anglo-Saxon missions in India.
D.Phil., Sussex, 1976.

490. FOSTER, J. The Christian Church of the T'ang Dynasty.
M.A., Birmingham, 1938.

491. FULTON, A. Through earthquake, wind and fire: Church and mission in Manchuria 1867-1950.
M.Litt., Trinity College, Dublin, 1969.

492. GASH, I.J. An historical survey and assessment of the ecclesiastical and missionary policy of the East India Company.
B.Litt., Oxford, 1968.

493. GEHANI, T.G. A critical review of the work of Scottish Presbyterian missions in India 1878-1914.
Ph.D., Strathclyde, 1967.

494. GRAYSON, J.H. The emplantation of religion, the development of Buddhism and Christianity in Korea.
Ph.D., Edinburgh, 1979.

495. HAIRE, J.M. The character and ideological struggle of the Church: Halmahern, Indonesia, 1941-1979.
Ph.D., Birmingham, 1981.

496. HARTLEY, S.E. Work among the educated classes of nineteenth century India: the thought and work of Thomas Ebenezer Slater.
M.Litt., Lancaster, 1977.

497. INGHAM, K. The achievements of Christian missionaries in India 1794-1833.
D.Phil., Oxford, 1949.

498. ION, A.H. British and Canadian missionaries in the Japanese Empire, 1905-1925.
Ph.D., Sheffield, 1978.

498A. McCARTHY, M. The role of the Christian mission schools on the development of education in Singapore, 1918-1974. 2 vols.
Ph.D., National University of Ireland (Cork), 1982.

499. McKAY, M.J. Faith and facts in the history of the China Inland Mission, 1832-1905.
M.Litt., Aberdeen, 1981.

500. McLELLAN, J.M. Latin monasteries and nunneries in Palestine and Syria in the time of the Crusades.
Ph.D., St Andrew's, 1974.

Part 1: General and Theoretical Studies

501. MATHER, B.H. The Gossner mission to Chota-Nagpur 1845-1875: a crisis in Lutheran Anglican missionary policy.
M.A., Durham, 1968.

502. ODDIE, G.A. The Rev. James Long and Protestant missionary policy in Bengal 1840-1872.
Ph.D., School of Oriental and African Studies, London, 1964.

503. ORR, J.M. The contribution of Scottish missionaries to the rise of responsible Churches in India.
Ph.D., Edinburgh, 1967.

504. PIGGIN, F.S. The social background, motivation and training of British missionaries in India 1789-1858.
Ph.D., London School of Economics and Political Science, 1974.

505. PORTER, R.S. The Christian conscience and industrial welfare in China, 1920-1941.
Ph.D., School of Oriental and African Studies, London, 1977.

506. POTTS, E.D. British Baptist missions and missionaries in India 1793-1837.
D.Phil., Oxford, 1963.

507. PRATT, J.H. An examination of certain Chinese institutions, customs, aesthetic concepts and achievements with a view to determining how they could be naturalized in the practice and teaching of the Christian Church in China.
B.Litt., Oxford, 1935.

508. ROONEY, J. The history of the Catholic Church in East Malaysia and Brunei (1880-1976).
Ph.D., School of Oriental and African Studies, London, 1981.

509. SENGUPTA, K. The Christian missionaries in Bengal, 1795-1833.
Ph.D., School of Oriental and African Studies, London, 1966.

510. SHAW, G. The place of Ashrams in the Christian enterprise in India.
M.A., Birmingham, 1963.

511. SILVA, J.W. A study of theology of Church government and the practices of Church administration with special reference to the Churches of Asia.
Ph.D., Edinburgh, 1979.

511A. STONE, I.R. Education and the Seychelles: the government and the missions, 1839-1944.
B.Phil., Open University, 1977.

512. THAIKOODAN, J. Education in Kerala and the missionary contribution to it during the first half of the nineteenth century.
M.Phil., Institute of Education, London, 1967.

513. WERFF, L L van der The strategy of Christian mission to the Muslim: Anglican and Reformed contributions in India and the Near East from Henry Martyn to Samuel Zwemer 1800-1938.
Ph.D., Edinburgh, 1968.

514. WEYMONT, M.E. The Church of South India: progress, practice and problems 1960-1970.
M.A., Durham, 1975.

515. WILLIAMSON, H.R. All for China: an account of the life and labour of Mrs E H Edwards of Taiyanfu, Shensi.
M.A., London, 1922.

516. WILSON, D.K. The history and the problems of Christian education in the Protestant mission schools of Ceylon.
B.Litt., Oxford, 1954.

517. WILSON, D.K. Methodism in North Ceylon: its history and influence 1814-1890.
Ph.D., London, External, 1969.

PART 2

NATIONAL AND REGIONAL STUDIES
ON IMMIGRANTS, MINORITIES
AND RACE RELATIONS

AFRICA

I. GENERAL STUDIES

518. ABDULAI, O.N. The United Nations and the later stages of decolonization in Africa 1965-1975.
Ph.D., Keele, 1979.

519. CAPLAN, L. Some problems of social change with particular reference to the effects of labour migration on the tribal life of selected African peoples.
M.A., School of Oriental and African Studies, London, 1963.

520. FAFOWORA, O.O. A comparative study of British attitudes and policy towards secessionist movement in the Congo (1960-1963) and in Nigeria (1966-1969).
B.Litt., Oxford, 1977.

521. JAMES, L. The Indian problem in Eastern and Southern Africa.
M.A., Liverpool, 1940.

522. JASSAT, E.M. A sociological analysis of the interrelation of the economic and political activities of Indian traders in East and South Africa from the mid-nineteenth to the mid-twentieth centuries.
Ph.D., Keele, 1977.

523. KRECH, S. An examination of some religious movements in Sub-Saharan Africa and their relations to the incipient forms of nationalism.
B.Litt., Oxford, 1970.

524. McLEAN, M. A comparative study of assimilationist and adaptationist policies in British Colonial Africa 1925-1953 (with special reference to the Gold Coast and Tanganyika).
Ph.D., Institute of Education, London, 1978.

524A. MAZRUI, A.A.'A. The idea of self-government and the idiom of nationalism in some Commonwealth African countries, 1957-63.
D.Phil., Oxford, 1961.

525. MOSLEY, P. The settler economies: studies in the economic history of Kenya and Southern Rhodesia, 1900-1963.
Ph.D., Cambridge, 1980.

526. SALOLE, G.M. Change in ethnic group identity: a comparison of Shoa (Ethiopia) and the Zongo (Ghana).
M.A., Manchester, 1979.
(A comparison of the 'stranger' neighbourhood (Zongo) of Kumasi, Ghana and the Shoa Province of Ethiopia.)

527. SWAISLAND, H.C. The Aborigines Protection Society and British Southern and West Africa.
D.Phil., Oxford, 1968.

II. NORTH AND NORTH-EASTERN AFRICA

528. KWAPONG, A.O.A. Epilydes and Autochthones: a survey of the relations between the immigrants and the Libyans of North Africa, 631-111 B.C.
Ph.D., Cambridge, 1960.

Part 2: National and Regional Studies

528A. SKELTON-SMITH, I. Social status and occupation: an investigation of some caste-like groups in north-east Africa.
M.A.(Econ), Manchester, 1979.

A. ALGERIA

529. HUMPHREY, J.C. 'Nationalism' and the colonial situation in Algeria under French rule, 1830-1962.
D.Phil., York, 1976.

B. EGYPT

530. BARAKAT, E.E. The status of aliens in Egypt since 1937 with a sketch of the historical development of their position and a comparison of the present law in Egypt with the British law as to aliens.
B.Litt., Oxford, 1950.

531. EBEID, A.H. National politics and popular education in Egypt 1919-1958.
D.Phil., Oxford, 1965.

532. EL-BATRAWI, A.M. The racial history of Egypt and Nubia from predynastic to present times.
Ph.D., University College, London, 1940.

533. EL-FEKI, M.M.M. Makram Ebeid, a Coptic leader in the Egyptian national movement: a case study in the role of the Copts in Egyptian politics 1919-1952.
Ph.D., School of Oriental and African Studies, London, 1977.

534. HASSAN, A.M. Race, culture and nationalism in Egypt to the Roman period.
Ph.D., Cambridge, 1981.

535. HOLT, A.E. The non-Muslim communities in Cairo, 969-1517 A.D.
M.A., Hull, 1974.

536. ISAAC, S.B. The Coptic community in Egypt: a sociological study.
Ph.D., Wales, 1957.

537. KITROEFF, A. Britain and the Greeks in Egypt during the Second World War.
M.A., Keele, 1979.

537A. SEIKALY, S.M. The Copts under British rule, 1882-1914.
Ph.D., School of Oriental and African Studies, London, 1968.

C. ETHIOPIA

538. CORLETT, J.A. Despised occupational groups in Ethiopia.
B.Litt., Oxford, 1974.

539. GADAMU, F. Ethnic associations in Ethiopia and the maintenance of urban/rural relationships with special reference to the Alemgara-Walamo road construction association.
Ph.D., London School of Economics and Political Science, 1972.

540. RUBENS, M.L. Non-white reaction to the Italo-Ethiopian crisis, 1934-1936.
B.Litt., Oxford, 1978.

541. SCHOENBERGER, M.A. The Falashas of Ethiopia: an ethnographic study.
M.Litt., Cambridge, 1976.

D. LIBYA

542. AL-MAHJUBI, G. The riddle of the sands: an account of schooling the Libyans 642(22)-1951(1371).
Ph.D., Sheffield, 1982.
(includes analysis of cultural and educational clashes between Libyans and Italians, 1911-1939)

543. APPLETON, L. Italian educational policy towards the Muslims in Libya, 1911-1928.
M.Phil., King's College, London, 1980.

544. EL-BADRI, S. Alien educational influence in Libya with special reference to the period of Italian occupation.
M.Ed., Hull, 1981.

E. SUDAN

545. BAKHIET, G.M.A. British administration and Sudanese nationalism 1919-1939.
Ph.D., Cambridge, 1966.

546. EL-BASHIR, A.Al-R.A. Problem of settlement of immigrants and refugees in Sudanese society.
D.Phil., Oxford, 1978.

547. KARADAWI, A.A. Political refugees: a case study from the Sudan, 1964-1972.
M.Phil., Reading, 1977.

548. SHUKRY, M.F. The Khedive Ismail and slavery in the Sudan.
Ph.D., Liverpool, 1935.

549. ZAHIR AL SADATY, F. Political mobilization in a Western Sudanese immigrant group in Khartoum.
Ph.D., Manchester, 1972.

F. TUNISIA

549A. LEE, W.S. French policy and the Tunisian nationalist movement, 1950-1954.
D.Phil., Oxford, 1964.

III. WEST AFRICA

550. CHICK, J.D. The 'white press' a study of the role of foreign owned newspapers in Ghana, Nigeria, Sierra Leone, 1946-1965.
Ph.D., Manchester, 1967.

551. HANNA, M.I. Lebanese emigrants in West Africa: their effect on Lebanon and West Africa.
D.Phil., Oxford, 1959.

552. HUNT, G.P. Transmission of knowledge in a West Africa immigrant religious group.
M.Phil., University College, London, 1973.

553. NWORAH, K.K.D. Humanitarian pressure groups and British attitudes to West Africa 1895-1915.
Ph.D., King's Colleg, London, 1966.

554. SPIEGLER, J.S. Aspects of Nationalist thought among French-speaking West Africans 1921-1939.
D.Phil., Oxford, 1968.

555. to 557. No entries.

A. GHANA

558. EADES, J.S. Enterprise in a migrant community: a study of Yoruba migrants in Northern Ghana with special reference to Tamale.
Ph.D., Cambridge, 1975.

559. KIMBLE, D.B. The rise of nationalism in the Gold Coast.
Ph.D., London, 1961.

560. RENEHAM, M.A. The Denkyira and the British 1823-1874: successful efforts of an African group to gain inclusion in the British protectorate of the Gold Coast.
Ph.D., Birmingham, 1978.

561. SACKEY, J.A. Language, education and European contact in Ghana since 1471.
M.Phil., Leeds, 1972.

562. SARFO, K. Nationalism in the Gold Coast, 1850-1925.
Ph.D., Reading, 1977.

563. SCHILDKROUT, E. Ethnicity, kinship and politics among Mossi immigrants in Kumasi.
Ph.D., Cambridge, 1970.

564. SHORT, A.W. Continuity and change in West African foreign relations: problems of some stranger communities in Ghana in the nineteenth and twentieth centuries.
Ph.D., Aberdeen, 1978.

B. LIBERIA

565. HAYES, R.C. The relation of ethnic politics to the creation of the modern geography of Liberia.
M.Litt., Oxford, 1980.

565A. LOWENKOPF, M. Political modernisation and integration in Liberia.
Ph.D., London, External, 1969.

C. NIGERIA

566. ANIKPO, M.O.C. Patterns in ethnic integration: a study of Ibo ethnic identification in Jos, Nigeria.
Ph.D., Cambridge, 1980.

567. CHIDOLUE, A.B. Federalism: a Nigerian experiment.
Ph.D., Cambridge, 1969.

568. HERSKOVITS, J.F. Liberated Africans and the history of Lagos colony to 1886.
D.Phil., Oxford, 1960.

Part 2: National and Regional Studies

569. LINDAU, B. Urbanization and Islamization in a West African country: a study of their interest in traditional and modern urban areas in Nigeria.
M.Litt., Edinburgh, 1975.

D. SENEGAL

570. O'BRIEN, R.R.C. The French of Senegal: the behaviour and attitudes of a white minority in Africa.
Ph.D., London School of Economics and Political Science, 1969.

571. TREFFGARNE, C.B.W. Language usage and policies in Senegambia: local responses to the anglophone/francophone division of a multilingual region.
Ph.D., Institute of Education, London, 1978.

E. SIERRA LEONE

572. BENNIE, M.J. Government and politics of Sierra Leone, with special reference to the influence of the Creole community.
M.Phil., Nottingham, 1977.

573. BUTCHER, D.A.P. The role of Fulbe in the urban life and economy of Lunsar, Sierra Leone: being a study of the adaptation of an immigrant group.
Ph.D., Edinburgh, 1965.

574. GRACE, J.J. The problem of domestic slavery in British West Africa, with particular reference to the Sierra Leone.
Ph.D., Aberdeen, 1972.

575. STEPHEN, D.A.V. A history of the settlement of liberated Africans in the colony of Sierra Leone in the first half of the nineteenth century.
M.A., Durham, 1962.

IV. EAST AFRICA

576. CHIN, E.Y.Y. Geographical aspects of Chinese contacts with East Africa during the medieval period.
Ph.D., School of Oriental and African Studies, London, 1979.

577. DE SOUZA, F.R.C. Indian political organisations in East Africa.
Ph.D., London School of Economics and Political Science, 1959.

578. MANGAT, J.S. Indian settlement in East Africa c. 1886 to 1945.
Ph.D., London, 1967.

579. PETTERSON, D.R. Geographical aspects of the development of white settlement patterns in British Tropical East Africa since 1870.
Ph.D., London School of Economics and Political Science, 1952.

580. POCOCK, D.F. Indians in East Africa with particular reference to their social and economic situation and relationships.
D.Phil., Oxford, 1955.

A. KENYA

581. ANDERSON, D.M. Herder, settler and colonial rule: a history of the peoples of the Baringo Plains, Kenya c. 1890-1940.
Ph.D., Cambridge, 1982.

582. CLAYTON, A.H.L.Q. Labour in the East African Protectorate 1895-1918.
Ph.D., St Andrew's, 1971.

583. DUDER, C.J.D. The soldier settlement scheme of 1919 in Kenya.
Ph.D., Aberdeen, 1978.

584. EL-SAFI, M.A.G.H. The Somalis in the East African Protectorate and Kenya Colony 1895-1963.
Ph.D., Edinburgh, 1972.

585. FIELDING, I.J. The geographical background of white settlement in the Kenya Highlands.
M.Sc., London School of Economics and Political Science, 1947.

586. FROST, R.A. Trusteeship, discrimination and attempts to promote inter-racial cooperation in Kenya 1945-1963.
D.Phil., Oxford, 1973.

587. MAINI, P.L. The Indian problem in Kenya.
M.Sc., London School of Economics and Political Science, 1944.

588. REDLEY, M.G. The politics of a predicament: the white community in Kenya, 1918-1932.
Ph.D., Cambridge, 1977.

588A. ROGERS, P.H. The Kikuyu and the British 1890-1905: a reassessment.
M.A., Warwick, 1977.

589. SALIM, A.I. The Swahili speaking communities of the Kenya coast 1895-1965.
Ph.D., School of Oriental and African Studies, London, 1968.

590. SORRENSON, M.P.K. Land policy, legislation and settlement in the East African Protectorate 1895-1915.
D.Phil., Oxford, 1963.

591. TANGRI, R.K. A political history of the Asians in Kenya.
M.Sc., Edinburgh, 1967.

592. WOODCOCK, A.C. The problems of the European community in Kenya.
M.A., Leeds, 1949.

593. WYLIE, D.S. Critics of colonial policy in Kenya with special reference to Norman Leys and W. McGregor Ross.
M.Litt., Edinburgh, 1975.

594. ZWANENBERG, R.M.A. van Primitive colonial accumulation in Kenya 1919 to 1939: a study of the processes and determinants in the development of a wage labour force.
D.Phil., Sussex, 1971.

B. TANZANIA/TANGANYIKA

595. BOWRING, W.J.W. Foreign settlers and agricultural development in Tanganyika under British rule 1920-1961.
Ph.D., London School of Oriental and African Studies, 1977.

596. HOBBS, M.E.J. The contribution of education to the development of a plural society in Africa (with special reference to Tanganyika).
M.A., Bristol, 1957.

C. UGANDA

597. CHARSLEY, S.R. Patterns of social organisation in an area of mixed immigration in Uganda.
Ph.D., Manchester, 1969.

597A. DOUGLAS, J.M. Domestic servants in Kampala: anomaly or status symbol?
M.Phil., Edinburgh, 1979.
(A study of ethnic inter-group relations.)

598. EL-SHEIKH, M.A.R. The Egyptians in Uganda 1870-1889.
M.A., Exeter, 1979.
(Reaction of the Kingdoms of Bunyoro and Buganda to Egyptian advance to the Great Lakes.)

599. ENGHOLM, S.F. Immigrant influences upon the development of policy in the Protectorate of Uganda, 1900-1952, with particular reference to the role of the Legislative Council.
Ph.D., London (Makerere College), 1968.

600. FORTT, J.M. The distribution of African population, native and immigrant, in Buganda: a geographical interpretation.
M.A., London, External, 1953.

601. KING, A.G. A history of West Nile district, Uganda: political penetration into ethnic groups 1860-1900.
D.Phil., Sussex, 1972.

602. KUPER, J.S. The Goan community in Kampala, Uganda.
Ph.D., London, External, 1973.

603. MORRIS, H.S. Immigrant Indian communities in Uganda.
Ph.D., London School of Economics and Political Science & Makerere College, 1963.

604. SOFER, C. Some aspects of race relations in an East African township.
Ph.D., London School of Economics and Political Science, 1953.
(Jinja)

605. SOUTHWOLD, M. Community and State in Buganda.
M.A., Cambridge, 1960.

V. CENTRAL AFRICA

606. BOOTH, J.R. Race relations in the Rhodesias with special reference to the idea of partnership.
M.Sc., London School of Economics and Political Science, 1962.

607. MANDAZA, I.M.D.J. White settler ideology, African nationalism and the 'coloured' question in Southern Africa: Southern Rhodesia/Zimbabwe, Northern Rhodesia/Zambia and Nyasaland/Malawi 1900-1976.
D.Phil., York, 1979.

608. PERRINGS, C.A. Black labour in the copper mines of Northern Rhodesia and the Belgian Congo, 1911-1941: industrial strategies and the evolution of an African proleteriat.
Ph.D., School of Oriental and African Studies, London, 1976.

609. SANDERSON, F.E. Nyasaland migrant labour in British Central Africa 1890-1939.
M.A., Manchester, 1961.

A. MALAWI/NYASALAND

610. KRISHNAMURTHY, B.S. Land and labour in Nyasaland, 1891-1914.
Ph.D., School of Oriental and African Studies, London, 1964.

611. TANGRI, R.K. The development of modern African politics and the emergence of a nationalist movement in colonial Malawi, 1891-1958.
Ph.D., Edinburgh, 1970.

B. ZAIRE/CONGO

612. KORNFIELD-GILMAN, R. Relations between Zaireans and Europeans in the city of Kisangansi: a symbolic interactionist approach.
Ph.D., Manchester, 1974.

C. ZAMBIA/NORTHERN RHODESIA

613. GANN, L.H. The development of Northern Rhodesia under the British South African Company 1894-1914: a study in white penetration, growth of administration and racial relations.
B.Litt., Oxford, 1956.

614. GANN, L.H. The growth of a plural society: social, economic and political aspects of Northern Rhodesian development, 1890-1953, with special reference to the problem of racial relations.
D.Phil., Oxford, 1964.

615. MEEBELO, H.S. African reaction to European rule in the Northern Province of Northern Rhodesia, 1895-1939: a study of the genesis and development of political awareness among a colonial people.
Ph.D., London, External, 1969.

616. MILIMO, M.C. Relations between the Lozi, their subject tribes and the colonial administration, 1890-1941.
D.Phil., Oxford, 1982.

617. MUBITANA, K. Ethnicity and integration in urban Zambia: Wiko initiations and the use of masks in a modern African town.
M.Sc., Edinburgh, 1970.

618. STEGMANN, G.M. European mine workers and development of Zambia 1930-1950.
M.Litt., Cambridge, 1979.
(includes consideration of colour bar in employment)

619. WILMER, S.E. African opposition to federations in Northern Rhodesia, 1950-1953.
B.Litt., Oxford, 1974.

D. ZIMBABWE/RHODESIA

620. CHADUKA, N.L. Britain and Southern Rhodesia, 1923 to 1939: British opinion and the politics of 'African affairs'.
M.A., Liverpool, 1971.

621. CLARKE, D.G. The political economy of discrimination and underdevelopment in Rhodesia with special reference to African workers, 1940-1973.
Ph.D., St Andrew's, 1975.

622. FELTOE, G. Law, ideology and coercion in Southern Rhodesia.
M.Phil., Kent, 1979.

623. FITZHENRY, R. Social sources of the politics of resistance and repression in Southern Africa: the case of Southern Rhodesia 1945-1964.
M.Phil., Southampton, 1971.

623A. HOLMAN, N.M.S. The Rhodesian Front and African affairs: policy and administration.
M.Sc., Edinburgh, 1975.

624. KWIDINI, D.J. The missionary factor in Rhodesian native policy, 1910-1939.
M.Litt., Cambridge, 1971.

625. LEE, M.E. Politics and pressure groups in Southern Rhodesia, 1898-1923.
Ph.D., London (University of Rhodesia), 1974.

626. McEWEN, P.J.M. The assimilation of European immigrants in Southern Rhodesia.
Ph.D., Edinburgh, 1963.

627. McGREGOR, R. Native segregation in Southern Rhodesia: a study of social policy.
Ph.D., London, External, 1940.

628. MACHINGAIDZE, V.E.M. The development of settler capitalist agriculture in Southern Rhodesia with particular reference to the role of the state, 1908-39.
Ph.D., School of Oriental and African Studies, London, 1980.

629. MAKAMBE, E.P. The African immigrant factor in Southern Rhodesia 1890-1930: the origin and influence of external elements in a colonial setting.
D.Phil., York, 1979.

630. MASHINGAIDZE, E.K. The influence of African migrants in Rhodesia's native affairs 1890-1945.
D.Phil., York, 1973.

631. NKALA, J.C. The United Nations international law and the Rhodesian independence crisis.
Ph.D., Keele, 1978.

632. SIBANDA, C.J. Conflict amongst European landowners and land policy in Southern Rhodesia 1890-1945.
M.Sc., Cambridge, 1982.

633. STEELE, M.C. The challenge of Rhodesia to European liberal thought.
M.Litt., Edinburgh, 1968.

634. TAYLOR, J.J. The emergence and development of the Native Department in Southern Rhodesia 1894-1914.
Ph.D., London, External, 1975.

635. VAN ONSELOW, C. African mine labour in Southern Rhodesia, 1900-1933.
D.Phil., Oxford, 1975.

636. WHITEHEAD, R.M. The Aborigines' Protection Society and the safeguarding of AFrican interests in Rhodesia 1889-1930.
D.Phil., Oxford, 1976.

VI. SOUTHERN AFRICA

637. BEINART, W.J. Production, labour migrancy and the chieftancy: aspects of the political economy of Pondoland, c.1860-1930.
Ph.D., School of Oriental and African Studies, London, 1979.

638. BLACK, P.A. A critical assessment of the economic strategy to develop the homelands of South Africa.
M.Litt., Glasgow, 1976.

639. BONNER, P. African participation in the Anglo-Boer War of 1899-1902.
M.A.*, London, 1967.

640. BOZZOLI, B. The roots of hegemony: ideologies, interests and the legitimation of South African capitalism 1890-1940.
D.Phil., Sussex, 1975.

641. BROMILEY, W.P. The development of the white community in Natal, 1845-1872.
Ph.D., London, 1937.

642. BROOKS, A.K. Fron class struggle to national liberation: the Communist Party of South Africa, 1940 to 1950.
M.A., Sussex, 1968.

643. CARTER, D.J. Organized non-violent rejection of the law for political ends: the experience of blacks in South Africa.
Ph.D., Durham, 1978.

Part 2: National and Regional Studies

644. CLACK, G. The changing structure of industrial relations in South Africa with special reference to the racial factors and social movements.
Ph.D., London School of Economics and Political Science, 1962.

645. DAVIES, R.H. The political economy of white labour in South Africa 1880-1960.
D.Phil., Sussex, 1977.

646. EDGECOMBE, D.R. The influence of the Aborigines' Protection Society upon British policy towards black African and Cape Coloured affairs in South Africa 1886-1910.
Ph.D., Cambridge, 1976.

647. EDWARDS, I.E. The colonial policy of the Liverpool administration with special reference to British settlement in South Africa.
M.A., Wales, 1931.

648. EDWARDS, I.E. Colonial policy and slavery in South Africa, 1806-1826.
B.Litt., Oxford, 1937.

649. EISENBERG, P.S. Bantu education in the Union of South Africa.
B.Litt., Oxford, 1958.

650. GAITSKELL, D.L. Female mission initiatives: black and white women in three Witwatersrand churches, 1903-1939.
Ph.D., School of Oriental and African Studies, London, 1981.

651. GELDENHUYS, D.J. The effects of South Africa's racial policy on Anglo-South African relations 1945-1961.
Ph.D., Cambridge, 1977.

652. GINWALA, F.N. Class consciousness and control: Indian South Africans 1860-1946.
D.Phil., Oxford, 1975.

653. GOODFELLOW, D.M. Culture contact between Bantu and European in South East Africa as illustrated by the life of Sir Theophilus Shepstone.
Ph.D., London School of Economics and Political Science, 1932.

654. GRIFFITHS, H. A study of British opinion on the problem and policies of Union of South Africa from the end of the Second World War until South Africa's withdrawal from the Commonwealth.
M.Sc., London School of Economics and Political Science, 1963.

655. HATTON, J.D. Race and racism in the Union of South Africa.
M.A., National University of Ireland, 1948.

655A. HEMSON, D. Class consciousness and migrant workers: dock workers of Durban.
Ph.D., Warwick, 1979.

656. HUNTER, M.M. The effect of contact with Europeans upon a South Eastern Bantu group.
Ph.D., Cambridge, 1934.

657. HUTCHINSON, B.A. European and the Bantu family.
Ph.D., London, External, 1945.

658. JOHNSTONE, F.A. Class and race relations in the South African gold-mining industry, 1910-26.
D.Phil., Oxford, 1972.

659. KAPLAN, D.E. Class conflict, capital accumulation and the state: an historical analysis of the state in twentieth century South Africa.
D.Phil., Sussex, 1978.
(How far racially exclusive character of the state modified by 'foreign' capital?)

660. LAMBERT, R.V. Black working class consciousness and resistance in South Africa 1950-1961: a historical materialist analysis.
M.A., Warwick, 1978.

661. LEE, P. Earl Grey's native policy in South Africa with special reference to Natal.
M.A., Sheffield, 1930.

662. LEVY, N. The foundation of cheap labour system in the South African gold-mining industry (1887-1906).
Ph.D., London School of Economics and Political Science, 1977.

663. McCRACKEN, E.M. The growth and distribution of white population of South Africa from the second British occupation (1806) until 1951.
Ph.D., Queen's University, Belfast, 1962.

664. MARKS, S.E. Black and white in self-governing Natal: an assessment of the 1906-1908 disturbances.
Ph.D., School of Oriental and African Studies, London, 1967.

665. MARTIN, S.J.R. British images of the Zulu, c.1820-1879.
Ph.D., Cambridge, 1982.

666. MASHASHA, F.J. The road to colonialism: concessions and the collapse of Swazi independence, 1875-1926.
D.Phil., Oxford, 1977.

667. MASON, D.J. Class, race and national liberation: some implication of the policy dilemmas of the International Socialist League and Communist Party of South Africa, 1915-1931.
M.Sc., Bristol, 1972.

668. NASSON, W.R. Race and civilisation in the Anglo-Boer War of 1899-1902.
M.A.*, York, 1977.

669. NGAVIRUE, Z. Political parties and interest groups in South West Africa: a study of a plural society.
D.Phil., Oxford, 1973.

670. NIEUWENHUYSEN, J.P. The development of the African Reserves in South Africa, with special reference to the period since 1948.
Ph.D., London School of Economics and Political Science, 1963.

671. O'MEARA, D. Class, capital and ideology in the development of Afrikaner nationalism, 1934-1948.
D.Phil., Sussex, 1979.

672. PAHAD, E. The development of Indian political movements in South Africa, 1924-1946.
D.Phil., Sussex, 1972.

673. PILLAY, P.D. The imperial government and British Indians in the Transvaal.
Ph.D., King's College, London, 1967.

674. PORTER, A.N. British imperialism and its public: Chamberlain, Milner and South Africa, 1895-1899.
Ph.D., Cambridge, 1971.

675. PRINGLE, A.D. A contribution to the study of the Bantu race (Zulus) in Natal with reference to (1) their mode of living, racial customs and social conditions and (2) their physical and mental diseases.
M.D., Aberdeen, 1916.

676. PURKIS, A.J. The politics, capital and labour of railway building in the Cape Colony, 1870-1885.
D.Phil., Oxford, 1978.

677. RICH, P. The dilemmas of South African liberalism: white liberals, racial identity and the politics of social control in the period of South African industrialisation, 1887-1943.
Ph.D., Warwick, 1980.

678. RICHARDSON, P.G.L. The provision of Chinese indentured labour for the Transvaal goldmines, 1903-8.
Ph.D., London, 1978.

679. RUSSELL, M. Texture and structure in race relations: a comparison of interpersonal relations in race relations in two Southern African communities under conditions of apartheid and non-racialism.
Ph.D., East Anglia, 1977.
(A study of two white communities - in Durban and Afrikaner cattle farmers in Botswana and their racial attitudes.)

680. SACHS, A. The administration of justice in a racially stratified society: South Africa, 1652 to 1970.
D.Phil., Sussex, 1972.

681. SANSOM, C.J. The British Labour Movement and South Africa, 1918-1955: Labourism and the imperial tradition.
Ph.D., Birmingham, 1982.

682. SHARP, J.S. Community and boundaries: an enquiry into the institution of citizenship in two Cape Coloured Reserves, South Africa.
Ph.D., Cambridge, 1978.

683. SHILLINGTON, K.T.J. Land loss, labour and dependence: the impact of colonialism on the Southern Tswana c.1870-1900.
Ph.D., School of Oriental and African Studies, London, 1981.

684. SIEBERT, W.S. An analysis of the relative pay of white and non-whites in South Africa.
Ph.D., London School of Economics and Political Science, 1975.

685. SINGH, R.N. Indian and coloured education in the Cape.
M.A., Institute of Education, London, 1962.

686. SOFER, C. Some recent trends in the status history of the coloured people of South Africa.
M.Sc., London School of Economics and Political Science, 1949.

687. STEBBING, J.R. Race relations in the Union of South Africa: their influence on the problem of the High Commission territories.
B.Litt., Oxford, 1954.

688. STONE, J. Some sociological aspects of the integration of British immigrants in South Africa.
D.Phil., Oxford, 1970.

689. TAYAL, M.J. Gandhi: the South African experience.
D.Phil., Oxford, 1978.

690. TRAPIDO, S. White conflict and non-white participation in the politics of the Cape of Good Hope, 1853-1910.
Ph.D., Institute of Commonwealth Studies, London, 1970.

691. TURRELL, R.V. Capital, class and monopoly: the Kimberley diamond fields, 1871-89.
Ph.D., London, 1982.

692. WAGENBERG, R.H. Commonwealth reactions to South Africa's racial policy, 1948-1961.
Ph.D., London School of Economics and Political Science, 1966.

693. WALSHE, A.P. The African National Congress of South Africa: aspects of ideology and organisation between 1912 and 1951.
D.Phil., Oxford, 1968.

694. WARWICK, P. African societies and the South African War, 1899-1902.
D.Phil., York, 1978.

695. WILSON, F.A.H. An analysis of the forces operating in the labour market of the South African gold mines, 1936-1965.
Ph.D., Cambridge, 1967.

696. WITCOMB, J.D. Emigration from Great Britain to South Africa, 1820 to 1840.
M.A., Birmingham, 1963.

697. WOLFSON, J.G.E. The ideology and provision of racially segregated education in South Africa 1948 to 1972: a study of some aspects of Bantu education.
M.Ed., Birmingham, 1976.

698. WORDEN, N.A. Rural slavery in the Western districts of Cape Colony during the eighteenth century.
Ph.D., Cambridge, 1982.

VII. MALAGASY REPUBLIC/MADAGASCAR

699. MUTIBWA, P.M. The Malagasy and Europeans: a study of Madagascar's foreign policy 1861-1895.
D.Phil., Sussex, 1970.

ASIA

I. AFGHANISTAN

700. BARTH, T.F.W. The political organization of Swat Pathans.
Ph.D., Cambridge, 1958.

701. EVANS-VON KRBEK, J.H.P. The social structure of a Pakhton speaking community in Afghanistan.
Ph.D., Durham, 1977.
(The Safi of Afghaniya unable to maintain Pakhton identity in face of centralisation.)

702. JONES, S. The implications of ethnic divisions in Afghanistan with particular reference to the Hazara Mongols.
B.Litt., Oxford, 1976.

II. BANGLADESH

703. BEST, N.J. Bangladesh: a divided Pakistan.
M.A., Ulster, 1975.

704. KHAN, A.R. Internal relations in the South-Asian subcontinent since the emergence of Bangladesh: conflict or cooperation?
M.Litt., Aberdeen, 1976.

705. KHAN, A.R. Nationalism in Bangladesh.
Ph.D., Aberdeen, 1979.

706. RAHMAN, M. The emergence of Bangladesh as a sovereign state.
Ph.D., Institute of Commonwealth Studies, London, 1976.

III. BURMA

707. CHAKRAVARTI, N.R. The political and economic conditions of Indians in Burma, 1900-1941.
Ph.D., School of Oriental and African Studies, London, 1969.

708. SAIHOO, P. The Shan of Burma: an ethnographic survey.
B.Litt., Oxford, 1959.

IV. CAMBODIA

709. WILLMOTT, W.E. Chinese society in Cambodia with special reference to the systems of congregations in Phnom-Penh.
Ph.D., London School of Economics and Political Science, 1964.

Part 2: National and Regional Studies

V. CHINA

A. GENERAL STUDIES

710. FORBES, A.D.W. Muslim secessionist movements in N.W. China during the Koomintang period: the Hui rising of Ma Chaung-Yin and the Republic of Turkestan of Akhmedjan Kasim.
Ph.D., Leeds, 1981.

711. GASKELL, A. The colonization and settlement of Manchuria.
M.A., Liverpool, 1932.

712. HADDEN, M.A. The problem of the European child in Shanghai (China).
M.D., Trinity College, Dublin, 1933.

713. KEITH, R.C. The pattern of national political integration in China: the role of greater administrative regions.
Ph.D., School of Oriental and African Studies, London, 1977.

714. MOSELEY, G.V.H. Policy towards ethnic minorities on the southern frontier of the People's Republic of China.
D.Phil., Oxford, 1971.

715. SOUZA, G.B. Portuguese trade and society in China and the South China Sea, c.1630-1754.
Ph.D., Cambridge, 1981.

B. EMIGRATION

716. CAMPBELL, P.C. Chinese coolie emigration to countries within the British Empire.
M.Sc., London, 1922.

717. CHENG, T.C. The education of overseas Chinese: a comparative study of Hong Kong, Singapore and the East Indies.
M.A., Institute of Education, London, 1949.

718. DAVIDI, A. Some cultural changes in Chinese minority communities in South-East Asia: a study in political geography with special reference to Singapore.
Ph.D., School of Oriental and African Studies, London, 1975.

719. FRANKEL, J. The governments of South East Asia and the Chinese.
Ph.D., London School of Economics and Political Science, 1951.

720. FREEDMAN, M. Kinship local grouping and migration: a study in social realignment among Chinese overseas.
Ph.D., London, External, 1956.

721. HUANG, T. The legal status of Chinese abroad.
Ph.D., London School of Economics and Political Science, 1936.

722. HUNTER, P.A. The status of Chinese women in South East Asia.
M.A., London School of Economics and Political Science, 1965.

723. MILES, G.J. The Chinese in South Eastern Asia and the East Indies.
M.A., Birkbeck College, London, 1932.

724. NIEW SHENG TENG The population geography of the Chinese communities in Malaysia, Singapore and Brunei.
Ph.D., School of Oriental and African Studies, London, 1970.

725. WONG, S-L. The economic enterprise of the Chinese in South East Asia: a sociological reference to West Malaysia and Singapore.
B.Litt., Oxford, 1975.

726. WONG, S-L. Industrial entrepreneurship and ethnicity: a study of the Shanghainese cotton spinners in Hong Kong.
D.Phil., Oxford, 1979.

VI. FORMOSA

727. CARRINGTON, G.W. Foreigners in Formosa, 1841-1874.
D.Phil., Oxford, 1973.

VII. INDIA

A. GENERAL STUDIES

728. BHATT, R.S. Some aspects of the minority problem in India.
M.A., London School of Economics and Political Science, 1936.

729. CHATTOPADHAYAY, A.K. Slavery in the Bengal Presidency under East Indian Company rule 1772-1843.
Ph.D., School of Oriental and African Studies, London, 1963.

730. HJEJLE, B. The social policy of the East India Company with regard to sati, slavery, thagi and infanticide, 1772-1858.
D.Phil., Oxford, 1958.

731. KHAN, R.A. Government of India policy towards Portuguese possessions in India 1947-1957.
M.Sc.(Econ)*, London School of Economics and Political Science, 1961.

732. LUIS, G.T. Protection of minority interests under the Indian constitution.
Ph.D., School of Oriental and African Studies, London, 1970.

B. EMIGRATION

733. COLACO, L. (Sister Lucille) Labour emigration from India to the British colonies of Ceylon, Malaya and Fiji during the years 1850-1921.
M.Sc., London School of Economics and Political Science, 1957.

734. CUMPSTON, I.M. The problem of the Indian immigrant in British colonial policy after 1834.
D.Phil., Oxford, 1950.

735. GUNDARA, J.S. Implication of British extra-territorial jurisdiction over Indians in nineteenth century Zanzibar.
Ph.D., Edinburgh, 1975.

736. RAYNER, W.R. The settlement of Indians in the margins of Indian Ocean.
M.A., Birkbeck College, London, 1934.

737. SIRCAR, K. Migration of Indian labour to British plantations in Mauritius, Natal and Fiji 1834-1914.
M.Sc., London School of Economics and Political Science, 1964.

C. REGIONALISM AND NATIONALISM

738. AHMAD, W. The formation of Government of India Act, 1935.
Ph.D., Cambridge, 1970.

739. ARNOLD, D.J. Nationalism and regional politics: Tamilnad, India 1920-1937.
D.Phil., Sussex, 1973.

740. AROORAN, K.NAMBI The Tamil resistance and Dravidian nationalism 1905-1944 with special reference to the works of Maraimalai Atikal.
Ph.D., School of Oriental and African Studies, London, 1976.

741. BERGSTROM, G.W. His Majesty's government's policies towards India: the critical years, 1927-1939.
D.Phil., Oxford, 1970.

742. BROWN, J.M. Gandhi in India, 1915-1920: his emergence as a leader and the transformation of politics.
Ph.D., Cambridge, 1968.

743. GHOSH, S. The influence of western particularly English, political ideas on Indian political thought with special reference to the political ideas of the Indian National Congress, 1885-1919.
Ph.D., School of Oriental and African Studies, London, 1950.

744. GORDON, A.D. British Indian relations in the 1930's and in particular the 1935 Act.
Ph.D., Cambridge, 1940.

745. GORDON, R.A. Aspects in the history of the Indian National Congress with special reference to the Swarajya Party, 1919-1927.
D.Phil., Oxford, 1970.

746. JONES, I.M. The origins and development to 1892 of the Indian National Congress.
M.A., School of Oriental and African Studies, London, 1946.

Part 2: National and Regional Studies

747. KANNANGARA, A.P. Nationalism in Bengal, 1903-1911: a study of Bengali reaction to the partition of the Province with special reference to the social groups involved.
D.Phil., Oxford, 1971.

748. KRISHNA, G. The Indian National Congress, 1918-1923.
D.Phil., Oxford, 1960.

749. McLANE, J.R. The development of nationalist ideas and tactics and the policies of the government of India 1897-1905.
Ph.D., London, 1961.

750. MASANI, Z.M. Radical nationalism in India 1930-1942: the role of the All India Congress Socialist Party.
D.Phil., Oxford, 1976.

751. RIZVI, S.A.G. British policy and the political impasse in India during the vice-royalty of Lord Linlithgow, 1936-43.
D.Phil., Oxford, 1976.

752. SANDERS, I.L. Indian nationalism with special reference to Nehru's career and influence.
M.Sc., London School of Economics and Political Science, 1959.

753. SEAL, A. The emergence of Indian nationalism.
Ph.D., Cambridge, 1963.

754. SUNTHARALINGAM, R. Politics and change in the Madras Presidency 1884-1894: a regional study of Indian nationalism.
Ph.D., School of Oriental and African Studies, London, 1966.

755. TAYLOR, D.D. Indian politics and the election of 1937.
Ph.D., School of Oriental and African Studies, London, 1972.

756. TOMLINSON, B.R. Nationalism and Indian politics: the Indian National Congress 1934-1942.
Ph.D., Cambridge, 1975.

756A. WILSON, J.C. Gandhiites and Socialists: the struggle for control of the Indian National Congress, 1931-1939.
Ph.D., School of Oriental and African Studies, London, 1978.

757. WOLF, T.W. Political conflict and regionalism, Orissa 1938-1948.
M.Phil., Institute of Commonwealth Studies, London, 1978.

D. MINORITIES

a) Christian and European Communities

758. CROWTHER, K.J. Portuguese society in India in the sixteenth and seventeenth centuries.
D.Phil., Oxford, 1959.

759. DUNNE, M.A. An enquiry into the purpose and development of Catholic education in Madras (1850-1950).
M.Phil., Institute of Education, London, 1968.

760. DYSON, K.K. The journals and memoirs of British travellers and residents in India in the late eighteenth and nineteenth centuries prior to the mutiny.
D.Phil., Oxford, 1975.

761. EMMOTT, D.H. Christian schools in Bengal prior to 1857.
M.A., Bristol, 1960.

762. FULLER, C.J. Nayars and Christians in Travancore.
Ph.D., Cambridge, 1975.

763. GEORGE, G. The Syrian Christians of Kerala and their education.
M.A., Institute of Education, London, 1959.

764. GHOSH, S. The social condition of the British community in Bengal, 1757-1800.
Ph.D., School of Oriental and African Studies, London, 1966.

764A. KANJAMALA, A. Religion and modernisation: a case study of interaction between Christianity, Hinduism and modernization in Northern Orissa, 1947-1977.
Ph.D., Lancaster, 1978.

765. KAUFMANN, S.B. Popular Christianity caste and Hindu society in South India 1800-1915: a study of Travancore and Tironelveli.
Ph.D., Cambridge, 1980.

766. MACMILLAN, M.O. Social and political attitudes of British expatriates in India 1880-1920.
D.Phil., Oxford, 1975.

767. PEARSON, R. A social history of the European community in Calcutta.
M.Sc.(Econ.)*, London, External, 1955.

768. RENFORD, R.K. The non-official British in India, 1883-1920.
Ph.D., School of Oriental and African Studies, London, 1979.

769. SPEAR, T.G. English social life in India in the eighteenth century.
Ph.D., Cambridge, 1932.

770. SWAI, B. The British in Malabar, 1792-1806.
Ph.D., Sussex, 1975.

771. TIWARI, R. The social and political significance of Anglo-Indian schools in India.
M.A., Institute of Education, London, 1965.

b) Muslims

772. AHMED, R. The Bengal Muslims: c.1871-1906: the redefinition of identity.
D.Phil., Oxford, 1977.

773. AHMED, S. Some aspects of the history of the Muslim community in Bengal, 1884-1912.
Ph.D., School of Oriental and African Studies, London, 1960.

774. ALEEM, M.A. The social and economic development of Islamic society in North India 1290-1320.
Ph.D., School of Oriental and African Studies, London, 1952.

774A. ASAD, T. Some aspects of change in the structure of the Muslim family in the Punjab under British rule.
B.Litt., Oxford, 1962.

775. AZIZ, K.K. British and Muslim India: a study of British public opinion vis-a-vis the development of Muslim nationalism in India 1905-1947.
Ph.D., Manchester, 1960.

776. BAHADOORSINGH, I.J. Communal representation and Indian self-government.
B.Litt., Oxford, 1944.

777. BOND, J.A. Islam in India since the partition of the subcontinent: issues in self definition.
M.Phil., Sussex, 1978.

778. CHUGTAI, M. Muslim politics in the Indo-Pakistan sub-continent, 1858-1916.
D.Phil., Oxford, 1961.

779. EADE, P.J.K. Identity amongst Muslims in West Bengal, India and its relationship with political, social and economic change.
B.Litt., Oxford, 1971.

780. GREWAL, J.S. British historical writing from Alexander Dow to Mountstuart Elphinstone on Muslim India.
Ph.D., School of Oriental and African Studies, London, 1963.

781. HASAN, M. The Indian National Congress and the Indian Muslims, 1916-1928.
Ph.D., Cambridge, 1977.

782. HUSSAIN, M.D. A study of nineteenth century historical work on Muslim rule in Bengal: Charles Stuart to Henry Beveridge.
M.Phil., School of Oriental and African Studies, London, 1976.

783. IQBAL, S.J. The development of Muslim political philosophy in Indo-Pakistan Subcontinent.
Ph.D., Cambridge, 1955.

784. KARIM, A.K.N. The modern Muslim political elite in Bengal.
Ph.D., London School of Economics and Political Science, 1965.

785. KHATOON, L. Some aspects of the social history of Bengal with special reference to the Muslims, 1854-1884.
M.A., School of Oriental and African Studies, London, 1956.

786. MITRA, M. Political propaganda and inter-communal relation in India, 1919-1947.
M.A., London School of Economics and Political Science, 1957.

Part 2: National and Regional Studies

787. NAHAR, S. Some aspects of the Hindu-Muslim relationship in India, 1876-1892.
M.Phil., School of Oriental and African Studies, London, 1967.

788. NAZ, S. Muslim politics in India 1857-1922 with special reference to the influence of Sir Syed Ahmad Khan.
B.Phil., St. Andrew's, 1969.

789. NOORUZZAMAN, A.H.M. Rise of the Muslim middle class as a political factor in India and Pakistan 1858-1947.
Ph.D., School of Oriental and African Studies, London, 1965.

790. PAGE, D.J.H. Prelude to partition: all India Moslem politics, 1920-1932.
D.Phil., Oxford, 1974.

791. RAHMAN, M. The All-India Muslim League in Indian politics 1906-1912.
Ph.D., School of Oriental and African Studies, London, 1968.

792. RIZVI, J.M. Muslim politics and government policy: studies in the development of Muslim organisation and its social background in North India and Bengal, 1885-1917.
Ph.D., Cambridge, 1969.

793. ROBINSON, F.C.R. The politics of U.P. Muslims, 1906-1922.
Ph.D., Cambridge, 1971.
(Uttar Pradesh)

794. SINGH, A.I. The origins of the partition of India, 1936-1947.
D.Phil., Oxford, 1981.

795. TALBOT, I.A. The growth of the Muslim League in the Punjab, 1937-1946.
Ph.D., Royal Holloway College, London, 1981.

796. WAHI, T. British scholarship on Muslim rule in India: the work of William Erskine, Sir Henry M. Elliot, John Dawson, Edward Thomas, J. Talboys Wheeler and Henry G. Keene.
Ph.D., School of Oriental and African Studies, London, 1975.

797. WASTI, S.R. Lord Minto and the Indian nationalist movement, with special reference to the political activities of Indian Muslims 1905-1910.
Ph.D., School of Oriental and African Studies, London, 1962.

798. ZAIDI, S.Z.H. The partition of Bengal and its annulment: a study of the schemes of territorial redistribution of Bengal 1902-1911.
Ph.D., School of Oriental and African Studies, London, 1965.

799. ZAKARIA, R.A. Muslims in India: a political analysis (from 1885-1906).
Ph.D., School of Oriental and African Studies, London, 1948.

c) Sikhs

800. BRIEF, D. The Punjab and recruitment to the Indian army, 1846-1918.
M.Litt., Oxford, 1979.

801. CHAUDHRI, J.J.M. A typical support structure of leadership in Punjab: the faction.
Ph.D., Manchester, 1969.

802. KAPUR, R.A. Religion and politics among the Sikhs in Punjab, 1873-1925.
D.Phil., Oxford, 1978.

d) Untouchables

803. KALOTA, R.S. A history of the education of the 'Shudra Untouchables' before and under the British rule in India 2000 B.C. to 1947 A.D.
M.Ed., Durham, 1950.

804. PARASHER, A. A study of attitudes towards 'Mlecchas' and other outsiders in Northern India (c.A.D. 600).
Ph.D., School of Oriental and African Studies, London, 1978.

805. SEN-GUPTA, L. Constitutional change and depressed classes: the representations from the depressed classes in the United Provinces to the Indian Statutory Commission, 1928, and their outcome.
M.A., Sussex, 1968.

806. SHARMA, R.S. The position of the S'udras in ancient India to A.D. 500.
Ph.D., School of Oriental and African Studies, London, 1956.

VIII. INDO-CHINA

807. MARGOT, A.G. The Chinese in Indo-China.
B.Litt., Oxford, 1970.

808. WALKER, A.R. The Laku of the Yunnan-Indochina borderlands: ethnic group and village community.
D.Phil., Oxford, 1973.

IX. INDONESIA

809. AWAR, K. Indonesian problems of development and use of a national language.
Ph.D., School of Oriental and African Studies, London, 1976.

X. JAPAN

810. KIM, O.P.M. Outcaste relations in four Japanese villages: a comparative study.
M.Litt., Oxford, 1979.
(A study of the Burakumin minority group.)

811. WEINER, M.A. The origins and early development of the Korean minority in Japan 1910-1925.
Ph.D., Sheffield, 1982.

XI. KOREA

812. KU, D.Y. Korean resistance to Japanese colonialism: the March First movement of 1919 and Britain's role in its outcome.
Ph.D., London School of Economics and Political Science, 1980.

XII. LAOS

813. DAVIS, G.E. External intervention and the mobilization of the ethnic minorities in Laos, 1945-1973.
Ph.D., London School of Economics and Political Science, 1975.

XIII. MALAYSIA

A. GENERAL STUDIES

814. ABDUAL RAZAK. A. The administration of Muslim law in Malaysia.
M.Phil., Kent, 1978.

815. ABRAHAM, C.E.R. Race relations in West Malaysia with special reference to modern political and economic development.
D.Phil., Oxford, 1976.

816. BUTCHER, J.G. A social history of the British in Malaya 1880-1941, with special reference to the Federated Malay States.
Ph.D., Hull, 1976.

817. DOBBY, E.H.C. The political geography of Malaya.
Ph.D., Birkbeck College, London, 1945.

818. FREEDMAN, M. A sociology of race relations in south east Asia with special reference to British Malaya.
M.A., London School of Economics and Political Science, 1948.

819. GHOSH, K.K. Decentralization of power in the Federated Malay States, 1920-1929.
Ph.D., School of Oriental and African Studies, London, 1977.

819A. HAMZAH, A.B. Al-Imam: its role in Malay society, 1906-1908.
M.Phil., Kent, 1981.

820. HARDSTONE, P.C.N. Malaysia: a case study in the creation of state nationalism.
Ph.D., Queen's University, Belfast, 1975.

Part 2: National and Regional Studies

821. JEYARATNAM, K. Communalism and the political process in the Federation of Malaya.
Ph.D., London School of Economics and Political Science, 1960.

822. KESSLER, C.S. Islam and politics in Malay society: Kelantan 1886-1969.
Ph.D., London School of Economics and Political Science, 1975.

823. LEE SOW LING Education and national unity in a bicultural society: Malaya.
M.Phil., Institute of Education, London, 1968.

824. NEMENZO, F. Revolution and counter-revolution: a study of British colonial policy as a factor in the growth and disintegration of national liberation movements in Burma and Malaya.
Ph.D., Manchester, 1965.

825. OSMAN, S. The national unity policy and ethnic relations in Malaysia, with special reference to Malacca town.
Ph.D., Bristol, 1981.

826. SAID, A.R. Solo legal practice in a changing Malaysian society: ethnic and class elements in lawyers' responses to state intervention.
Ph.D., Keele, 1979.

827. SAW, S.H. The demography of Malaya with special reference to race differentials.
Ph.D., London School of Economics and Political Science, 1963.

828. SHANG, A.E.L. Political development and class formation in an ethnically divided country: a case study of Peninsular Malaya before and after independence.
M.A., Sussex, 1976.

829. SIMANJUNTAK, B. Malayan federalism, 1945-1963: a study of federal problems in a plural society.
D.Phil., Oxford, 1966.

830. VILLIERS, C.S. Education and nation building in a plural society: the Malayan case.
M.A.(Econ.), Manchester, 1972.

831. WAN, A.H. bin, O. Ethnogenesis: a study of the Malayans of Peninsular Malaysia.
Ph.D., Bristol, 1980.

B. IMMIGRANTS AND MINORITIES

i) Chinese

832. EDMONDS, M.J. An anthropological study of the role of the Chinese in Malayan society since the end of Second World War.
M.A., London School of Economics and Political Science, 1967.

833. LEWIS, G.E.D. A comparative study of the intelligence and educability of Malays and Chinese in Malaya and its significance in relation to educational policy.
Ph.D., Institute of Education, London, 1949.

833A. NEWELL, W.H. A comparative study of informal relationships in a Chinese village in Malaya and North India.
Ph.D., Manchester, 1958.

834. TING, C.P. The Chinese in peninsular Malaysia: a study of race relations in a plural society.
Ph.D., Warwick, 1976.

ii) Indians

835. AMPALAVANAR, R. Politics and the Indian community in West Malaysia and Singapore, 1945-1957.
Ph.D., School of Oriental and African Studies, London, 1978.

836. CALMAN, D.A. Indian labour migration to Malaya, 1867-1910.
B.Litt., Oxford, 1955.

837. SANDHU, K.S. Indians in Malaya: some aspects of their arrival and settlement with special reference to the period of British rule, 1786-1957.
Ph.D., University College, London, 1966.

838. SELVARATNAM, V. Metropolitan control and South Indian proletariat on the Malaysian plantation frontier: the persistence and powerlessness of poverty.
Ph.D., Manchester, 1976.

iii) Indonesians

839. BAHRIN, T.S. The Indonesians in Malaya.
M.A., Sheffield, 1964.

iv) Thais

839A. KERSHAW, R.G. The Thais of Kelantan: a socio-political study of an ethnic outpost.
Ph.D., School of Oriental and African Studies, London, 1969.

XIV. MAURITIUS

840. DHANDA, P. History of Indian indentured immigration into Mauritius.
M.Phil., Birkbeck College, London, 1970.

XV. PAKISTAN

840A. ALI, M. Regionalism and political integration in Pakistan.
Ph.D., Edinburgh, 1971.

840B. HASAN, M. The transfer of power to Pakistan and its consequences.
Ph.D., Cambridge, 1967.

XVI. SINGAPORE

841. CHENG, L-K. The Chinese in Singapore: their socio-economic geography with special reference to Pang structure.
Ph.D., School of Oriental and African Studies, London, 1979.

842. DJAMOUR, J. The Malay family in Singapore.
Ph.D., London School of Economics and Political Science, 1955.

843. HUANG, S.K.S. Marriage and divorce in Singapore Chinese society - a Christian critique.
B.Phil., St Andrew's, 1973.

844. TOPLEY, M.D. The organisation and social function of Chinese women's Chai t'ang in Singapore.
Ph.D., London, External, 1958.

XVII. SRI LANKA

845. ARIYARATNE, R.A. Communal conflict in Ceylon politics and the advance towards self-government, 1917-1932.
Ph.D., Cambridge, 1973.

846. BANKS, M.Y. The social organisation of the Jaffna Tamils of North Ceylon with special reference to kinship, marriage and inheritance.
Ph.D., Cambridge, 1957.

847. DE SILVA, I.W. Cultural conflicts and education in Ceylon since independence.
Ph.D., London, External, 1971.

848. DUTTA, A. Effect of international labour migration on trade and real income: a case study of Ceylon, 1920-1938.
Ph.D., London School of Economics and Political Science, 1960.

849. FERNANDO, Q.G. The minorities in Ceylon 1926-1931 with special reference to the Donoughmore Commission.
Ph.D., London School of Oriental and African Studies, London, 1973.

850. GOONERATNE, D.D.M. The Sinhalese in Ceylon: a study in historical and social geography.
M.A., Liverpool, 1930.

851. GREENSTREET, D.K. The nationalist movement in Ceylon between 1910-1931 with special reference to communal and elective problems.
Ph.D., London School of Economics and Political Science, 1959.

852. INDRAPALA, K. Dravidian settlement in Ceylon and the beginnings of the kingdom of Jaffna.
Ph.D., School of Oriental and African Studies, London, 1966.

853. JAYASURIYA, T.D. The bilingual problem in Ceylon.
M.A., London, 1921.

854. LANGTON, P.J. Communities in Ceylon: the ethnic perspective on Sinhalese-Tamil relations.
M.Litt., Oxford, 1979.

855. SAVERIMUTTU, N.M. Relations between Roman Catholics and Hindus in Jaffna, Ceylon, 1900-1926: a study of religious encounter.
Ph.D., School of Oriental and African Studies, London, 1978.

856. STIRRAT, R.L. The kinship and social organisation of a Roman Catholic fishing village in Ceylon.
Ph.D., Cambridge, 1975.

857. WESUMPERUMA, D. The migration and conditions of immigrant labour in Ceylon 1880-1910.
Ph.D., School of Oriental and African Studies, London, 1975.

858. WILSON, S.J. Language policy and eduction: Ceylon.
M.Ed., Birmingham, 1962.

XVIII. THAILAND

858A. KUWINPANT, P. Marketing in north-central Thailand: a study of socio-economic organisation in a Thai market town.
Ph.D., Kent, 1977.
(includes a study of the role of the Chinese)

859. SAIHOO, P. Social organization of an inland Malay village community in Southern Thailand with emphasis on the pattern of leadership.
D.Phil., Oxford, 1974.

AUSTRALASIA

I. GENERAL STUDIES

860. FORSYTH, W.D. Migration to Australia and New Zealand: post war experience, present position and future possibilities.
B.Litt., Oxford, 1939.

II. AUSTRALIA

861. BALFOUR, R.A.C.S. Emigration from the Highlands and Western Islands of Scotland to Australia during the nineteenth century.
M.Litt., Edinburgh, 1973.

862. CROWLEY, F.K. British migration to Australia, 1860-1914.
D.Phil., Oxford, 1951.

863. GRAVES, A.A. Pacific Island labour in the Queensland sugar industry, 1862-1906.
D.Phil., Oxford, 1979.

864. HARRIS, M. British migration to Western Australia 1829-1850.
Ph.D., London School of Economics and Political Science, 1934.

865. MADGWICK, R.B. The quality of immigration into eastern Australia.
D.Phil., Oxford, 1935.

866. RICHARDSON, A. British emigrant to Australia: a study of some psycho-social differences between emigrant and non-emigrant skilled manual workers.
Ph.D., Bedford College, London, 1956.

866A. TAYLOR, G.P. Land policy and the development of settlement in Queensland, 1868-1894.
Ph.D., Birkbeck College, London, 1966.

III. NEW ZEALAND

867. BROWN, L.B. Some psychological characteristics of applicants for assisted emigration to New Zealand.
Ph.D., Bedford College, London, 1955.

868. CLEAVE, P.J. The language and political interests of Maori and Pakeha communities in New Zealand in the nineteenth century.
D.Phil., Oxford, 1979.

869. COURIE, J.A. The effect of civilization on the Maori race with special reference to health and disease.
M.D., Glasgow, 1913.

870. DALTON, B.J. The control of native affairs in New Zealand: a constitutional experiment and its consequences, 1855-1870.
D.Phil., Oxford, 1956.

Part 2: National and Regional Studies

871. GREVILLE, S.E. Briton and Maori: a comparative study of the relations between the races 1840-1848.
M.A., London, 1910.

872. HARRÉ, J.N.
Māori-Pākehaā mixed marriages in New Zealand.
Ph.D., London School of Economics and Political Science, 1964.

872A. HOPA, N.K. The 'Rangatira' or chief in traditional Maori society.
B.Litt., Oxford, 1966.

872B. HOPA, N.K. Urban Maori sodalities: a study in social change.
D.Phil., Oxford, 1977.

873. MADDEN, A.F. The influence of the evangelical spirit on a policy of trusteeship towards native races, as illustrated by the records of certain missionary societies dealing with New Zealand, 1814-1854.
B.Litt., Oxford, 1939.

873A. METGE, A.J. The changing structure of Maori society: a study in social process in urban and rural areas of northern New Zealand.
Ph.D., London School of Economics and Political Science, 1958.

874. TURNBULL, M.R.M. The colonisation of New Zealand by the New Zealand Company (1839-1843): a study of the Wakefield system in operation including some comparison with emigration to other Australasian colonies.
B.Litt., Oxford, 1951.

875. WINIATA, W. The changing role of the leader in Maori society: a study in social change and race relations.
Ph.D., Edinburgh, 1955.

IV. PACIFIC ISLANDS AND PACIFIC OCEAN REGION

876. ASHTON, C.P.M. The study of European colonial and ruling minorities: with special reference to the Australians of Papua and New Guinea.
B.Litt., Oxford, 1969.

877. BICKERTON, Y.J. Alcoholism and ethnicity in Hawaii.
D.Phil., Sussex, 1975.

878. ELLISS, J.D. Some problems concerning the Chinese in Oceania.
M.A., London School of Economics and Political Science, 1956.

879. FIRTH, S.G. German recruitment and employment of labourers in the Western Pacific before the First World War.
D.Phil., Oxford, 1972.

880. HEMPENSTALL, P.J. Indigenous resistance to German rule in the Pacific colonies of Samoa, Ponape, and New Guinea, 1884-1914.
D.Phil., Oxford, 1974.

881. HUGHES, C.A.A. Racial issues in Fiji.
D.Phil., Oxford, 1965.

882. INGLIS, C.B. Social structure and patterns of economic action: the Chinese in Papua New Guinea.
Ph.D., London School of Economics and Political Science, 1978.

883. KESBY, J.D. British missionaries in the South west Pacific, 1842-1900; their policies and evaluation with regard to the indigenous people.
B.Litt., Oxford, 1963.

884. MACCLANCY, J.V. Issues in the analysis of the ethnography of the New Hebrides.
B.Litt., Oxford, 1978.

885. MA'IA'I, F. Bilingualism in Western Samoa: its problems and implications for education.
Ph.D., Institute of Education, London, 1960.

886. MAYER, A.C. Indian rural society in Fiji.
Ph.D., London School of Economics and Political Science, 1953.

887. MOHAN, M. Demographic structure in Fiji Island.
B.Litt., Oxford, 1964.

888. PARNABY, O.W. The policy of the Imperial Government towards the recruitment and use of Pacific Island labour with special reference to Queensland, 1863-1901.
D.Phil., Oxford, 1953.

889. SHEPPARD, C.A. The Cook Islands through European eyes: an assessment of the evidence.
B.Litt., Oxford, 1972.

890. TREAIS-SMART, D.J. United States policy in the Pacific area, 1898-1922 with special reference to China and the Open Door.
M.A., Birmingham, 1956.

891. WILKINSON, J.F. A study of a political and religious division of Tanna, New Hebrides.
Ph.D., Cambridge, 1979.
(Study of the rivalry between Presbyterian Church and the Cargo cult in the Island.)

CARIBBEAN

I. GENERAL STUDIES

892. ALLEN, T.N. The Caribbean and Bermuda: a British frontier of settlement 1600-1700.
M.Phil., Birkbeck College, London, 1979.

893. FARQUHAR, D. Christian missions in the Leeward Islands, 1810-50: an ecclesiastical and social analysis.
D.Phil., Oxford, 1972.

894. GULLICK, C.J.M.R. The changing society of the black Caribs: a study of the origins, and political, economic and social history up to 1960 of a minority group namely those Black Caribs who originated in St. Vincents and were deported to Ruatan and thence spread along the Central American coast as far as the Mosquito Coast and British Honduras.
B.Litt., Oxford, 1970.

895. PAYNE, A.J. The position of the Caribbean community, 1961-1976: regional integration in the third world.
Ph.D., Manchester, 1978.

896. RIVIERE, W.E. The emergence of free-labour economy in the British West Indies, 1800-1850.
Ph.D., Cambridge, 1962.

897. ROMAIN, R.I. Negro education in the British West Indies: attitudes and policy after emancipation, 1834-1850.
Ph.D., Cambridge, 1962.

II. BARBADOS

898. BECKLES, McD. Indentured and free labour in Barbados, 1660-1750.
Ph.D., Hull, 1980.

898A. BELLE, G.A.V. The politics of development: a study in the political economy of Barbados.
Ph.D., Manchester, 1977.
(includes a study of attempts by the planters to maintain the old order after the abolition of the slave economy.)

III. BERMUDA

899. BYRON, M.T. An interpretative analysis of the origin, growth and social significance of Bermuda's bi-racial school system with a comparative reference to integrated education in the United States of America and the British West Indies.
M.A., London, External, 1959.

IV. CUBA

900. MARTINEZ-ALIER, V. Marriage class and colour in nineteenth century Cuba.
D.Phil., Oxford, 1971.

V. DESIRADÉ (GUADELOUPE)

901. NAISH, J.M. Race and rank in a Caribbean island: Desiradé.
Ph.D., University College, London, 1975.

GUYANA (See under Latin America)

VI. HAITI

902. GEGGUS, D.P. The British occupation of Saint-Dominigue, 1793-98.
D.Phil., York, 1979.

VII. JAMAICA

902A. BRATHWAITE, E. The development of the Creole community in Jamaica, 1770-1820.
D.Phil., Sussex, 1968.

903. CAMPBELL, M.C. Edward Jordon and the free coloureds: Jamaica, 1800-1865.
Ph.D., London, External, 1972.

904. CATHERALL, G.A. British Baptist involvement in Jamaica, 1783-1865.
Ph.D., Keele, 1971.

905. DUNCKER, S.J. The free coloured and their fight for civil rights, Jamaica, 1800-1830.
M.A., London, External, 1961.

906. HALL, D.G.H. The economic development of the British West Indies, 1790-1850 with special reference to the transition from slave to free labour in Jamaica.
M.Sc.(Econ.), London School of Economics and Political Science, 1952.

907. HENRIQUES, L.F. The social structure of Jamaica with special reference to racial distinctions.
D.Phil., Oxford, 1948.

908. KILPATRICK, J.W. Protestant missions in Jamaica being a critical survey of mission policy from 1754 to the present day.
Ph.D., Edinburgh, 1944.

909. KIRK-DUNCAN, B.A.C. The origins and development of the Church of England in Jamaica to 1916.
Ph.D., Trinity College, Dublin, 1964.

910. LONG, A.V. Post-emancipation problems in Jamaica, 1838-47.
B.Litt., Oxford, 1952.

911. RAMSELL, P.J. Jamaica - place of exile: the Ras Tafarians and emergent ideologies in West Kingston.
M.A., Manchester, 1977.

912. RECKORD, M. Missionary activity in Jamaica before emancipation.
Ph.D., King's College, London, 1964.

VIII. TRINIDAD

913. BECKLES, G.L.A. The prevalence of characteristics referrant of cardio-vascular disease among urban women of different ethnic origins: Trinidad.
M.Sc., Wales (School of Medicine), 1982.

914. CARTER, S.P.A. Social attitudes of Trinidad youth: a study of ethnic and social awareness.
Ph.D., Bedford College, London, 1979.

915. GOODENOUGH, S.S. Race, status and residence, Port of Spain, Trinidad.
Ph.D., Liverpool, 1976.

916. GOODRIDGE, C.A. Land, labour and immigration in Trinidad, 1783-1833.
Ph.D., Cambridge, 1970.

917. LAURENCE, K.M. Spanish in Trinidad: survival of a minority language in a multilingual society.
Ph.D., London, External, 1970.

918. LAURENCE, K.O. Immigration into Trinidad and British Guiana, 1834-1871.
Ph.D., Cambridge, 1958.

919. MALIK, Y.K. East Indians in Trinidad: a study in minority politics.
D.Phil., Oxford, 1971.

920. MOHAMMED, N. Indian indentured immigration into the West Indies 1870-90 with particular reference to Trinidad.
M.A., London, 1974.

Part 2: National and Regional Studies

921. NEWSON, L.A. Aboriginal and Spanish colonial Trinidad: a study in cultural evolution.
Ph.D., University College, London, 1972.

922. SHIELS, R. Indentured immigration into Trinidad, 1891-1916.
B.Litt., Oxford, 1968.

923. WINFORD, D. Sociolinguistic description of two communities in Trinidad.
D.Phil., York, 1972.

EUROPE

I. GENERAL STUDIES

924. CASTLES, G. & CASTLES, S. Immigrant workers and class structure in Western Europe.
D.Phil., Sussex, 1971.

925. ERGUN, T. Some economic implications of migration to Western Europe since 1945, with special reference to Turkey.
M.Sc., Loughborough, 1975.

926. HUMPHREYS, V.E. Social security for migrant workers in the European Community.
L.L.M., Wales (Aberystwyth), 1975.

927. KNOWLES, F.E. Linguistic and ethnic minorities in Central and Eastern Europe with special reference to the history of the German language since the Second World War.
M.Sc., Salford, 1967.

II. AUSTRIA/AUSTRO-HUNGARIAN EMPIRE

928. HANAK, H.H. British opinion about the dissolution of the Hapsburg monarchy and independence for the Czecks and Slovaks, 1914-1918.
M.A., School of Slavonic and South Eastern European Studies, London, 1959.

929. OKEY, R.F.C. Cultural and political problems of the Austro-Hungarian administration of Bosnia-Herzegovina.
D.Phil., Oxford, 1972.

930. OKLADEK, F. The return movement of Jews to Austria (with special reference to the return of Jews from Israel).
M.Sc., London, External, 1965.

931. THEOBALD, J.R.P. The response of the Jewish intelligentsia to Vienna to the rise of anti-Semitism with special reference to Karl Kraus.
Ph.D., Southampton, 1975.

III. CYPRUS

932. BAHCHELI, T.S. Communal discord and stake of interested governments in Cyprus 1955-1970.
Ph.D., London School of Economics and Political Science, 1973.

932A. DIKIGOROPOULOS, A.I. Cyprus "betwixt Greeks and Saracens", A.D. 147-965.
D.Phil., Oxford, 1962.

933. SANT CASSIA, P. Patterns of politics and kinship in a Greek-Cypriot community, 1920-1980.
Ph.D., Cambridge, 1982.
(Paphos)

Part 2: National and Regional Studies

IV. CZECHOSLOVAKIA

934. APPLEBY, B.L. The relations between the Slovaks and the central government of the First Czechoslovak Republic 1918-1938.
M.Litt., Glasgow, 1975.

935. GUY, D.E. The attempt of Socialist Czechoslovakia to assimilate its gypsy population.
Ph.D., Bristol, 1977.

936. RIFF, M.A. The assimilation of the Jews of Bohemia and the rise of political anti-Semitism, 1848-1918.
Ph.D., School of Slavonic and South Eastern European Studies, London, 1975.

937. ROSAK, E. Czech-Slovak relations from 1896 to 1914.
Ph.D., London, 1982.

938. SKILLING, H.G. The German-Czech national conflict in Bohemia, 1879-1893.
Ph.D., School of Slavonic and East European Studies, London, 1940.

939. WALLACE, L.V. The Czech exiles and the Thirty Years' War.
M.A., School of Slavonic and South Eastern European Studies, London, 1953.

940. ZEMAN, Z.A.B. The Czechs and the Hapsburg Monarchy, 1914-1918.
D.Phil., Oxford, 1956.

V. DENMARK

941. DJURSAA, M. Danish Nazism: the membership of 'Danmarks National Socialistiske Arbedjer Parti', 1930-1945.
Ph.D., Essex, 1979.

VI. FINLAND

942. GRÖNFORS, M.J. Finnish gypsies and the police: an examination of a racial minority and its relationship with law enforcement agents.
Ph.D., London School of Economics and Political Science, 1979.

943. INGOLD, T. The social organisation of a Finnish Lapp community: the Skolts of Sevettijärvi.
Ph.D., Cambridge, 1976.

VII. FRANCE

944. CALMANN, M.J. The carrière at Carpentras.
M.A., Warwick, 1977.
(A study of the Jewish ghetto in Carpentras, Provence)

945. GRIFFIN, C.C.M. Italians into south-east France.
D.Phil., Sussex, 1974.

946. HAINSWORTH, P.A. The policy of the Communist Party (P.C.F.) towards Catholics in France 1958-1967.
Ph.D., Bristol, 1976.

947. JONES, A.M. Spatial and social mobility of foreign immigrants in Marseilles 1962-1975.
D.Phil., Oxford, 1980.

947A. JONES, P.C. The segregation and integration of provincial and international migrants in Lyon, France, 1962-1975.
Ph.D., Sheffield, 1982.

948. KOHNSTAMM, J. Family structure and behaviour and ghetto life in the Jewish community of L'Isle-sur-Sorgue, 1680-1780.
Ph.D., East Anglia, 1982.

949. LOVECY, J. Regionalism, regional development politics and the 'economic concertée': a case study of Brittany.
D.Phil., Sussex, 1980.

949A. McCEARNEY, J. The writing of a reactionary: Charles Maurras until 1900.
Ph.D., Glasgow, 1974.

950. MELOT, S.M. The political outlook of Drieu La Rochelle, 1930-1945.
M.Litt., Bristol, 1976.
(A fascist thinker and writer.)

951. NICHOLLS, D.J. The origins of Protestantism in Normandy: a social study.
Ph.D., Birmingham, 1977.

952. OTT, S.J. An ethnographic study of a French Basque mountain community.
D.Phil., Oxford, 1978.
(Saint-Engrâce, Seule Province)

953. RABINOWITZ, L.I. The social life of the Jews of Northern France in the XII-XIV centuries as reflected in the rabbinical literature of the period.
Ph.D., London, External, 1937.

954. WHITE, A.W.J. North African immigration to the Paris region, 1946-1975: the housing problem.
M.Phil., Queen Mary College, London, 1981.

955. WEINTRAUB, F.J. Aesthetics and politics in the works of Charles Maurras.
Ph.D., Nottingham, 1978.

VIII. GERMANY

956. APPLEGATE, J.M. Sociolinguists and National Socialism: an historical study of English language writing on the sociology of National Socialism 1933-1945.
B.Litt., Oxford, 1975.

957. BILLINGHAM, A.L. The Silesian expellees in West Germany, 1945-1959.
M.A., Birmingham, 1961.

958. BUSS, P.H. The non-Germans in the German armed forces, 1939-1945.
M.A., Kent, 1975.

959. CARR, W. The development of the consciousness of German nationality in Schleswig-Holstein, 1815-1848.
Ph.D., Sheffield, 1955.

960. CLARK, R.I. Neo-Nazism in West Germany.
M.Phil., Aston, 1981.

961. CONWAY, I.C. The educational role of the Hitlerjugend movement in Germany, 1922-1945.
M.A., Sheffield, 1973.

962. DICKINS, E.P. The attitudes of three writers of 'Innere Emigration' to national socialism: Emil Wiechert, Werner Bergengruen and Erich Kästner.
Ph.D., Keele, 1974.

963. FRIEDMAN, I. Germany and Zionism, 1897-1917.
Ph.D., London School of Economics and Political Science, 1965.

964. GOTLIEB, H.B. England and the nature of the Nazi regime: a critical assessment of British opinion, 1933-1939.
D.Phil., Oxford, 1953.

965. HUTCHINSON, G.P. The Nazi ideology of Alfred Rosenberg: a study of his thought, 1917-1946.
D.Phil., Oxford, 1977.

966. JENSEN-BUTLER, B.B. Theories of fascism: a study of some interpretations of the rise of the Nazi Party in Germany.
M.A., Durham, 1974.

967. KING, C.E. Minor Christian religious groups in the Third Reich: their strategies for survival.
Ph.D., C.N.A.A., 1980.

968. MARA, P. German education under National Socialism (1933-1939): its historical determinants.
M.A., London, External, 1972.

969. MASON, T.W. National Socialist policy towards the working classes in Germany before 1939.
D.Phil., Oxford, 1972.

970. MÜHLBERGER, D.W. The rise of National Socialism in Westphalia, 1920-1933.
Ph.D., School of Slavonic and South Eastern European Studies, London, 1975.

971. NOAKES, J.D. The N.S.D.A.P. in lower Saxony, 1921-1933: a study of National Socialist organisation and propaganda.
D.Phil., Oxford, 1968.

971A. OKADA, K. The Labour movement's reaction to Hitler.
M.Phil., Sheffield, 1982.

972. PRIDHAM, G.F.M. The National Socialist Party in Southern Bavaria, 1925-1933: a study of its development in a predominantly Roman Catholic area.
Ph.D., School of Slavonic and South Eastern European Studies, London, 1969.

973. PULZER, P.G.J. Anti-Semitism in Germany and Austria, 1867-1918.
Ph.D., Cambridge, 1960.

Part 2: National and Regional Studies

974. REICHMANN, E.G. The social sources of National Socialist anti-Semitism.
Ph.D., London School of Economics and Political Science, 1945.

975. RIDLEY, H.M. National socialism and literature: a study of five authors in search of an ideology.
Ph.D., Cambridge, 1968.

976. SLOAN, K. Education in Nazi Germany, 1933-1945.
M.Phil., Leeds, 1972.

977. TAYLOR, J.A. The Third Reich in German drama, 1933-1936.
Ph.D., Birkbeck College, London, 1978.

978. TAYLOR, S. The Thousand Year Reich: a critique of millenarian interpretation of National Socialism.
Ph.D., Liverpool, 1980.

979. WELLS, A.R. German public opinion and Hitler's policies, 1933-9.
M.A., Durham, 1968.

979A. WHEELER, L.M. The S.S. and the administration of Nazi-occupied eastern Europe, 1939-45.
D.Phil., Oxford, 1981.

980. WILLIAMSON, R.J. Alternative strategies?: reactions in the two Germanies to the World Council of Churches' programme to combat racism, 1969-1975.
Ph.D., Birmingham, 1981.

981. WILMOT, L.H. National Socialist youth organisations for girls: a contribution to the social and political history of the Third Reich.
D.Phil., Oxford, 1980.

982. WISELEY, W.C. The German settlement of the 'incorporated territories' of the Wartheland and Danzig-West Prussia, 1939-45.
Ph.D., School of Slavonic and East European Studies, London, 1955.

983. WISTRICH, R.S. Socialism and the Jewish question in Germany and Austria, 1880-1914.
Ph.D., University College, London, 1975.

IX. GREAT BRITAIN

A. GENERAL STUDIES

a) Emigration

984. BASTIN, R. Cunard and the Liverpool emigrant traffic, 1860-1900.
M.A., Liverpool, 1971.

985. CARROTHERS, W.A. Emigration from the British Isles, 1815-1921.
Ph.D., Edinburgh, 1921.

986. CLEMENTS, R.V. English trade unions and the problem of emigration, 1840-1880.
B.Litt., Oxford, 1954.

987. JOHNSTON, H.J.M. The emigration policies and experiments of the British Government after the Napoleonic Wars, 1815-1830.
Ph.D., King's College, London, 1970.

988. JONES, M.A. The role of the United Kingdom in the transatlantic emigrant trade, 1815-1875.
D.Phil., Oxford, 1956.

989. PAGE, N.M.G. A study of emigration from Great Britain, 1802 to 1860.
Ph.D., London School of Economics and Political Science, 1931.

990. SCHOLES, A.G. Education for Empire settlement: a study of juvenile migration.
Ph.D., Edinburgh, 1930.

991. WERTIMER, S. Migration from the United Kingdom to the Dominions in the inter-war period with special reference to the Empire Settlement Act of 1922.
Ph.D., London School of Economics and Political Science, 1952.

b) Medieval and Early Modern Immigrant Communities and English attitudes

992. AILES, J.A. Foreign Protestant communities under the law, 1570-1630.
M.Phil., Kent, 1978.
(French, Dutch & Walloon Communities in England)

993. ALJUBOURI, D.A.H. The medieval idea of the Saracen as illustrated in English literature, spectacle and sport.
Ph.D., Leicester, 1972.

994. BALLENTYNE, A.W.G. 'Gerardus de Atyes et tota sequela': a study into the establishment in thirteenth century England of a 'notorious body of foreigners'.
M.Litt., Cambridge, 1979.

995. BEARDWOOD, A. The position of foreign merchants in England at the time of Edward III mainly from the legal standpoint.
B.Litt., Oxford, 1927.

996. BEARDWOOD, A. The legal and economic relations between alien merchants and the central government in England 1350-77.
D.Phil., Oxford, 1929.

997. BOLTON, J.L. Alien merchants in England in the reign of Henry VII, 1422-1461.
B.Litt., Oxford, 1971.

998. BRATCHEL, M.E. Alien merchant communities in London, 1500-1550.
Ph.D., Cambridge, 1975.

999. KNIGHT, M.J. Aliens in English politics, 1204-1224.
M.A., Nottingham, 1959.

1000. ROKER, L.F. The Flemish and Dutch community in Colchester in the sixteenth and seventeenth centuries.
M.A., London, External, 1963.

1001. RUSSELL, E. The societies of Bardi and Peruzzi and their dealings with Edward III.
M.A., Manchester, 1912.

1002. SCOULOUDI, I. Alien immigration into and alien communities in London 1558 to 1640.
M.Sc., London School of Economics and Political Science, 1936.

1003. WILLIAMS, L.H. The alien contribution to the social and economic development of England and Wales in the sixteenth century.
M.A., Wales, 1953.

1004. WYATT, T.G. The part played by aliens in the social and economic life of England during the reign of Henry VIII.
M.A., Birkbeck College, London, 1952.

c) Politics, Law and Race Relations

(i) General Studies

1004A. BROWNE, S.A. Freedom of movement of aliens and Commonwealth citizens in English law.
L.L.M., Southampton, 1965

1005. CARSON, J. The law in British race relations: an analysis of the political background to immigration and anti-discrimination legislation and some proposals for statutory reform.
B.Litt., Oxford, 1971.

1006. DEAKIN, N. The immigration issue in British politics, 1948-1964, with special reference to three selected areas.
D.Phil., Sussex, 1973.
(Southall, Brixton, Stepney)

1007. DICKEY, A.F. Organised racial incitement and the law in England, 1945-1965.
Ph.D., Kent, 1973.

1008. DUNCAN, N.C. British party attitudes to immigration and race with particular reference to special areas, 1955-1971.
Ph.D., Manchester, 1977.

1009. DUNN, R. Coloured immigrants and elections in Britain: case studies of Birmingham and Inner London.
M.A.*, Lancaster, 1972.

1010. GAINER, B. The alien invasion: the origins of the Aliens Act.
Ph.D., Cambridge, 1969.

1011. GREENWOOD, P.N. The English stereotype of the Scottish, Welsh and Irish.
M.Sc., Exeter, 1978.

1012. LITTLE, K.L. The anthropology of some coloured communities in Great Britain with comparative material on colour prejudice.
Ph.D., London, 1945.

1012A. SILVERSTEEN, R.A. A critical analysis of the justifications for limitations on freedom of expression under the incitement to racial hatred section of the Race Relations Act, 1976.
M.Phil., Oxford, 1980.

1013. WALKER, I. An analysis of questions in the House of Commons in the fields of race relations and Commonwealth immigration, 1959-1964.
M.Sc., Bradford, 1974.

(ii) Fascist and Right-Wing Political Movements and ideas

1014. BAKER, D.L. The making of a British fascist: the case of A.K. Chesterton.
Ph.D., Sheffield, 1982.

1015. BENEWICK, R.J. The British Fascist movement, 1932-1940: its development and significance.
Ph.D., Manchester, 1964.

1016. BREWER, J.D. The British Union of Fascists, Sir Oswald Mosley and Birmingham: an analysis of the content and context of an ideology.
M.Soc.Sc., Birmingham, 1976.

1017. FIELDING, N.G. The National Front: a sociological study of political organisation and identity.
Ph.D., London School of Economics and Political Science, 1977.

1018. MARSH, Q.R.H. The National Front, 1976-1977.
M.Phil., Bradford, 1978.

1019. MORRELL, J.E. Arnold Leese: his life and work, his ideas and his place in British Fascism.
M.A., Sheffield, 1975.

1020. RAWNSLEY, S.J. Fascism and Fascists in Britain in the 1930s: a case study of Fascism in the North of England in a period of economic and political change.
Ph.D., Bradford, 1982.

1021. SCHOEN, D.E. Enoch Powell and Powellism, 1962-1975.
D.Phil., Oxford, 1976.

(iii) Pressure Groups

1022. HEINEMAN, B.W. The campaign against racial discrimination.
B.Litt., Oxford, 1968.

1023. MULLARD, C.P. Race, power and resistance: a study of the Institute of Race Relations, 1952-1972.
Ph.D., Durham, 1980.

1024. WILLMINGTON, S. The activities of the Aborigines' Protection Society as a pressure group on the formulation of colonial policy, 1868-1880.
Ph.D., Wales (Lampeter), 1973.

(iv) Media

1025. DOWNING, J.D.H. Some aspects of the presentation of industrial relations and race relations in some major British news media.
Ph.D., London, External, 1975.

1026. MACKELVIE, M.J. The treatment of the Brixton riots in a selection of British newspapers 11/4/81-18/4/81.
M.A.*, Sheffield, 1982.

1027. NICHOLSON, J.R. An imperial frame of mind: imperialist and racialist attitudes in the British periodical press, 1851-1914.
Ph.D., Keele, 1982.

d) Regional Studies

1028. ATKINSON, A.M. Coloured immigrants and their families: a study of assimilation in an inner urban area of Newcastle-upon-Tyne.
M.Ed., Newcastle, 1972.

1029. BENSON, S.W. Inter-racial households in a multi-ethnic community.
Ph.D., Cambridge, 1975.
(Mixed marriages in Brixton)

1030. BIRKS, D.M. Some aspects of the geography of coloured immigrants in Bradford.
M.Phil., Hull, 1979.

1031. BUCKMAN, J. The economic and social history of alien immigrants to Leeds, 1880-1914.
Ph.D., Strathclyde, 1968.

1032. DIMMOCK, G.W. Racial hostility in Britain with particular reference to the disturbances in Cardiff and Liverpool in 1919.
M.A.*, Sheffield, 1976.

1033. DOHERTY, J.M. Immigrants in London: a study of the relationship between spatial structure and the social structure.
Ph.D., London School of Economics and Political Science, 1973.

1034. ELDRIDGE, J.E.T. Race relations in Leicester University.
M.A., Leicester, 1959.
(study of race relations in the student body)

1035. HITCH, P.J. Migration and illness in a northern city: an investigation into the relationship between ethnic group membership, area of residence, residential mobility, social class and hospitalisation for diagnosed mental disorder.
Ph.D., Bradford, 1975.

1036. JOHNSON, A.W. Metropolitan areas and racial discrimination.
M.A., Southampton, 1973.

1037. KING, J.R. Immigrants in Leeds: an investigation into their socio-economic characteristics, spatial distribution, fertility trends and population growth.
Ph.D., Leeds, 1977.

1038. LAWRENCE, D. Black migrants: white natives: a study of race relations in Nottingham.
Ph.D., Nottingham, 1975.

1039. MANYONI, J.R. Ethnic and cultural minorities in Reading: a study of social relations and status of minority groups in an English town.
B.Litt., Oxford, 1969.

1040. PICKARD, O.G. Midland immigrations.
M.Com., Birmingham, 1940.

1041. PRATT, M.J. Mugging as a social problem: an analysis of this form of robbery with particular reference to the Metropolitan Police District.
Ph.D., Birkbeck College, London, 1979.

1042. SARRAFF, R.G. New ethnic minorities and planning sensitivity.
M.Sc., Strathclyde, 1978.
(Inner city planning and coloured immigrants.)

1043. WOOD, G.J. The Commonwealth Citizens' Advisory Panel of the Bradford Problem and After-Care Service.
M.Sc., Bristol, 1972.

e) Employment and industry

1043A. ANISULOWO, S.A. Cyclical variations in industrial accidents among immigrant workers in Great Britain.
M.Soc.Sc.*, Birmingham, 1969.

1044. AURORA, G.S. Indian workers in England: a sociological and historical survey.
M.Sc.(Econ.), London School of Economics and Political Science, 1960.

1045. DESAI, R.H. The social organisation of Indian migrant labour in the United Kingdom with special reference to the Midlands.
M.A., School of Oriental and African Studies, London, 1960.

1046. DESAI, R.H. Some aspects of social relations between the Indian immigrants in the United Kingdom and the host society with particular reference to economic activities.
Ph.D., School of Oriental and African Studies, London, 1962.

1047. DEX, S. British black and white young employment differentials: an application of Markov chains to socio-economic process.
Ph.D., Keele, 1977.

1048. FOSSICK, S. Factors affecting the distribution of coloured immigrants in industry in Birmingham.
M.Soc.Sc., Birmingham, 1966.

1049. MSGENA, B.V. Black immigrants in the British labour market.
Ph.D., Bath, 1980.

1050. PATTERSON, S. Immigrants in industry.
Ph.D., London School of Economics and Political Science, 1970.

1051. WRIGHT, P.L. The coloured worker in British industry with special reference to the Midlands and North of England.
Ph.D., Edinburgh, 1966.

Part 2: National and Regional Studies

f) Housing

1052. FLEISS, A. The importance of owner-occupation: housing and the immigrant community in Gravesend.
D.Phil., Sussex, 1974.

1053. FLETT, H. Black people and council housing: a study of Manchester.
Ph.D., Bristol, 1980.

1054. LEE, T.R. Concentration and dispersal: a study of West Indian residential patterns in London, 1961-1971.
Ph.D., School of Oriental and African Studies, London, 1975.

1055. LORD, A.H. Housing of Asians in Wardleworth: a study of the effects of Asian immigration on Wardleworth, an older residential area of Rochdale.
M.Sc., Salford, 1975.

1056. STAFFORD, F.A. Housing policies and the coloured immigrant: a study of North Westminster.
M.Sc., Edinburgh, 1970.

1057. WARD, R.H. Residential succession and race relations in Moss Side Manchester.
Ph.D., Manchester, 1975.

g) Educational issues

(i) General and comparative studies

1058. ANKRAH-DOVE, L. Social and political orientation of adolescents in London secondary schools with special reference to immigrants.
Ph.D., School of Oriental and African Studies, London, 1975.

1059. BATE, W. An examination of personality variables and teacher attitudes amongst British, Malay, Chinese and Indian student teachers.
M.Ed., Bristol, 1970.

1060. BHATNAGAR, J.K. A study of the adjustment of immigrant children in a London school.
Ph.D., Institute of Education, London, 1969.

1061. BRAZIL, D.E. The effect of the community school on parental attitudes to a multi-racial school in an educational priority area.
M.Ed., Birmingham, 1976.

1062. CARNIE, J.W. The development of junior school children's ideas of people of different race and nation.
Ph.D., London, External, 1972.

1063. CHAPLEN, E.F. The identification of non-native speakers of English likely to under-achieve in university courses through inadequate command of the language.
Ph.D., Manchester, 1971.

1064. CLARE, D.W. A comparative study of public library provision for immigrant communities in some towns of the West Midlands.
M.A.*, Sheffield, 1975.

1065. D'SOUZA, M.B. Intergroup attitude of adolescents in multi-ethnic schools of London.
D.Phil., Oxford, 1977.

1066. DURKACZ, V.E. Language in Celtic education: a comparative view of the language question, Gaelic, Irish and Welsh, 1688-1872.
Ph.D., Dundee, 1980.

1067. DUROJAIYE, S.M. A comparison of the spoken English of some West Indian and Asian immigrant secondary pupils with that of their English schoolmates.
M.Ed., Manchester, 1968.

1068. ELZUBEIR, M.A. Correlates of ethnic minority school performance: a case study of West Indian and Asian pupils attending a Welsh comprehensive school.
Ph.D., Wales (Cardiff), 1982.

1069. FEAKES, B.A. A study in the changing of attitudes towards foreign people by educational means.
M.A., Institute of Education, London, 1953.

1070. FINER, A.R. A preliminary comparative study of the motor development of infants and children born in Britain of West Indian, Indian and English parents.
M.Sc., Leicester, 1974.

1071. GLOVER, D. Roman Catholic education and the state: a sociological analysis.
Ph.D., Sheffield, 1979.

1072. GRUBB, M. Analysis of career advisory service records on immigrant school-leavers.
M.Sc., Keele, 1973.

1073. HAMMOND, H.K. Overseas students in Wolverhampton: an enquiry into the social adjustment and attitudes of selected students.
M.A., Nottingham, 1971.

1074. HARTLEY, H.P. A psychological investigation of the self-concept of a selected group of immigrant and British adolescents.
M.Ed., Birmingham, 1977.

1075. HILL, D. Attitudes of ethnic minorities in Britain among adolescents.
Ph.D., Birmingham, 1974.

1076. HILTON, J. The employment expectations and aspirations of white and coloured school-leavers in the Manchester area.
M.A., Manchester, 1972.

1077. HOLES, C.D. An investigation into some aspects of the English language problems of two groups of overseas postgraduate students at Birmingham University.
M.A., Birmingham, 1973.

1078. IDRUS, F. The problems of overseas students in further education.
M.Ed., Aberdeen, 1975.

1079. JONES, H.K. Some problems of the education of immigrant children in Bradford.
M.A., London, External, 1970.

1080. KANDELA, R.E. The transition from school to work: the job aspirations and employment situation of a group of immigrant school leavers.
M.Phil., Leicester, 1977.

1081. LEDERMAN, S. An investigation into some factors relevant to the social acceptance of immigrant boys in secondary schools.
M.A., Institute of Education, London, 1968.

1082. LOUDEN, D.M. A comparative study of self-concept, self-esteem and locus of control in minority group adolescents in English multi-racial schools.
Ph.D., Bristol, 1977.

1082A. LUCAS, F.E. Playmate choice and language usage in infant schools with differing immigrant intakes.
M.Ed., Manchester, 1971.

1083. MACDONALD, M.I. Language acquisition by a multi-cultural group: a comparative study of a sample of Jamaican, Greek, Turkish and British students attending a London College of Further Education in an attempt to assess their progress in achieving a command of standard British English.
Ph.D., Institute of Education, London, 1975.

1084. McLEAN, A.C. The use of television in the teaching of English to immigrant children.
M.Litt., Strathclyde, 1974.

1085. MARETT, V.P. Immigrants in further education colleges.
M.Ed., Leicester, 1976.

1086. MARSTERS, T.L. A critical account of the provision made in the United Kingdom for overseas students coming to improve their English.
M.Phil., Institute of Education, London, 1968.

1087. MARVELL, J. Religious beliefs and moral values of immigrant children.
M.Ed., Leicester, 1973.

1088. MILLER, H.J. A study of the effectiveness of a variety of teaching techniques for reducing colour prejudice in a male student sample (aged to 21).
M.Phil., Institute of Education, London, 1968.

1089. MOORES, K. Differential development of spatial ability in immigrant and English children.
M.Ed., Manchester, 1975.

1090. PHILLIPS, E.R. The consolidation of Catholic education policy in England and Wales, 1950-1959.
Ph.D., London, External, 1979.

Part 2: National and Regional Studies

1091. POOL, O. The needs of immigrant communities in adult eduction.
M.Phil., Nottingham, 1975.

1092. RABY, A.L. Career aspirations and attitudes of middle and low stream pupils in an urban multiracial comprehensive school.
Ph.D., Aston, 1979.

1093. RANGACHAR, C. An experimental study of school children with regard to some racial mental differences.
M.Ed., Leeds, 1930.

1094. ROGERS, B. An examination of some correlates of racial prejudice amongst fourth form Birmingham secondary modern school children.
M.Ed., Birmingham, 1967.

1095. RUDD, E.M. Tests of English for immigrant children in British junior schools: a study of the background and nature of the need and suggested test specifications.
M.Ed., Birmingham, 1971.

1096. SARDAR, Z.M. An experiment in modifying attitudes of British children towards an Indian teacher.
M.Phil., Institute of Education, London, 1971.

1097. SCOTT, B. A comparison of the determinants of behaviour in mono-racial and inter-racial classrooms.
M.A., Sussex, 1972.

1098. SHEARD, E.R. Information for immigrants: the situation in the Sheffield area.
M.Sc.*, Sheffield, 1977.

1099. SPRINGHALL, J.O. Youth and empire: a study of the propagation of imperialism to the young in Edwardian Britain.
D.Phil., Sussex, 1968.

1100. ST. RIMAIN, C. The social relations and adjustment problem of coloured immigrant pupils in the primary schools of Newcastle-upon-Tyne.
M.Ed., Newcastle, 1973.

1101. STANWORTH, H. The assimilation of immigrant children in a Midlands town: a sample survey.
M.Phil., Leicester, 1975.

1102. TOMLINSON, S. Decision making in special education (ESN-M) with some reference to the children of immigrant parentage.
Ph.D., Warwick, 1979.

1103. WILLIAMS, S. Race relations in educational theory: a study based on observations made in two schools.
M.Phil., Surrey, 1975.

1104. WITHRINGTON, M.P. A study of the linguistic and cultural needs of overseas students studying in Britain with referenc to course design.
M.Ed.*, Wales (Cardiff), 1982.

(ii) Asian children and education

1105. ASHBY, B.E. Cultural background an educational response: an investigation int the differences of ability and attainment of Asian immigrant pupils and native Scots in Glasgow schools.
M.Ed., Edinburgh, 1968.

1106. ATKINSON, D. An investigation into the effect of educational provision on English language acquisition of junior age Asian children.
M.Sc., Lancaster, 1978.

1107. BARI, A.F.M.A. A comparative study of attitude and reasoning ability of a group of East Pakistani immigrant children in Britain and East Pakistan children in East Pakistan in the age group 13-14 years.
M.Phil., Institute of Education, London, 1973.

1108. CLOW, D. Library provision for Pakistani immigrants in Sheffield: the children.
M.A.*, Sheffield, 1972.

1109. DOSANJH, J.S. A study of the problems in educational and social adjustment of immigrant children from the Punjab in Nottingham and Derby.
M.Ed., Nottingham, 1968.

1110. DOSANJH, J.S. A comparative study of Punjabi and English child rearing practices with special reference to lower juniors (7-9 years).
Ph.D., Nottingham, 1976.

1111. DUDLEY, M.P. Library provision for Pakistani immigrants in Sheffield: the adults.
M.A.*, Sheffield, 1972.

1112. ELLMAN, L.J. The social situation of Muslim adolescents.
M.Phil., York, 1973.

1113. FITTER, R.S. Reading errors made by Pakistani and Indian children in junior schools in Newcastle-upon-Tyne.
M.Ed., Newcastle, 1974.

1113A. GANGULY, S.R. The ego-attitudes of second language learning of Asian adolescent bilinguals in England.
Ph.D., Brunel, 1980.

1114. GHIKA, P.D. Punjabi immigrant pupils in a Scottish primary school.
M.Ed., Dundee, 1977.

1115. GHUMAN, A.S. A cross-cultural study of the basic thinking process of English, 'British' Punjabi and indigenous Punjabi boys.
Ph.D., Birmingham, 1974.

1116. HALSALL, P. South Asians in the schools: a study into the changing distribution of an ethnic minority group in the London Borough of Hillingdon.
M.Sc.*, Wales (Cardiff), 1982.

1117. HAYNES, J.M. The children of immigrants: a study of educational progress of 7-9 years old Indian children.
Ph.D., Institute of Education, London, 1971.

1118. JACKSON, R. A comparative study of political socialisation with special reference to English and Asian children in English secondary schools.
Ph.D., Institute of Education, London, 1972.

1119. KALLARACKAL, A.M. Prevalence of maladjustment in Indian immigrant children.
Ph.D., Leicester, 1975.

1120. KANGA, A.S. Some aspects of linguistic interference in the speech of Gujarati-speaking immigrant children in Leeds schools.
M.A., Leeds, 1967.

1121. KANITKAR, H.A. The social organisation of Indian students in the London area.
Ph.D., School of Oriental and African Studies, London, 1972.

1122. No entry

1123. MARTELL, B. Asian children in English secondary schools: an enquiry into some aspects of their background, adjustment, social and educational problems.
M.Phil., Reading, 1975.

1124. MUKHERJI, B. An enquiry into the social adjustment of Asian students in Nottingham colleges.
M.Phil., Nottingham, 1980.

1125. NAYLER, H. Information provision to Asian communities in Huddersfield.
M.A.*, Sheffield, 1981.

1126. PAIGE, J.P. The relation between Punjabi immigrants and selected schools in Coventry.
M.Phil., School of Oriental and African Studies, London, 1977.

1127. RASHID, A.K.M.H. The comprehensibility of Punjabi teachers in British schools: a phonological enquiry into their spoken performance.
M.Phil., University College, London, 1976.

1128. REED, P.A. Moslem adolescent boys in Batley.
M.Phil., York, 1974.

1129. SAINT, C.K. The scholastic and sociological adjustment problems of the Punjabi speaking children in Smethwick.
M.Ed., Birmingham, 1964.

1130. SHARMA, R. The measured intelligence of immigrant children from the Indian subcontinent resident in Hertfordshire.
Ph.D., Institute of Education, London, 1971.

1131. SINGH, A.K. Indian students in Britain: a survey of their adjustment and attitudes.
Ph.D., London School of Economics and Political Science, 1962.

1132. SPIER, A.B. A study of some aspects of personality structure in adolescent immigrants from India and Pakistan.
M.Sc., Lancaster, 1977.

1133. VALIANT, G.L. The role of mass media among Muslim and white adolescents: a study of media use and gratification as it relates to cultural, social and psychological background.
Ph.D., Leeds, 1978.

1134. WALKER, S.K. Home and school expectations for second generation Asian youth in Manchester.
M.Ed., Manchester, 1977.

1135. WATSON, E.M. The performance of eight to eight and a half year old British and Pakistani children on scales from the British Ability Scales.
M.Sc., Manchester, 1977.

(iii) Jewish children and education

1136. COHEN, R.L. The influence of Jewish radical movements on adult education among Jewish immigrants in the East End of London 1881-1914.
M.Ed., Liverpool, 1977.

1137. HERSHON, C.J. The evolution of Jewish elementary education in England with special reference to Liverpool.
Ph.D., Sheffield, 1973.

1138. HUGHES, A.G. An investigation into the comparative intelligence and attainments of Jewish and non-Jewish school children.
Ph.D., London, 1928.

1139. QUINN, P.L.S. The Jewish schooling system of London, 1656-1936.
Ph.D., Institute of Education, London, 1958.

1140. STEINBERG, M.B.B. Provision for Jewish schooling in Great Britain, 1939-1960.
M.A., Institute of Education, London, 1963.

(iv) West Indian/African children and education

1141. AHLIJAH, W.O.C.K. A comparative study of the pattern of delinquent behaviour in West Indian immigrant children in a remand home.
M.Phil., Institute of Psychiatry, London, 1971.

1141A. ANDERSON, E. The reading behaviour of a group of children of families of West Indian origin.
M.Phil., Nottingham, 1979.

1142. CAREY, A.T. The social adaptation of colonial students in London with special reference to West Indians and West Africans.
Ph.D., Edinburgh, 1955.

1143. CROFTS, D. The importance of context in the classroom language of English and West Indian children.
M.Ed., Manchester, 1978.

1144. CURRAN, H.V. Cultural influences on learning: an investigation into the cognitive processes of Nigerian immigrant school children.
Ph.D., Birkbeck College, London, 1980.

1145. EDWARDS, V.K. Language and comprehension in West Indian children.
Ph.D., Reading, 1977.

1146. FIGUERUA, P.E. West Indian school leavers in London: a sociological study in ten schools in a London borough, 1966-1967.
Ph.D., London School of Economics and Political Science, 1975.

1147. GRACE, A.M. Attainments v. home background of West Indian immigrant children.
M.Ed., Nottingham, 1973.

1148. GREEN, P.A. Attitudes of teachers of West Indian immigrant children.
M.Phil., Nottingham, 1972.

1149. HALL, J. West Indians and libraries: an enquiry into the needs of the West Indian community in Sheffield and the potential role of the Public Library in helping satisfy some of those needs, with particular reference to the Havelock area of the city.
M.A.*, Sheffield, 1981.

1150. HILL, D.M. The attitudes of West Indian and English adolescents in Britain.
M.Ed., Manchester, 1968.

1151. HOUGHTON, V.P. The abilities of West Indian and English infant school children.
M.Ed., Nottingham, 1967.

1152. JONES, P.J.T. An evaluation of the effect of sport on the integration of West Indian school children.
Ph.D., Surrey, 1977.

1153. KITZINGER, S.H.E. An analysis of the problems of assimilation of African and West Indian students in Oxford and Cambridge.
B.Litt., Oxford, 1954.

1154. NICOL, A.R. Psychiatric disorder in the children of Caribbean immigrants.
M.Phil., Institute of Psychiatry, London, 1971.

1155. NORRIS, R.A. The vocabulary of disadvantaged children: a comparative study of the vocabulary ability of children of English and West Indian origin.
M.A., Birmingham, 1975.

1156. OLOMOLATYE, F.'O.O. A study of the impact of emigration on the attitudes of West Indian immigrants to school.
Ph.D., Institute of Education, London, 1979.

1157. PAYNE, J.F. A comparative study of the mental ability of 7 & 8 year old British and West Indian children in a West Midland town.
M.A., Keele, 1968.

1158. PHIZACKLEA, A-M. The political socialisation of black adolescents in Britain.
Ph.D., Exeter, 1975.

1159. TIDRICK, K. Need for achievement in relation to class and colour among Jamaican students.
Ph.D., London, External, 1971.

1160. WEIR, K. The language problems of the West Indian pupil in the junior school.
M.Ed., Liverpool, 1977.

Europe - Great Britain

B. IMMIGRANTS AND MINORITIES: SPECIFIC COMMUNITY STUDIES

a) Comparative Studies

1161. BENEDICT, B. Muslim and Buddist associations in London.
Ph.D., London School of Economics and Political Science, 1954.

1162. BENTLEY, S. The structure of leadership among Indians, Pakistanis and West Indians in Britain.
M.Sc., Bradford, 1971.

1163. BLAXTER, L. Leadership in Indian and Italian immigrant communities.
M.Phil., Sussex, 1968.

1164. COLLINS, S.F. Moslem and Negro groupings on Tyneside: a comprehensive study of social integration in terms of intra group and inter group relations.
Ph.D., Edinburgh, 1952.

1165. COZIN, M.L. A religious sect in Korea and Great Britain.
M.Phil., University College, London, 1975.

b) Chilean Community

1166. WILSON, J.P. Library services for the Spanish speaking: resources in Sheffield and a survey of the Chilean community.
M.A.*, Sheffield, 1982.

c) Chinese Community

1167. BRADLEY, W.C.A.A. The Chinese in Ei: study of adjustment of the restaurant group.
M.Phil., Edinburgh, 1973.

1168. CHEUNG, C.H.W. The Chinese way: a social study of the Hong Kong Chinese community in a Yorkshire city.
M.Phil., York, 1975.

1169. FREEBERNE, J.D.M. The Chinese community in Britain with special reference to housing and education.
Ph.D., School of Oriental and African Studies, London, 1980.

Part 2: National and Regional Studies

1170. MAY, J. The British working class and the Chinese, 1870-1911: with particular reference to the seaman's strike of 1911.
M.A.*, Warwick, 1973.

1171. NG, K.C. Some aspects of the social organization of the Chinese engaged in the restaurant business in London.
M.A., London School of Economics and Political Science, 1965.

1172. O'NEILL, J.A. The role of family and community in the social adjustment of Chinese in Liverpool.
M.A., Liverpool, 1973.

d) Cypriot Community

1173. BERK, F. A study of the Turkish-Cypriot community in Haringey with particular reference to its background, its structure and changes taking place within it.
M.Phil., York, 1973.

1174. LADBURY, S.A. Turkish Cypriots in London: economy, society, culture and change.
Ph.D., School of Oriental and African Studies, London, 1979.

1175. NEARCHOU, V. The Cypriot community of London.
M.A., Nottingham, 1960.

1176. OAKLEY, R.E. Cypriot migration and settlement in Britain.
D.Phil., Oxford, 1972.

1177. PSARIAS, V. Greek Cypriot immigration in Greater Manchester.
M.Phil., Bradford, 1979.

e) French Community

1177A. BELLENGER, D.T.J. The French ecclesiastical exiles in England, 1789-1815.
Ph.D., Cambridge, 1978.

1177B. GWYNN, R.D. The ecclesiastical organization of French Protestants in England in the later seventeenth century with special reference to London.
Ph.D., University College, London, 1976.

1178. LUGET, P.J.F. A study of the educational aspect of the Huguenot settlements in England.
M.A., Institute of Education, London, 1952.

1179. MARTINEZ, P.K. Paris Communard refugees in Britain, 1871-1880.
D.Phil., Sussex, 1981.

1180. MURDOCH, T.V. Huguenot artists, designers and craftsmen in Great Britain and Ireland, 1680-1760.
Ph.D., London, 1982.

1181. NICHOLLS, A.W. French refugees in England from the Restoration to the death of William III.
B.Litt., Oxford, 1923.

1182. SULLY, G.H. The Huguenots and the Church of England.
M.A., Leeds, 1954.

1183. WILKINSON, E.M. French emigrés in England, 1789-1802: their reception and impact on English life.
B.Litt., Oxford, 1953.

f) German Community

1184. SHERMAN, A.J. British government policies towards refugees from the Third Reich, 1933-39.
D.Phil., Oxford, 1970.

g) Gypsies/Travellers

1185. ACTON, T.A. A sociological analysis of the development of attitudes towards the changing place of gypsies in the social and cultural structure in England and Wales from the Moveable Dwellings Act agitation to the Romanestan controversy.
D.Phil., Oxford, 1974.

1186. BINNS, D. Personality characteristics and attitudes of gypsy and non-gypsy children.
M.Ed., Manchester, 1978.

1187. BROOKS, P.M. Travellers: a study of 'mobility' from a 'race' to a 'class'.
B.Sc.*, Bristol, 1979.

1188. CONNELL, R.K. Planning for gypsies: aspects of current policies and procedures.
Dip. Town & Regional Planning, Leeds Polytechnic, 1976.

1189. FREESTON, D.G. The social problems of gypsies and travellers.
B.Sc.*, Southampton, 1964.

1190. MAYALL, D. Itinerant minorities in England and Wales in the nineteenth and early twentieth centuries: a study of gypsies, tinkers, hawkers and travellers.
Ph.D., Sheffield, 1981.

1191. MONTGOMERY, D.P. Planning for gypsies.
Dip. Town Planning*, Nottingham, 1964.

1192. OKELY, J.M. The Travellers: a study of some gypsies in England.
D.Phil., Oxford, 1977.

1193. REHFISCH, F. The Tinkers of Perthshire and Aberdeenshire.
M.A., Edinburgh, 1958.

1194. TRIGG, E.B. An historical and anthropological study of magic and religion among the gypsies of Britain.
D.Phil., Oxford, 1968.

1195. WORRALL, R.V. Gypsies, education and society: case studies in conflict.
M.Ed., Birmingham, 1978.

h) Irish Community

1196. BEECHEY, F.E. The Irish in York, 1840-1875.
D.Phil., York, 1977.

1197. COOTER, R.J. The Irish in Co. Durham and Newcastle, 1840-1880.
M.A., Durham, 1973.

1198. GRANATH, A. The Irish in mid-nineteenth century Lancashire, 1830-71.
M.A.*, Lancaster, 1975.

1199. HYNES, M.P. Differential integration of Irish immigrants in Birmingham.
Ph.D., Cambridge, 1982.

1200. JACKSON, J.A. The Irish in London: a study of migration and settlement in the past 100 years.
M.A., London School of Economics and Political Science, 1958.

1201. KERR, B.M. Irish immigration into Great Britain, 1798-1838.
B.Litt., Oxford, 1939.

1202. LOWE, W.J. The Irish in Lancashire, 1847-1871.
Ph.D., Trinity College, Dublin, 1975.

1203. McDERMOTT, M. Irish Catholics and the British Labour Movement: a study with particular reference to London, 1918 to 1970.
M.A., Kent, 1979.

1204. McDONAGH, A.M. Irish immigrants and labour movements in Coatbridge and Airdrie, 1891-1931.
B.A.*, Strathclyde.

1204A. O'CONNELL, B. The Irish Nationalist Party in Liverpool.
M.A., Liverpool, 1972.

1205. O'REILLY, G.W. Irish immigration and urban schooling in the nineteenth century.
M.A., King's College, London, 1980.

1206. PAPWORTH, J.D. The Irish in Liverpool, 1835-71: family structure and residential mobility.
Ph.D., Liverpool, 1982.

1207. TREBLE, J.H. The place of the Irish Catholics in the social life of the North of England, 1829-51.
Ph.D., Leeds, 1969.

1208. WALTER, B.M. The geography of Irish migration to Britain since 1939, with particular reference to Luton and Bolton.
D.Phil., Oxford, 1979.

1209. WILSON, F.L. Irish immigration in Great Britain during the first half of the nineteenth century.
M.A., Manchester, 1946.

Part 2: National and Regional Studies

i) Italian Community

1209A. PAROLIN, G. Foreign Catholics: the religious practice of the Emilian community in London.
M.A., Kent, 1979.

1210. WICKS, M.C.W. A history of the Italian exiles in London, 1816-1848.
Ph.D., Edinburgh, 1930.

j) Jewish community and anti-Semitism

1211. BAYLISS, G.M. The outsider aspects of the political career of Sir Alfred Mond, first Lord Melchet.
PhD., Wales (Swansea), 1970.

1212. BENNETT, J.J. East End newspaper opinion and Jewish immigration, 1885-1905.
M.Phil., Sheffield, 1979.

1213. BIRAM, F. The problems of urban minorities: a socio-historical study of the Jewish question in East London, 1870-1939 with special reference to educational and cultural issues.
M.A., King's College, London, 1980.

1214. BLUME, H.S.B. A study of anti-semitic groups in Britain, 1818-1940.
M.Phil., Sussex, 1971.

1214A. BUSH, J.F. Labour, politics and society in East London during the First World War.
Ph.D., Queen Mary College, London, 1978.
(includes a study of how the war helped to draw Jewish workers into East London politics.)

1215. CARRIER, J.W. Working-class Jews in present-day London: a sociological study.
M.Phil., London School of Economics and Political Science, 1969.

1216. COHEN, S. Plea rolls of the Exchequer of the Jews (Michaelmas Term 1277-Hilary 1279).
Ph.D., Birkbeck College, London, 1951.

1217. DAKIN, E. The position and history of the Jews in England in the thirteenth century.
M.A., Wales, 1913.

1218. ELMAN, P. Jewish finance in England, 1216-1290, with special reference to royal revenue.
M.A., London School of Economics and Political Science, 1935.

1219. FACHLER, M. A study of London Jewish families in the light of Zbrowski and Landes' examination of family relationships in the Eastern European Jewish shtetl.
M.Phil., Brunel, 1976.

1220. FERNANDO, S.J.M. Socio-cultural factors in depressive illness: a comparative study of Jewish and non-Jewish patients in East London.
M.D., Cambridge, 1975.

1221. GARRARD, J.A. The political left-wing (the Liberals and the emergent Labour Party) and the issue of alien Jewish immigration 1880-1910.
M.Sc., Manchester, 1965.

1222. GOTTLIEB, P. Social mobility of the Jewish immigrant.
M.Phil., Nottingham, 1971.

1223. HARRIS, S. The identity of some Bristol Jews.
M.Sc., Bristol, 1970.

1224. KATZ, D.S. Philo-Semitism in England, 1603-1655.
D.Phil., Oxford, 1978.

1225. KRAUSZ, E. Aspects of social control in a minority community: the Leeds Jewish community.
M.Sc.(Econ.), London, External, 1960.

1226. KRAUSZ, E. A sociological field study of Jewish suburban life in Edgeware, 1962-1963 with special reference to minority identification.
Ph.D., London School of Economics and Political Science, 1965.

1227. LUNN, K.J. The Marconi scandal and related aspects of British anti-Semitism, 1910-1914.
Ph.D., Sheffield, 1975.

1228. O'BRIEN, R. The establishment of the Jewish minority in Leeds.
Ph.D., Bristol, 1975.

1229. QUINN, P.L.S. The re-entry of the Jews into England and Ireland.
Ph.D., National University of Ireland, 1966.

1230. ROBB, J.H. A study of anti-Semitism in a working class area.
Ph.D., London School of Economics and Political Science, 1952.
(London)

1231. RUMYANECK, J. The economic and social development of the Jews in England, 1730-1860.
Ph.D., London School of Economics and Political Science, 1933.

1232. SALBSTEIN, M.C.N. The emancipation of the Jews in Britain with particular reference to the debate concerning the admission of Jews to Parliament, 1828-1860.
Ph.D., King's College, London, 1975.

1233. SHAPIRA, I. The relief of the Jewish disabilities in England, 1829-1858.
M.A., Queen Mary College, London, 1934.

1234. SHAROT, S.A. The social elements in the religious practices and organisation of English Jewry with special reference to the United Synagogues.
D.Phil., Oxford, 1969.

1235. SUSSER, B. The Jews of Devon and Cornwall from the Middle Ages to the early twentieth century.
Ph.D., Exeter, 1978.

1236. VOLZ-LEBZELTER, G.C. Political anti-semitism in England, 1918-1939.
D.Phil., Oxford, 1977.

1237. WALDENBURG, L.M. The history of Anglo-Jewish attitudes towards immigration and racial issues since 1952.
M.A., Sheffield, 1972.

k) Maltese Community

1238. DENICH, G.E. The London Maltese: collective responsibility and community structures.
Ph.D., London School of Economics and Political Science, 1972.

1239. ZAMMIT, E.L. The behaviour pattern of Maltese migrants in London with reference to Maltese social institutions.
B.Litt., Oxford, 1977.

l) Polish Community

1240. ZUBRZYCKI, J. The adjustment of Polish immigrants in Great Britain.
M.Sc.(Econ.), London School of Economics and Political Science, 1953.

m) South Asian Immigrants

(i) General Studies

1241. ASLAM, M. The practice of Asian medicine in the United Kingdom.
Ph.D., Nottingham, 1979.

1242. BAROT, R. The social organistion of a Swaminarayan sect in Britain.
Ph.D., School of Oriental and African Studies, London, 1981.

1243. BETTS, G.S. Working-class Asians in Britain: economic, social and political changes, 1959-1979.
M.Phil., School of Oriental and African Studies, London, 1981.

1244. CANDAMITTO, V. Buddhist organisations in Great Britain.
M.A., Durham, 1973.

1245. CLARKE, P.B. The Ismaili Khojas: a sociological study of an Islamic sect in London.
M.Phil., King's College, London, 1975.

1245A. DAHYA, B.U-D. South Asian urban immigrations with special reference to Asian Muslim immigrants in the English Midlands.
M.Sc., School of Oriental and African Studies, London, 1967.

1246. EDGAR, J.R. A study of public libraries and Asian immigrants in Britain.
M.A., Strathclyde, 1973.

1247. HALLAM, R.N.M. The Shia Imami Ismailia community in Britain.
M.Phil., School of Oriental and African Studies, London, 1971.

Part 2: National and Regional Studies

1248. HOMANS, H.Y. Pregnant in Britain: a sociological approach to Asian and British women's experience.
Ph.D., Warwick, 1980.

1249. HUNT, S.P. Adaptation and nutritional implications of food habits among Uganda Asians settling in Britain.
Ph.D., Queen Elizabeth College, London, 1977.

1250. JAFAREY, S. Inter-generational tensions among South Asians settled in the Potteries.
M.A., Keele, 1980.

1251. JOSHI, M. Role conflict in young Asians living in Britain.
M.Sc.*, Wales (UWIST), 1982.

1252. MAHMUD, S. The measurement of social support amongst immigrant Asian women.
M.Phil., Edinburgh, 1978.

1253. MOHAN, P.R.L. Asian doctors in England and their professional experiences and social life (a case study in Sandwell).
M.Soc.Sc., Birmingham, 1979.

1254. NATH, J. Some aspects of the life of Indians and Pakistanis in Newcastle with special reference to women.
M.A., Durham, 1971.

1256. O'KEEFE, B.M. Hindu family life in East London.
Ph.D., London School of Economics and Political Science, 1980.

1257. PINTO, R.T. A study of psychiatric illness among Asians in the Camberwell area.
M.Phil., Institute of Psychiatry, London, 1971.

1258. SHAH, S. Aspects of the geographic analysis of Asian immigrants in London.
D.Phil., Oxford, 1980.

1259. TURNER, D.M. A study of home tuition of Asian women immigrants in West Yorkshire.
Ph.D., Liverpool, 1977.

(ii) Bangladeshi Community

1259A. AHMED, S.H. Entrepreneurship and management practices among immigrants from Bangladesh in the United Kingdom.
Ph.D., Brunel, 1981.

(iii) Bengali Community

1260. BARTON, S.W. The Bengali Muslims of Bradford: a study of their observance of Islam, with special reference to the function of the Mosque and the work of Imam.
M.Phil., Leeds, 1981.

1261. ISLAM, M.M. Bengali migrant workers in Britain: a study of their position in the class structure.
Ph.D., Leeds, 1977.

(iv) Pakistani Community

1262. HOSSAIN, A.S.M.T. The social and economic background of male Pakistani immigrants attending venereal disease clinic in the United Kingdom.
M.Phil., St. Thomas's Hospital Medical School, London, 1970.

1263. HUSSAIN, A.B.Md.A. Factors influencing satisfaction with life in Britain among Pakistani immigrants in Leeds and Bradford.
M.Phil., Leeds, 1969.

1264. IFTIKHAR, A. Effects of cultural attitudes on the adjustment of Pakistani students in Britain.
M.A., Bedford College, London, 1964.

1265. JEFFERY, P.M. Pakistani families and their networks in Bristol and Pakistan.
Ph.D., Bristol, 1973.

1266. KHAN, M.A. Islam and Muslim in Liverpool.
M.Phil., Liverpool, 1980.

1267. MALIK, M.A. Ventilatory capacity and prevalence of respiratory symptoms in Pakistani immigrants in different occupations.
M.Sc., Manchester, 1971.

1268. RASHID, S. The socialization and education of Pakistani teenage girls in London.
M.Phil., School of Oriental and African Studies, London, 1981.

1269. SAIFULLAH-KHAN, V.J.M. Pakistani villagers in a British city: the world of the Mirpuri villager in Bradford and in his village.
Ph.D., Bradford, 1975.

1270. No entry

1271. WERBNER, P. Ritual and social networks: a study of Pakistani immigrants in Manchester.
Ph.D., Manchester, 1979.

(v) Sikh Community

1272. AGNIHOTRI, R.K. Process of assimilation: a socio-linguistic study of Sikh children in Leeds.
D.Phil., York, 1980.

1273. BATH, K.S. The distribution and spatial patterns of Panjabi population in Wolverhampton.
M.A., Wales (Aberystwyth), 1972.

1274. BHACHU, P.K. Marriage and dowry among selected East African Sikh families in the United Kingdom.
Ph.D., School of Oriental and African Studies, London, 1981.

1275. GIRDHAR, D.S. A study of second generation Asian women in Britain, with special reference to Sikhs.
M.A., Warwick, 1980.

1276. NESBITT, E.J. Aspects of Sikh trdition in Nottingham.
M.Phil., Nottingham, 1981.

1277. SINGH HINDBALRAJ Bhatra Sikhs in Bristol: development of an ethnic community.
M.Sc.*, Bristol, 1977.

1278. THOMPSON, M.A. A study of generation differences in immigrant groups with particular reference to Sikhs.
M.Phil., School of Oriental and African Studies, London, 1970.

n) Turkish Community

1279. GRYSKIEWICZ, N. A study of the adaptation of Turkish migrant workers to living and working in the United Kingdom.
Ph.D., Birkbeck College, London, 1979.

o) Ukrainian Community

1280. PETRYSHYN, W.R. Britain's Ukrainian community: a study of the political dimension in ethnic community development.
Ph.D., Bristol, 1981.

p) West Indian/African Communities

1281. BANTON, M.P. Negro immigrants in a Dockland area.
Ph.D., Edinburgh, 1954.
(study relates to London docks)

1282. BUTTERWORTH, A.E. An anthropological critique of sociological studies of coloured Commonwealth immigrants in Britain with special reference to West Indians.
M.A.(Econ.), Manchester, 1974.

1283. CASHMORE, E.E.H. A sociological analysis of the origins, development and current state of the Rastafarian movement in Jamaica and England.
Ph.D., London School of Economics and Political Science, 1979.

1284. FISCIAN, C.E. Minority group prejudice: a study of some sociological and psychological correlates of anti-English prejudice among West Indian immigrants in London.
Ph.D., London School of Economics and Political Science, 1960.

1285. HILL, C.S.H. The West Indian immigrant and the Church.
M.A., London, External, 1964.

1286. JERROME, D.M. Continuity and change in the social organisation of the Ibos in London.
Ph.D., School of Oriental and African Studies, London, 1975.

Part 2: National and Regional Studies

1287. JONES, C.J. Immigration and social adjustment: a case study of West Indian food habits in London.
Ph.D., London School of Economics and Political Science, 1971.

1288. KINDER, C.R. The effectiveness of voluntary organizations in integrating the West Indian immigrant in Moss Side, Manchester.
B.Litt., Oxford, 1970.

1289. LINDSTROM, V.R. An analysis of kinship and friendship in networks of West Indians in South London.
M.Phil., C.N.A.A., 1975.

1290. MACLENNAN, B.W. An analysis of group therapy techniques with negro adolescent girls.
Ph.D., London, External, 1960.

1291. MANLEY, D.R. The social structure of the Liverpool negro community with special reference to the development of formal associations.
Ph.D., Liverpool, 1959.

1292. MILDON, I.W. West Indians in Croydon: a study of dispersal and second-phase family settlement.
M.Phil., Sussex, 1975.

1293. NDEM, E.B. Negro immigrants in Manchester: an analysis of social relations within and between the various coloured groups and of their relation to the white community.
M.A., University College, London, 1954.

1294. OKPARA, E. Cultural variations in career aspirations: a study of Nigerian college students in the U.K.
Ph.D., Birkbeck College, London, 1977.

1295. PEACH, G.C.K. Socio-geographic aspects of West Indian migration to Great Britain.
D.Phil., Oxford, 1965.

1296. PEARSON, D.G. West Indians in Easton: a study of their social organisations with particular reference to participation in formal and informal associations.
Ph.D., Leicester, 1975.

1297. POLLARD, P.H. The formation of social relationships among Jamaican and Trinidadian immigrants in a North London borough.
M.Phil., University College, London, 1971.

1298. PRYCE, K.N. West Indian life styles in Bristol.
Ph.D., Bristol, 1975.

1299. RICHMOND, A.H. Assimilation and adjustment of a group of West Indian negroes in England: a case study of inter-group relations.
M.A., Liverpool, 1951.

1300. RWEGELERA, G.G.C. Mental illness in Africans and West Indians of African origin living in London.
M.Phil., Institute of Psychiatry, London, 1971.

1301. RYAN, S. Rastafarianism and the speech of adolescent blacks in London.
M.A., Birmingham, 1981.

1302. TROYNA, B. The significance of reggae music in the lives of black adolescent boys in Britain: an exploratory study.
M.Phil., Leicester, 1978.

1303. VAUGHN, J. The negro problem in Reading.
B.Litt., Oxford, 1960.

1304. WATSON, G. The sociology of black nationalism: identity, protest and the concept of 'Black power' among West Indian immigrants in Britain.
D.Phil., York, 1972.

C. SCOTLAND

(i) General Studies

1305. BAIN, D. The Scottish National Party from 1966 to the 1970 General Election: a study in electoral polarisation in British general elections.
M.Sc., Strathclyde, 1973.

1306. CHAPMAN, M.K. The nature of Scottish Gaelic folk culture.
B.Litt., Oxford, 1977.

1307. CONDRY, E.F. Culture and identity in the Scottish Highlands.
D.Phil., Oxford, 1980.

1308. DREXLER, M.J. Attitudes to nationality in Scottish historical writings from Barbour to Boece.
Ph.D., Edinburgh, 1979.

1309. ELDER, J.M. The ideology of the Scottish National Party.
M.Litt., Glasgow, 1979.

1310. GRIMBLE, I.A. A survival of a Celtic society in the Mackay county formerly called Strathnaver in Northern Scotland from the sixteenth century.
Ph.D., Aberdeen, 1964.

1311. HARDING, A.W. Sgoilean Chriosd, 1811-1861: a study of the Edinburgh Society for the Support of Gaelic Schools.
M.Litt., Glasgow, 1979.

1312. PIGGOTT, C.A. A geography of religion in Scotland.
Ph.D., Edinburgh, 1979.

1313. STEWART, J.A. Peoples of the Clanranald: a traditional Gaelic kindred in decline, 1644-1851.
Ph.D., Edinburgh, 1982.

1314. THOMPSON, W. Glasgow and Africa: connexions and attitudes, 1870-1900.
Ph.D., Strathclyde, 1970.

1315. WEBB, K. The context of nationalism in Scotland.
M.Sc., Strathclyde, 1973.

1316. WITHERS, C.W.J. The position of the Gaelic language in Scotland 1698-1881: its spatial extent and social usage.
Ph.D., Cambridge, 1982.

(ii) Emigration

1317. MACDERMID, G.E. The religious and ecclesiastical life of the north-west Highlands, 1750-1843: the background of the Presbyterian emigrants to Cape Breton, Nova Scotia.
Ph.D., Aberdeen, 1967.

1318. RINN, J. Factors in Scottish emigration: a study of Scottish participation in the indentured and transportation systems of the New World in the seventeenth and eighteenth centuries.
Ph.D., Aberdeen, 1979.

(iii) Immigration

1319. BENSKI, T. Inter-ethnic relations in a Glasgow suburb.
Ph.D., Glasgow, 1976.

1320. COLLINS, B.E.A. Aspects of Irish immigration into Scottish towns (Dundee and Paisley) during the mid-nineteenth century.
M.Phil., Edinburgh, 1979.

1321. DIXON, E.A.H. The American negro in Scotland in the nineteenth century.
M.Litt., Edinburgh, 1979.

1322. EASTON, E.G. A sociological survey of the Chinese community in Aberdeen.
M.Ed., Dundee, 1977.

1323. HANDLEY, J.E. The Irish in Scotland 1798-1845.
M.A., National University of Ireland, 1941.

1324. SRIVASTAVA, S.R. The Asian community in Glasgow.
Ph.D., Glasgow, 1975.

D. **WALES**

1325. BEACH, S.A. A statistical, ethnological and genetical investigation into racial differentiation among adult Welshmen.
M.Sc., Wales, 1953.

1326. BOURHIS, R.Y. Language and social evaluation in Wales.
Ph.D., Bristol, 1978.

1327. BUTT PHILIP, A.A.S. The political and sociological significance of Welsh nationalism since 1945.
D.Phil., Oxford, 1972.

1328. DANIEL, J.E. The geographical distribution of religious denominations in Wales in its relation to racial and social factors.
M.A., Wales, 1928.

Part 2: National and Regional Studies

1329. DAVIES, D.H. The Welsh National Party, 1925-1975: a search for identity.
M.Sc., Wales (Cardiff), 1979.

1330. DAVIES, J.A. An enquiry into the recent history of bilingualism and the educational implications in the Fishguard area of Pembrokeshire.
M.A., London, External, 1958.

1331. EVANS, E. Bilingual education in Wales with special reference to the teaching of Welsh.
M.A., Wales, 1924.

1332. HALLAS, D. Welsh nationalism: a geographical study.
M.Phil., Birkbeck College, London, 1975.

1333. HICKEY, J.V. The origin and growth of the Irish community in Cardiff.
M.A., Wales (Cardiff), 1959.

1334. HUGHES, J.E. Dan Isaac Davies a'i gyfraniad i addysg ddwyieithog yng Nghymru ynghyd a hanes sefydlu Cymdeithas yr Iaith Gymraeg (Dan Isaac Davies and his contribution to bilingual education in Wales together with a history of the establishment of the Welsh Language Society).
M.A., Wales (Bangor), 1978.

1335. OWEN, M.H. The attitude of parents and teachers of primary school children and ministers of religion to the teaching of Welsh as a second language in a selected area.
M.A., Wales (Cardiff), 1960.

1336. STEPHENSON, P.E. 'Radical Conservatism': the ideology of Plaid Genedlaethol Cymru, 1925-45.
M.Litt., Oxford, 1982.

1337. WILLIAMS, C. Language decline and nationalist resurgence in Wales.
Ph.D., Wales (Swansea), 1978.

1338. WILLIAMS, E.R. Welsh seaman, navigators and colonizers, Elizabethan and Jacobean together with some history of Welsh maritime and colonizing activity during the period.
M.A., Wales, 1915.

X. GREECE

1339. VGENOPOULOS, C.G. Post-war Hellenic emigration.
M.A., Sussex, 1977.

XI. HUNGARY

1340. GARAI, G. The policy towards the Jews, Zionism and Israel of the Hungarian Communist Party, 1945-1953.
Ph.D., London School of Economics and Political Science, 1979.

1341. MARSDEN, R.M. Hungarian Jews and the liberal party system, 1867-1914.
D.Phil., Oxford, 1978.

XII. IRELAND

1342. BARBOUR, W.N. The ministry of the Presbyterian Church in Ireland.
Ph.D., Queens' University, Belfast, 1965.

1343. BERESFORD, P.C.F.M. The Official IRA and Republican clubs in Northern Ireland 1968-1974 and their relation with other political and paramilitary groups.
Ph.D., Exeter, 1979.

1344. BOWEN, K.D. The Church of England in Eire since 1922: a study of the assimilation of an ethno-religious minority.
D.Phil., Oxford, 1978.

1344A. BOWMAN, J.F.V. De Valera and the Ulster question, 1917-1973.
Ph.D., Trinity College, Dublin, 1980.

1345. BROWN, J. The Presbyterian Church in Ireland and the Ulster Revival of 1859.
B.D., Trinity College, Dublin, 1965.

1346. BURTON, F.P. The social meanings of Catholicism in Northern Ireland.
Ph.D., London School of Economics and Political Science, 1976.

1347. CAMPISAND, M.S. The Unionists and the constitution, 1906-1911.
B.Litt., Oxford, 1977.

1348. CHERTKOW, P.S. Orangeism and Republicanism, 1948-1972: a study of two ideologically opposed movements in Irish politics.
Ph.D., London School of Economics and Political Science, 1975.

1349. COOKE, J.H. The development and distribution of Methodism in North Ireland: a demographic study.
M.A., Queen's University, Belfast, 1965.

1350. FERRY, E.B.M. The origin and development of craft among the wandering people of Ireland.
M.Soc.Sc., Ireland, 1972.

1351. FLANAGAN, M.T. Gaelic society, Norman settlers and Angevin kinship: a study of interaction in Ireland in the late twelfth century.
D.Phil., Oxford, 1980.

1352. GALWAY, R.N. The perception and manipulation of the religious identities in a Northern Ireland community.
M.A., Queen's University, Belfast, 1978. (Harmonious relations between Catholic and Protestant communities in an Irish village.)

1353. HANNA, S.G. The Moravian settlement at Gracehill, County Antrim.
M.A., Queen's University, Belfast, 1964.

1353A. HARBINSON, J.F. The Ulster Unionist Party, 1882-1970: its development and organisation.
Ph.D., Queen's University, Belfast, 1972.

1353B. HAYES, J.C. Bilingualism as an objective in education in Ireland, 1893-1941.
M.Ed., Trinity College, Dublin, 1982.

1354. HURLEY, J. The nationalism of Canon Sheehan.
M.A., National University of Ireland, 1956.

1355. IDIZKOWSKI, H.A. Internal colonialism and the emergence of the Irish police.
M.Phil., Edinburgh, 1977.

1356. LAW, D.T.S. Emigration and the flight from the land, 1901-1951.
M.A., National University of Ireland, 1953.

1357. McALLISTER, I. The ballot not the bullet: the Northern Ireland Social Democratic and Labour Party.
Ph.D., Strathclyde, 1977.

1358. McANALLEN, M.C. Minority interaction in a small Northern Irish village.
M.A., Queen's University, Belfast, 1977.

1359. McCARTHY, P.J. Itinerancy and poverty: a study on the sub-culture of poverty.
M.Soc.Sc., National University of Ireland, 1971.

1360. MACDONAGH, O.O.G.M. Irish overseas emigration and the state during the Great Famine.
Ph.D., Cambridge, 1952.

1361. MANNING, M.A. The Irish Blueshirt Movement.
M.A., National University of Ireland (Dublin), 1967.

1362. MARTIN, D. Migration within and emigration from the six counties of Northern Ireland between 1911 and 1937.
M.A., Queen's University, Belfast, 1977.

1363. MEGAHEY, A.J. The Irish Protestant Church and social and political issues 1870-1914.
Ph.D., Queen's University, Belfast, 1969.

1364. MURPHY, T.D. Derry and north-west Ulster, 1790-1914.
M.Litt., Trinity College, Dublin, 1980.

1365. NELSON, S. Ulster's uncertain defenders: a study of loyalists in political parliamentary and community organisations in Belfast 1969-1975.
Ph.D., Strathclyde, 1980.

1366. NOLAN, N.G. The Irish emigration: a study in demography.
Ph.D., National University of Ireland, 1936.

1366A. O'BRIEN, M.C. Foreigners' attitudes towards Irish people.
Ph.D., Trinity College, Dublin, 1980.

1367. O'NEILL, S.G. The politics of culture in Ireland, 1899-1910.
D.Phil., Oxford, 1982.

Part 2: National and Regional Studies

1368. PINTER, F.M. The exluded society: a study of Northern Ireland and other divided societies.
Ph.D., University College, London, 1975.

1369. ROBERTS, D.A. The Orange movement in Ireland 1886 to 1916: a study in the sociology of religion and politics.
Ph.D., London, External, 1975.

1370. RODGERS, R.J. Presbyterian missionary activities among Irish Roman Catholics in the nineteenth century.
M.A., Queen's University, Belfast, 1969.

1371. SAWYER, R.M. The origins and career of Roger Casement with particular reference to the development of his interest in the rights of dependent ethnic groups.
Ph.D., Southampton, 1979.

1371A. SCRATON, P. Images of deviance and the politics of assimilation: a study of labelling processes and their effect on a special education project for Irish gypsies.
M.A., Liverpool, 1977.

1372. SHOULDICE, F.J. Emigration, 1900-1950.
M.A., National University of Ireland, 1953.

1373. THORNBERRY, P. International law and the problem of the double minority in the North Ireland.
LL.M., Keele, 1976.

1374. WHYTE, J.H. Church and State in the Republic of Ireland.
Ph.D., Queen's University, Belfast, 1976.

1374A. WOODS, C.J. The Catholic church and Irish politics.
Ph.D., Nottingham, 1969.

XIII. ITALY

1375. CHAPMAN, B. The problem of regionalism in Italy: its historical background and present constitutional importance.
D.Phil., Oxford, 1952.

1376. INUMARU, K.F. The Japanese business community in Milan.
M.Litt., Cambridge, 1978.

1377. LUCE, H.F. The Italian Socialist Party and the rise of fascism.
M.Sco.Sc., Birmingham, 1975.

1378. MORGAN, P.J. The Italian Fascist Party, 1926-1932.
Ph.D., Reading, 1975.

1379. RAVINDRANATHAN, T.R. Bakunin and the Italians.
D.Phil., Oxford, 1978.

1380. SNOWDON, F.M. The social origins of fascism in Tuscany.
D.Phil., Oxford, 1975.

XIV. MALTA

1381. DELIA, E.P. The interrelationship between emigration and economic activity in Malta.
D.Phil., Oxford, 1980.

1382. PRICE, C.A. Maltese emigration, 1826-1885: an analysis and a survey.
D.Phil., Oxford, 1952.

1383. WETTINGER, G. Some aspects of slavery in Malta, 1530-1800.
Ph.D., London, External, 1972.

XV. NETHERLANDS

1384. WITTERMANS, T. The social organisation of Ambonese refugees in Holland.
Ph.D., London School of Economics and Political Science, 1955.

XVI. NORWAY

1385. HAYES, P.M. The career and political ideas of Vidkun Quisling.
D.Phil., Oxford, 1970.

XVII. POLAND

1386. CIECHANOWSKI, J.M. The political and ideological background of the Warsaw rising, 1944.
Ph.D., London School of Economics and Political Science, 1969.

1387. LEW, M.S. The works of Rabbi Moses Isserls as a source of the history of the Jews in Poland in the sixteenth century.
Ph.D., Jew's College, London, 1941.

1388. ROMAIN SRZEDNICKI, M.J.I. The sociology of religion in Poland: an enquiry into the approach to secularisation in the Communist State.
Ph.D., London School of Economics and Political Science, 1979.

XVIII. PORTUGAL

1389. SAUNDERS, A.C.deC.M. A social history of black slaves and freedmen in Portugal, 1441-1555.
D.Phil., Oxford, 1978.

XIX. ROMANIA

1390. SCHNEIDER, J.S. The Jewish question in Romania, prior to the First World War.
Ph.D., Southampton, 1982.

XX. SPAIN

1391. EPSTEIN, I. The Responsa of Rabbi Solomon ben Adreth of Barcelona, 1235-1310 as a source of the history of Spain: studies in the communal life of the Jews in Spain as reflected in the Responsa.
Ph.D., London, 1923.

1392. FREEDMAN, H. The life of the Jews in Spain in the times of Rabbi Asher B. Jechiel, as furnished by his Responsa.
Ph.D., London, 1930.

1393. GOWARD, N.J. Nationalism, ethnicity and ?Catalan culture: a regional and ethnographic study.
Ph.D., Kent, 1980.

1394. GUTWIRTH, E. Social tensions within fifteenth-century Hispano-Jewish communities.
Ph.D., University College, London, 1979.

1395. HITCHCOCK, R. An examination of the use of the term 'Mozarab' in eleventh and twelfth century Spain.
Ph.D., St. Andrew's, 1971.

1396. JACOB, J.G. The suffering of the Jews in Spain and Portugal in the fifteenth century as reflected in contemporary homilectical Hebrew literature.
Ph.D., Jew's College, London, 1961.

1397. LEVY, A. Court Rabbis in fourteenth and fifteenth century Castile.
Ph.D., University College, London, 1978.

1398. LOOMIE, A.J. Spain and the English Catholic exiles 1580-1604.
Ph.D., University College, London, 1957.

1399. LOURIE, E.R. Christian attitudes towards the Modijeras in the reign of Alfonso III of Aragon, 1285-1291.
D.Phil., Oxford, 1968.

1400. SAN ROMAN ESPINOSA, M.T. A comparative study of three gypsy urban settlements in Spain.
M.Phil., University College, London, 1975.

1401. TAHA, A.D. The Muslim conquest and settlement of North Africa and Spain.
Ph.D., Exeter, 1978.

1402. WASSERSTEIN, D.J. Civil wars in Muslim Spain: sources of conflict in the era of Al-Mansur and the party kings.
D.Phil., Oxford, 1982.

1403. YAMASEE, A.K. Contributions of the Spanish Arabs to western thought and education in the Middle Ages.
M.Phil., Institute of Education, London, 1972.

XXI. SWITZERLAND

1404. JENKINS, J.R.G. A geographical study of the Juru separatism in Canton Bern, Switzerland and its implications for the Swiss confederation.
D.Phil., Oxford, 1980.

1405. TROUST, J.C. Geneva and the first réfuge: a study of the social and economic effects of French and Italian refugees in Geneva in the sixteenth and early seventeenth centuries.
D.Phil., Oxford, 1968.

XXII. USSR/RUSSIA

1406. BARTLETT, R.P. Foreign settlement in Russia, 1760-1804: aspects of the government policy and its implementation.
D.Phil., Oxford, 1972.

1407. BOJCUN, J.M. Ukrainian nationalism and Soviet power in the Second World War.
M.Litt., Glasgow, 1977.

1408. FADNER, F.L. Development of pan-Slavist thought in Russia from Karazin to Danilevski 1800-1870.
Ph.D., School of Slavonic and East European Studies, London, 1949.

1409. FRANKEL, J. Socialism and Jewish nationalism in Russia, 1892-1907.
Ph.D., Cambridge, 1961.

1410. HENKO, J.P. The Ukrainian-Jewish political relationship during the period of the central Rada, March 1917-January 1918.
M.Litt., Oxford, 1981.

1411. KARIDIS, B. The Greek communities in Southern Russia in aspects of their formation and commercial enterprise, 1771-1829.
M.A., Birmingham, 1977.

1412. KRAWCHENKO, B.A. Social mobilization and national consciousness in 20th-century Ukraine.
D.Phil., Oxford, 1982.

1413. LANE, C.O. The impact of communist ideology and the Soviet order on Christian religion in the contemporary U.S.S.R. (1959-1974).
Ph.D., London School of Economics and Political Science, 1976.

1413A. MAHER, J.E. Nationality and society: a study of trends in national stratification among the union republics of the USSR.
Ph.D., Essex, 1981.

1414. MYKULA, W. Nationality policies and nationalism in the Soviet Ukraine 1920-1929.
B.Litt., Oxford, 1961.

1415. OGDEN, D.G. National Communism in Georgia 1921-1923.
Ph.D., School of Slavonic and East European Studies, London, 1977.

1416. ROSEN, K. A study of the Musar movement.
M.A., Manchester, 1943.
(Russian Jews)

1417. RUBESS, B.N. Janis Rainis and the problem of nationalism.
D.Phil., Oxford, 1982.
(Rainis (1865-1925) - a Latvian author and poet)

1418. SARAY, M. The Turkmens in the age of imperialism: a study of the Turkmen people and their incorporation into the Russian Empire.
Ph.D., Wales (Swansea), 1978.

1419. SAUNDERS, D.B. The political and cultural impact of the Ukraine on Great Russia c.1775-1835.
D.Phil., Oxford, 1978.
(beginnings of modern Ukrainian nationalism)

1420. SHUKMAN, H. The Jewish Bund and the Russian Social-Democratic Party, 1897-1903/5.
D.Phil., Oxford, 1961.

1421. URRY, J. The closed and open: social and religious change among the Mennonites in Russia, 1789-1889.
D.Phil., Oxford, 1978.

1422. WINAWER, H.M. The Jewish question in the district of Wilno in 1880-1914.
B.Phil., Oxford, 1948.

XXIII. YUGOSLAVIA

1423. McGHIE, D. Regional economic policy and regional economic development: a case study of Yugoslavia.
D.Phil., Sussex, 1980.

LATIN AMERICA

I. GENERAL STUDIES

1424. JIMINEZ DE SLIBE, M.A. Indian slavery in Venezuela and Brazil in the late sixteenth century.
M.A., Liverpool, 1977.

1425. KENNY, M. The integration of Spanish expatriates in Ibero-America and their influence on their communities of origin.
D.Phil., Oxford, 1968.

II. ARGENTINA

1426. BAILEY, J.P. The British community in Argentina.
Ph.D., Surrey, 1976.

1427. CADFAN, N.H. Hanes a llenyddiaeth cychwyniad a datblygiad mudiad y wladfa Gymreig ym Mhatagonia. (The history and literature of the origin and development of the Welsh colony in Patagonia.)
M.A., Wales, 1942.

1428. LORD, M.B. Italian immigration into the Argentine Republic.
M.A., Manchester, 1939.

1429. SKINNER, K.E.M. The relationship between the Welsh colonies in Chubut and the Argentine government with special reference to the work of Engineer Williams, 1875-1905.
Ph.D., Wales, 1977.

1430. VÁZQUEZ-PRESEDO, V. The role of foreign trade and migration in the development of the Argentine economy 1870-95.
D.Phil., Oxford, 1968.

1430A. WILLIAMS, G. Aspects of modernisation and sociocultural change within the Welsh colony in Patagonia.
Ph.D., Wales (Aberystwyth), 1972.

1431. WILLIAMS, R.B. Llenyddiaeth Gymraeg y Wladfa. (The Welsh literature of the colony in Patagonia.)
M.A., Wales, 1931.

III. BELIZE/BRITISH HONDURAS

1432. ASHDOWN, P.D. Race, class and the unofficial majority in British Honduras 1890-1949.
D.Phil., Sussex, 1979.

IV. BRAZIL

1433. GRIFFITHS, M. The development of religious pluralism in Brazil.
M.Litt., Glasgow, 1976.

1434. MASON, M. Contemporary colonisation processes in the North-east Mato Grosso, Brazil.
Ph.D., University College, London, 1978.

1434A. REID, H.A. Some aspects of movement, growth and change among the Hapdu Maku Indians of Brazil.
Ph.D., Cambridge, 1979.
(includes consideration of relations with non-Indians, work of Salesian missionaries.)

1435. STANIFORD, P. Political organisation in the North Brazilian community with special reference to Japanese immigrants.
Ph.D., London School of Economics and Political Science, 1967.

V. COLOMBIA

1436. FEARER, J. Ethnographic survey of the Indians of the Sierra Nevada de Santa Marta, Colombia.
B.Litt., Oxford, 1965.

1437. LONG, V. Acculturation and bilingualism in Guambia (Colombia).
Ph.D., St. Andrew's, 1980.

VI. GUYANA/BRITISH GUIANA

1438. DENNINGTON, G.L. Race relations between Africans and East Indians in British Guiana.
M.Sc.*, London, External, 1965.

1439. JAYAWARDENA, C. Social structure of a sugar estate community in British Guiana with special reference to theories of social conflict and control.
Ph.D., London School of Economics and Political Science, 1960.

1440. MANGRU, B. From Bengal to British Guiana: the emigration of Indian indentured labour, 1854-1884.
Ph.D., School of Oriental and African Studies, London, 1981.

1441. MENEZES, M.N. British policy towards the Amerindians in British Guyana, 1803-73.
Ph.D., University College, London, 1973.

1442. MOORE, R.J. East Indians and negroes in British Guiana, 1838-1880.
D.Phil., Sussex, 1970.

1443. O'CONNELL, V.E. Developments in the ideology of African ethnic groups in Guyana.
D.Phil., Oxford, 1972.

1444. RAMNARINE, T. The establishment and growth of the East Indian community in Guyana, 1880-1920.
D.Phil., Sussex, 1977.

1445. RIVIERE, P.G. An ethnographic survey of the Indians of the divide of the Guienese and Amazonian river systems.
B.Litt., Oxford, 1964.

1446. SINGH, T. Race, crime and culture: a study of Indians in Guyana.
Ph.D., Wales (Cardiff), 1979.

1447. SMITH, R.T. The negro family in rural British Guiana.
Ph.D., Cambridge, 1955.

1448. SUKDEO, I.D. Racial integration with special reference to Guyana.
D.Phil., Sussex, 1969.

VII. MEXICO

1449. ARIZPE-SCHLOSSER, L. Migration and ethnicity: the Mazahua Indians of Mexico.
Ph.D., London School of Economics and Political Science, 1975.

1450. KING, L.V. Indian schooling in Mexico, with particular reference to the Tzeltal-Tzotzil communities of the highlands of Chiapas.
B.Litt., Oxford, 1978.

VIII. NICARAGUA

1451. HOLM, J.A. The Creole English of Nicaragua's Miskito Coast: its sociolinguistic history and a comparative study of its lexicon and syntax.
Ph.D., University College, London, 1978.

IX. PERU

1452. ALTAMIRANO RUA, T. Regional commitment and political involvement amongst migrants in Lima: the case of regional associations.
Ph.D., Durham, 1980.

1453. GOLD, D.J. Sixteenth century European thought and its influence on Spanish colonial policy towards the Indians in Peru, 1532-42.
B.Litt., Oxford, 1978.

1454. HOGGARTH, P.F. Bilingualism in Calca, Department of Cuzco, Peru.
Ph.D., St. Andrew's, 1974.

1455. JONES, H.S. Educational aspects of the problem of racial integration in Peru.
M.A., London, External, 1961.

1456. SÁNCHEZ, R. Economy, ideology and political struggle in the Andean Highlands: a study of peasant protest in Southern Peru.
D.Phil., Sussex, 1977.

1457. SCAZZOCCHIO, F. Ethnicity and boundary maintenance among Peruvian Forest Quechua.
Ph.D., Cambridge, 1979-80.

X. VENEZUELA

1458. HENLEY, P.S. The internal social organisastion of the Panare of Venezuelan Guiana and their relations with the national society.
Ph.D., Cambridge, 1979.

MIDDLE EAST

I. GENERAL STUDIES

1459. AWAD, M. The conflict of nationalism and imperialism with particular reference to the Near and Middle East.
Ph.D., London, 1926.

1459A. COLLETT, P.R. Some psychological differences between Arabs and Englishmen and their implications for Arab-English encounters.
D.Phil., Oxford, 1973.

1460. GREENSHIELDS, T.H. The settlement of Armenian refugees in Syria and Lebanon 1915-1939.
Ph.D., Durham, 1979.

1461. RASHEED, N.S. Slave girls under the early Abbasids.
Ph.D., St. Andrew's, 1973.

II. BAHRAIN

1462. HOLES, C.D. A socio-linguistic study of the Arabic-speaking speech-community of Bahrain: language variation in relation to sect-membership, region and literacy.
Ph.D., Cambridge, 1981.

III. IRAN

1463. FARINPOUR, A.A. Regional development policy in developing countries: a case study of Iran.
M.Phil., Reading, 1975.

1464. SINGER, A.F.V. A study of the impact of social and cultural change upon ethnic identity in eastern Iran.
D.Phil., Oxford, 1976.

1465. SPOONER, B.J. Religion and political leadership in Persian Baluchistan: a study in the confusion of spiritual and temporal authority.
D.Phil., Oxford, 1967.

IV. IRAQ

1466. AHMAD, L.I. The role of the Turks in Iraq during the caliphate of Mu'tasim 218-27/833-42.
Ph.D., Manchester, 1965.

1467. AL-JABIRI, K.F.F. The 'Yezidis' in North Iraq.
B.Litt., Oxford, 1967.

1468. AL-JAMIL, K. Nationalism in Iraq 1936-1941: Rashid Ali and foreign involvement.
Ph.D., Keele, 1978.

1469. JAWAD, S.N. Iraq and the Kurdish question (1958-1970).
Ph.D., Wales (Aberystwyth), 1977.

1470. KHESHAK, S.H. The Kurds of Sulaimaniya Liwa.
Ph.D., Reading, 1958.

V. ISRAEL, PALESTINE: RELATIONS BETWEEN JEWS AND ARABS IN MIDDLE EAST

1471. ABDEL RAHMAN, A.W.A. British policy towards the Arab revolt in Palestine 1936-1939.
Ph.D., School of Oriental and African Studies, London, 1972.

1472. AL-KHFAJI, T.M.H. Arabs in Palestine before Muhammad.
M.A.*, Wales (Cardiff), 1982.

1473. BADRUD-DIN, A.A. The Arab League in Palestine, 1944-1949.
B.Litt., Oxford, 1960.

1474. BARER, R.G. Conflict and immigration in Israel, with special reference to rural cooperatives.
M.Soc.Sc.*, Birmingham, 1969.

1475. BERNSTEIN, D. The Black Panthers in Israel, 1971-72: contradiction and protest in the process of nation-building.
D.Phil., Sussex, 1976.

1476. BLACK, I.M. Zionism and the Arabs 1936-1939.
Ph.D., London School of Economics and Political Science, 1978.

1477. BROWN, D.W. Ideology and political relations in Israeli immigrant cooperatives (Moshvei Olim).
M.A.(Econ.), Manchester, 1974.

1478. BUDEIRI, M.K. The Palestine Community Party: its Arabization and the Arab-Jewish conflict in Palestine, 1929-1948.
Ph.D., London School of Economics and Political Science, 1977.

1479. CHARTERS, D.A. Insurgency and counter-insurgency in Palestine, 1945-1947.
Ph.D., King's College, London, 1980.

1480. COHEN, M.Y. Policies and politics in Palestine, 1936-1939: an analysis of British Zionist and Arab aspirations in Palestine and the Middle East.
Ph.D., London School of Economics and Political Science, 1972.

1481. COHEN, P.S. Leadership and politics amongst Israeli Yemenis.
Ph.D., London School of Economics and Political Science, 1962.

1482. DAUGHTREY, J. Cultural reversion among Arabs in Israel: a reappraisal; a study of the social and economic organisation of Arab villages.
M.A.(Econ.), Manchester, 1976.

1483. DESHEN, S.A. Religion and ethnicity in an Israeli local election.
Ph.d., Manchester, 1968.

1484. FREEMAN, P.G. The origins, course and intentions of the Palestinian Arab General Strike of 1936.
M.A., Ulster, 1975.

1485. FRISCHWASSER, H.F. The Palestine problem, 1900-1950: some geographical considerations.
B.Litt., Oxford, 1951.

1486. GOODSON, D.C. Palestine as a type region of the Mohammedan World.
M.A., Reading, 1936.

1487. HERRMAN, I.M. Anglo-Zionist relations from Herzl to the Balfour Declaration.
D.Phil., Oxford, 1972.

1488. JONES, G.L. The position of the Jewish community in Palestine in the first two centuries after the exile.
M.A., Wales, 1930.

1489. JONES, M.D. British and United States policy on Palestine after the Second World War.
Ph.D., London, 1982.

1490. KAMHAWI, L.W. Palestinian-Arab relations: a study of the political attitudes and activities of the Palestinians in the Arab host-states, 1949-1967.
Ph.D., University College, London, 1978.

1491. KAYYALI, A.W.S. The Palestinian Arab reactions to Zionism and the British mandate, 1917-1939.
Ph.D., School of Oriental and African Studies, London, 1970.

1492. KLUG, A.L. The politics and practices of the Israeli occupation and their impact on the economic, social and political structures of the West Bank, June 1967 to October 1973.
Ph.D., Birmingham, 1980.

1493. LEIFER, M. Zionism and Palestine in British opinion and policy 1945-1959.
Ph.D., London School of Economics and Political Science, 1960.

1494. LINTHWAITE, J.M. Zionism and British policy in Palestine.
M.Phil., Nottingham, 1981.

1495. LOURIE, J.I. Anthropometry of middle-caste Jews in Israel: studies of two groups of young immigrants of two different origins living under similar conditions.
Ph.D., University College, London, 1972.

1496. MANDEL, N.J. Turks, Arabs and Jewish immigration into Palestine 1882-1914.
D.Phil., Oxford, 1965.

1497. MANNERS, J. The United Nations and the Palestine problem, 1947-9.
M.A., Durham, 1974.

1498. MILLER, D. The absorption of immigrants in Israel.
B.Sc., Oxford, 1956.

1499. MINKOVITZ, M. A study of the settlement of a community of Moroccan Jews in an Israeli cooperative village.
Ph.D., Manchester, 1969.

1500. MOSSEK, M. Immigration policy in Palestine under Sir Herbert Samuel: British, Zionist and Arab attitudes.
Ph.D., London School of Economics and Political Science, 1975.

1501. NEWMAN, D. The role of Gush Emunin and Yishuv Kehillati in the West Bank, 1974-1980.
Ph.D., Durham, 1981.

1502. NOTTINGHAM, J.M. A study of the ideology of Palestinian Arab nationalism since 1948.
M.A., Durham, 1974.

1503. PARFITT, T.V. A study of the Jewish population in Palestine, 1800-1882.
D.Phil., Oxford, 1976.

1504. PORTUGALI, J. The effect of nationalism on the settlement pattern of Israel with special reference to Jerusalem.
Ph.D., London School of Economics and Political Science, 1977.

1505. RIEMER, S. Wages and immigrant absorption in Israel, 1948-1955.
Ph.D., Cambridge, 1962.

1506. ROSE, N.A. Gentile Zionism and Anglo-Zionist diplomacy, 1929-1939: some aspects of the role played by Gentile Zionists in relations between the British Government and the Jewish Agency.
Ph.D., London School of Economics and Political Science, 1968.

1507. ROUMANI, M.M. The contribution of the army to national integration in Israel: the case of Oriental Jews.
Ph.D., School of Oriental and African Studies, London, 1972.

1508. SARGENT, A.J. The British Labour Party and Palestine, 1917-1949.
Ph.D., Nottingham, 1981.

1509. SCHONTHAL, D.J.J. The Arab-Israeli conflict: primarily a sociological appreciation.
M.Sc.(Econ.), London School of Economics and Political Science, 1957.

1510. SHALLCROSS, H.M. Absorption: a study of the absorption of British groups in the Israeli Kibbutz.
M.Litt., Glasgow, 1974.

1511. SHEFFER, G. Policy making and British policies towards Palestine, 1929-39.
D.Phil., Oxford, 1971.

1512. SMITH, B.J. British economic policy in Palestine towards the development of the Jewish national home, 1920-9.
D.Phil., Oxford, 1978.

1513. TAGGAR, Y. The Mufti of Jerusalem and Palestine Arab politics, 1930-1937.
M.A., London School of Economics and Political Science, 1973.

1514. TSIMHONI, D. The British mandate and the Arab Christians in Palestine 1920-5.
Ph.D., School of Oriental and African Studies, London, 1976.

1515. USSISHKIN, A.N. Nazism and the German Christian communities in Palestine, 1917-29.
M.A., Queen Mary College, London, 1965.

1516. WASSERSTEIN, B.M.J. British officials and the Arab-Jewish conflict in Palestine, 1917-29.
D.Phil., Oxford, 1974.

1517. WEIL, S. Bene Israel Indian Jews in Lod, Israel: a study of persistence of ethnicity and ethnic identity.
D.Phil., Sussex, 1977.

1518. ZWEIG, R.W. British policy to Palestine, May 1939 to 1943: the fate of the White Paper.
Ph.D., Cambridge, 1978.

VI. JORDAN

1519. PLASCOV, A.O. The Palestinian refugees in Jordanian politics, 1948-1957.
Ph.D., School of Oriental and African Studies, London, 1978.

VII. LEBANON

1520. ADAMS, R.A. The social organisation of a Shi'ite community in Northern Lebanon.
Ph.D., Manchester, 1978.
(conflicts between Muslim Shi'ites and Christians)

1521. ATIYAH, N.W. The attitude of the Lebanese Sunnis towards the State of Lebanon.
Ph.D., School of Oriental and African Studies, London, 1975.

1522. BEDOYAN, H. The internal power structure and political leadership, of the Armenian and Druz communities in modern Lebanon (1943-72) and their political activities in three major crises.
D.Phil., Oxford, 1978.

1523. McDOWALL, D.B. The Druza revolt, 1925-7 and its background in the late Ottoman period.
B.Litt., Oxford, 1973.

1524. ZAMIR, M. The formation of modern Lebanon, 1918-1926.
Ph.D., London School of Economics and Political Science, 1980.

VIII. SYRIA

1525. ALI, J.S. The Christians of the Jazira, 17-132A.H./638-750 A.D.
Ph.D., Edinburgh, 1982.

1526. MIRZA, N.A. The Ismailis in Syria at the time of the Crusades.
Ph.D., Durham, 1964.

IX. TURKEY AND THE OTTOMAN EMPIRE

1527. ALEXANDRIS, A. The Greek minority in Turkey, 1918-1950: an aspect of Greco-Turkish relations.
Ph.D., King's College, London, 1979.

1528. COOPER, H. The Responsa of Rabbi Joseph ibn Leb: a study in the religious, social and economic conditions of the Jewish communities within the Ottoman Empire during the sixteenth to seventeenth centuries.
Ph.D., London, External, 1964.

1529. DUNLOP, D.M. The history of the Jewish Khazars.
D.Litt., Glasgow, 1955.

1530. KRIKORIAN, M.K. The participation of the Armenian community in Ottoman public life in Eastern Anatolia and Syria, 1860-1908.
Ph.D., Durham, 1963.

1531. NASSIBIAN, A. Britain and the Armenian question, 1915-23.
D.Phil., Oxford, 1981.

1532. WEEKS, D.C. The Armenian question and British policy in Turkey, 1894-1896.
M.A., King's College, London, 1951.

X. YEMEN

533. MAWI, N.El-H, H.M.A., El-A. Jews in Yemen in seventeenth-nineteenth centuries according to Hebrew sources in comparison with Arabic Yameni sources.
Ph.D., St. Andrew's, 1970.

NORTH AMERICA

I. GENERAL STUDIES

1534. DICKSON, R.J. An investigation into the causes, extent and character of emigration from the northern parts of Ireland to colonial America with particular reference to activities in Ireland of promoters of American lands.
Ph.D., Queen's University, Belfast, 1949.

1535. DIXON, J.T. Aspects of Yorkshire emigration to North America, 1760-1880.
Ph.D., Leeds, 1982.

1536. JOHNSON, S.C. A history of emigration from the United Kingdom to North America 1763-1912.
D.Sc., London, 1913.

1537. KEEP, G.R.C. The Irish migration to North America in the second half of the nineteenth century.
Ph.D., Trinity College, Dublin, 1952.

1538. LOCKHART, A. Some aspects of emigration from Ireland to the North American colonies 1660-1775.
M.Litt., Trinity College, Dublin, 1971.

1539. MACKINTOSH, J.D. Factors in emigration from the islands of Scotland to North America, 1772-1803.
M.Litt., Aberdeen, 1979.

1540. MOREHOUSE, F.M.I. Migration from the United Kingdom to North America 1840-1850.
Ph.D., Manchester, 1926.

1541. THOMAS, J.A. Anglican spiritual a[id] to foreign settlers and native peoples in 18th century America.
Ph.D., Southampton, 1956.

1542. WILSON, J.A. The depletion of natural resources of human talent in the United Kingdom: a special aspect of migration to North America, 1952-64.
Ph.D., Queen's University, Belfast, 1965.

II. CANADA

A. GENERAL STUDIES

1543. BARBER, M.J. The assimilation of immigrants to the Canadian Prairie Provinces, 1896-1918: Canadian perception and Canadian policies.
Ph.D., King's College, London, 1975.

1544. BIRBALSINGH, F.M. National identi[ty] and the Canadian novel in English, 1917-1967.
Ph.D., London, External, 1972.

1545. CAMERON, H.M.W. Wilmot Horton's experimental emigration to Upper Canada: his management of the emigration and his evaluation of the prospects and progress [of] his settlers.
B.Litt., Oxford, 1972.

1546. CHIASSON, R.J. Bilingualism in th[e] schools of Eastern Nova Scotia.
Ph.D., Institute of Education, London, 1959.

1547. GARCIA, D. Elaboration du système scolaire bi-confessional au Canada-Est, 1840-1867.
M.Phil., King's College, London, 1975.

1548. GOLDRING, P. British colonists and imperial interests in Lower Canada, 1820 to 1841.
Ph.D., Queen Mary College, London, 1978.

1549. GRIFFITHS, N.E.S. The Acadian deportation: causes and development.
Ph.D., London, External, 1970.

1550. LAWLESS, D.J. Motivation for migration to Canada: studies of applicants to London, Cologne and Dublin.
M.A., Birkbeck College, London, 1963.

1551. MACKENZIE, J.A. The courts and Canadian federalism: an historical, analytical, evaluative study of the interpretation of the British North America Act.
Ph.D., London School of Economics and Political Science, 1971.

1552. RICHMOND, A.H. The absorption of post-war immigrants in Canada.
Ph.D., London, External, 1965.

1553. STROTHARD, J.A. John Galt and the Canada Company: the early years of settlement, 1824-1829.
M.Phil., Edinburgh, 1979.

1554. STUBBS, G.M. The geography of cultural assimilation in the Prairie Provinces.
D.Phil., Oxford, 1967.

1555. WALPOLE, K.A. Emigration to British North America under the early Passenger Acts, 1803-1842.
M.A., London, 1929.

B. STUDIES OF SPECIFIC MINORITY AND IMMIGRANT GROUPS

a) Canadian Indians/Eskimos

1556. BOCKSTOCE, J.R. The changing society of the Eskimos in Canada's eastern Arctic.
B.Litt., Oxford, 1969.

1557. BUTT, A.J. The social organisation of the central and eastern Eskimo.
B.Litt., Oxford, 1951.

1558. DUNNING, R.W. Social and economic change among the Northern Ojibwa (Canada), with special reference to kinship and marriage.
Ph.D., Cambridge, 1957.

1559. DYCK, N.E. Advocacy brokerage and leadership: an examination of inter-band political organisation among Saskatchewan Indians.
Ph.D., Manchester, 1976.

1560. MILLOY, J.S. The era of civilization: British policy for the Indians of the Canadas, 1830-60.
D.Phil., Oxford, 1978.

1561. RICHES, D.J. A study of social change amongst the Killinirngmiut Eskimo of Canada's East Arctic.
Ph.D., London School of Economics and Political Science, 1975.

1562. SCRUTON, A.M. The education of American Indian children in British Columbia: a Holmesian case study.
M.Ed., Liverpool, 1978.

1563. SLATTERY, B. The land rights of indigenous Canadian peoples as affected by the Crown's acquisition of their territories.
D.Phil., Oxford, 1979.

b) English

1564. CELL, G.M. The English in Newfoundland 1577-1660.
Ph.D., Liverpool, 1964.

1565. HANDCOCK, W.G. An historical geography of the origins of English settlement in Newfoundland: a study of the migration process.
Ph.D., Birmingham, 1980.

c) French

1566. DESHAIES-LAFONTAINE, D. A socio-phonetic study of a Quebec-French community: Trois-Rivières.
Ph.D., University College, London, 1975.

1567. METCALFE, R.D. Aspects of French-Canadian nationalism.
B.Litt., Oxford, 1968.

1568. MITCHELL, M.J. Aspects of Quebec nationalism.
B.Litt., Oxford, 1974.

1569. SANCTON, A.B. Governing Montreal: the impact of French-English differences on metropolitan policies.
D.Phil., Oxford, 1978.

d) Irish

1570. TONER, P.M. The rise of Irish nationalism in Canada, 1858-84.
Ph.D., National University of Ireland (Galway), 1976.

e) Jews

1571. ANDREWS, H.P. The social structure of the Jewish community in an eastern Canadian city.
B.Litt., Oxford, 1954.

1572. SWITZER, K.B. Baron de Hirsch, the Jewish Colonization Association and Canada, 1891-1914.
Ph.D., London, 1982.

f) Scots

1573. CAMERON, J.M. A study of the factors that assisted and directed Scottish emigration to Upper Canada, 1815-1855.
Ph.D., Glasgow, 1971.

1574. KENNEDY, P.D. The Canadian identity as a focus for the study of Scots in Canada.
M.Litt., Edinburgh, 1977.

1575. McLEAN, M.L. 'In the new land a new Glengarry': migration from the Scottish Highlands to Upper Canada, 1750-1820.
Ph.D., Edinburgh, 1982.

g) Sikhs

1576. BHATTI, F.M. East Indian immigration to Canada, 1905-1973.
Ph.D., Surrey, 1975.

III. UNITED STATES OF AMERICA

A. GENERAL STUDIES

1577. ADAMS, M.C.C. Our masters and the rebels: the North and the myth of a martial South, 1861-5.
D.Phil., Sussex, 1973.

1578. CONWAY, A.A. New Orleans as a port of immigration.
M.A., University College, London, 1949.

1579. HAMPSHIRE, A.P. Mormonism in Illinois, 1839-1847: a study in the development of socio-religious conflict.
Ph.D., Durham, 1979.

1580. HART, D.R. Americanization and the education of the immigrant: a selected annotated biliography of the North Atlantic and North Central States 1880-1920.
M.A.*, Sheffield, 1979.

1581. KAPLANOFF, M.D. Making the South solid: politics and the structure of society in South Carolina 1790-1815.
Ph.D., Cambridge, 1980.

1582. LENNON, J.F. The Chicago foreign-language press and social issues, 1880-1920.
M.A., Manchester, 1975.

1583. MACLEOD, D.J. Racial attitudes in revolutionary and early national America.
Ph.D., Cambridge, 1970.

1584. MUNSLOW, A. The urban political assimilation of European immigrants in the United States 1870-1920.
Ph.D., Wales (Cardiff), 1979.

1585. MURPHY, M.J. British views of the American racial minorities: 1917-1945 with special reference to travel literature.
M.Phil., Nottingham, 1975.

1586. ROBERTS, H.W. The influence of the relations between groups upon the inner life of groups with special reference to black and white in the Southern States of the United States during the nineteenth century.
M.A., London School of Economics and Political Science, 1934.

1587. RUSSELL, J.de B. The theology of American protestantism and race relations.
Ph.D., Edinburgh, 1966.

1588. WENKERT, R. Accommodation and conflict between racial groups in an American community.
D.Phil., Oxford, 1971.

1589. WYNN, D.R. Trade unions and the 'new' immigration: a study of the United Mine Workers of America 1890-1920.
Ph.D., London School of Economics and Political Science, 1976.

B. **STUDIES OF SPECIFIC MINORITY AND IMMIGRANT GROUPS**

a) Afro-Americans

1590. ALLAN, P.M.L. Freedom and entertainment: Congress and courts, 1861-1865.
Ph.D., Glasgow, 1973.

1591. BARNES, R.P. "Blessings flowing free": the Father Divine Peace Mission movement in Harlem, New York City, 1932-1941.
D.Phil., York, 1979.

1592. BEARDSMORE, V. Moses, martyr and messiah: Abraham Lincoln and black emancipation: a study in the popular development and political use of myth, 1860-1880.
Ph.D., Kent, 1980.

1593. BURNS, J.R. Continuity and change: a comparative study of the Afro-Americans and the women's suffrage movement as minority groups in American society, 1900-1929.
M.Phil., Sheffield, 1979.

1594. CRANDALL, G.F. Black power in the deep South: a study of the Freedom movement in Alabama and Mississippi since the Civil Rights period.
D.Phil., Oxford, 1973.

1595. EVANS, D. The Harlem riot of 1933.
M.A., Sussex, 1975.

1596. FAIRCLOUGH, A. A study of the Southern Christian Leadership Conference and the rise and fall of the non-violent civil rights movement.
Ph.D., Keele, 1977.

1597. FINNIE, H.M. Scottish attitudes towards American Reconstruction, 1865-77.
Ph.D., Edinburgh, 1975.

1598. GOODMAN, M.H. The black bar: the black enlisted man in the Union Army, 1861-5.
Ph.D., Nottingham, 1976.

1599. GREER, C.S. Attitudes towards the Negro in New York City, 1890-1914.
M.A., London School of Economics and Political Science, 1968.

1600. McCALLUM, D.P.F. A unique experiment in Southern race relations?: Negroes, populists and the black political experience reconsidered.
M.A., Sussex, 1976.

1601. McINTOSH, W.L. The American negro faces European immigrtion in the United States, 1830-1924.
Ph.D., Cambridge, 1971.

1602. McKAY, D.H. Race and housing in the United States: a study of federal power and the 1968 Civil Rights Act.
Ph.D., Essex, 1974.

1603. MILES, M.G. A study of the negro in the Southern cities of the United States in the immediate post-Civil War period, 1865-1868.
M.A., Wales (Aberystwyth), 1969.

1604. SMITH, G.A. An American occupation: black American soldiers in Britain in World War II.
Ph.D., Keele, 1982.

1605. TREVAIL, J.J. British opinion on the Afro-American with special reference to prominent travellers, 1877-1932.
M.Litt., Edinburgh, 1975.

1606. WILSON, E.L. An analysis and interpretation of the life, writings and philosophy of Martin Luther King.
D.Phil., Oxford, 1981.

1607. WYNN, N.A. The Afro-American and the Second World War.
Ph.D., Open University, 1973.

1608. ZAROD, H. Recent forces of change affecting radical black American women.
Ph.D., Keele, 1980.

b) American Indians (including general studies of North American Indians)

1609. CALLOWAY, C.G. British relations with North American Indians from the end of the War of Independence to the end of war of 1812.
Ph.D., Leeds, 1978.

1610. EDNEY, J.R. Sir William Johnston and the Iroquois Indians in the French and Indian War, 1754-63.
M.A., Wales, 1978.

1611. FEAR, J.M. American Indian education: the reservation schools, 1870-1900.
Ph.D., University College, London, 1978.

1612. HASLOP, G.S.B. Anglo-native relations in North America in early Stuart times up to 1644.
M.A., Leeds, 1932.

1613. KUPPERMAN, K.O. British attitudes towards the American Indian, 1580-1640.
Ph.D., Cambridge, 1977.

1614. NICHOLSON, M.R. Iroquois and Europeans: a study of a seventeenth century contact situation.
M.A., London School of Economics and Political Science, 1955.

1615. PAGDEN, A.R.D. The American Indian as barbarian: a reassessment of some sixteenth centuy views on the nature of Amerindian man and his society.
D.Phil., Oxford, 1970.

1616. SEYMOUR, O.C. The religion of Cherokee Indians.
Ph.D., Edinburgh, 1934.

c) British/English immigrants

1617. BURCHELL, R.A. British immigration to California before 1870.
B.Litt., Oxford, 1969.

1618. BUSH, J.A. Early British immigrants to Virginia, 1615-1635.
B.Litt., Oxford, 1977.

1619. MARGRAVE, R.D. The emigration of silk workers from England to the United States of America in the nineteenth century with special reference to Coventry, Macclesfield, Paton, New Jersey and South Manchester, Connecticut.
Ph.D., London School of Economics and Political Science, 1981.

1620. PACKER, E.B. Middle-class British immigration to the trans-Mississippi West, 1870-1900.
M.Sc., London School of Economics and Political Science, 1967

1621. TAYLOR, P.A.M. Mormon emigration from Great Britain to the United States, 1840-70.
Ph.D., Cambridge, 1952.

1622. TRESCATHERIC, B. The Furness colony: the history of an emigration society in Great Britain and Minnesota from 1872 to c.1882.
M.Litt., Lancaster, 1981.

1623. TYACK, N.C.P. Migration from East Anglia to New England before 1660.
Ph.D., London School of Economics and Political Science, 1951.

1624. WAINWRIGHT, M.D. Agencies for the promotion or facilitation of emigration from England to the United States of America, 1815-1861.
M.A., Bedford College, London, 1952.

1625. WICKENDEN, H.J. Emigration from Taunton to New England, 1625-45.
M.A., Bristol, 1929.

d) Canadians

1626. BROOKES, A.A. Migration from the Maritime Provinces of Canada to Boston, Massachusetts, 1860-1900.
M.A., Hull, 1975.

e) Gypsies

1627. LOUIS, A.S. Social organisation of the Romany in America.
D.Phil., Oxford, 1972.

f) Irish

1628. ROLLO, D.A.T. Comparative aspects of Irish politics in Boston, New York and Glasgow.
M.Litt., Edinburgh, 1972.

g) Jews

1629. KHEDERI, H. Foreign policy and domestic pressures: a study of the Palestine controversy in American politics, 1945-1949.
M.A., Exeter, 1960.

1630. YUVAL-DAVIS, N. The new Jewish movement; Jewish nationalism and radical politics in the United States of America.
D.Phil., Sussex, 1979.

h) Mexicans

1631. GUNN, H.D. Some anthropological aspects of Mexican immigrant settlement in Dallas, Texas.
M.A., London School of Economics and Political Science, 1949.

i) Puerto Ricans

1632. JACKSON, P.A. A social geography of Puerto Ricans in New York.
D.Phil., Oxford, 1980.

j) Scots

1633. BAILES, E.S. The Scottish colonization of Georgia in America, 1732-42.
Ph.D., Edinburgh, 1978.

1634. EDWARDS, P.M. The Scottish role in Midlands America, with particular reference to Wyoming, 1875-1895.
Ph.D., St. Andrew's, 1972.

1635. JONES, D.L. The background and motives of Scottish emigration to the United States of America in the period 1815-1861 with special reference to emigrant correspondence.
Ph.D., Edinburgh, 1970.

1636. MOSS, B.G. The role of Scots and Scotch-Irishmen in the southern campaigns of the War of American Independence, 1780-1783.
Ph.D., St. Andrew's, 1979.

k) Welsh

1637. ROBERTS, E.K.R.R. A contribution to the study of emigration from North Wales to the United States of America, 1800-1850.
M.A., Liverpool, 1931.

ADDENDA

(entries not indexed)

1638. ABDUL-JALIL, M.A. The dynamics of ethnic identification and ethnic group relations among people of 'Dur' Northern Darfur, Sudan.
Ph.D., Edinburgh, 1980.

1639. AFONJA, S.A. Differential rates of industrial accidents between coloured and white workers in Great Britain.
Ph.D., Birmingham, 1972.

1640. AH HOON LAI. The problems of federal finance in plural societies: case studies of Malaya and Malaysia.
D.Phil., York, 1968.

1641. ALLEN, N.F. The migrant worker in the European Economic Community: immigration and discrimination.
M.Phil., CNAA, 1980.

1642. ANTONARAS, J. Le thème de l'Orient chez Molière.
M.A., Exeter, 1977.
[The original theme of Egyptians, Turks and Moors in Molière's comedies]

1643. BARNES, H.D. The incidence of various types of porphyria in South African Bantu as compared with that in the white population with a chemical-pathological study of representative cases.
Ph.D., London, University College Hospital Medical School, 1957.

1644. BELL, R.T. An analysis of the grammar of the English spoken by Indian immigrants in Smethwick.
M.A., Birmingham, 1966.

1645. BERNIER, T.A.I. International legal aspects of federalism.
Ph.D., London, London School of Economics, 1969.

1646. BIRD, J.C. Control of enemy alien in Great Britain, 1914-18.
Ph.D., 1981.

1647. BUCHANA, W.M. Bantu siderosis in Rhodesia.
M.D., Glasgow, 1968.

1648. CAMERON, A. The importance of social factors in the medical care of Arab refugees.
M.D., Edinburgh, 1953.

1649. CASTLE, W.M. Coronary heart disease risk factors in African and European men living in Salisbury, Rhodesia and the effect on the risk factors of different African living standards.
M.D., Birmingham, 1978.

1650. CLARKE, M. Social relations between British and overseas student nurses.
M.Phil., Surrey, 1976.

1651. COLLIS, R.J.M. The relationship between certain physical factors and psychiatric disorder among the Yoruba trib of Nigeria: an evaluation of the cultural influences involved.
M.D., Dublin, Trinity College, 1964.

1652. COMBE, J.C. Huguenots in the Ministry of the Churches in Ireland - their place and contribution.
Ph.D., Queen's Belfast, 1970.

1653. COULTER, T.T. An experimental and statistical study of the relationship of prejudice and certain personality variables.
Ph.D., Institute of Psychiatry, London, 1954.

1654. DANQUAH, S.A. Aspects of adjustment of overseas African students in the University of Wales, with special reference to psychological stress.
Ph.D., Wales, Swansea, 1972.

1655. DAVIES, T.C. The educational implications of the general interests of Welsh speaking children.
M.A., Wales, Bangor, 1971.

1656 DOBB, J.P.B. Music in the multi-racial society of West Malaysia.
Ph.D., London, School of Oriental and African Studies, 1972.

1657. DUNCAN, W.A. The resurgence of the ethnic religions and the mission of the Church.
Ph.D., Dublin, Trinity College, 1966.

1658. ENGIN, N. New Commonwealth immigration and welfare effects on the United Kingdom economy.
Ph.D., Surrey, 1976.

1659. FAULKNER, R.A. Some socio-psychological concomitants of inter-racial contact in an English primary school: a comparative study.
M.Sc., Bristol, 1972.

1660. FERMAN, G. The right of individual petition and the international protection of human rights: the case of the European Convention on Human Rights.
M.A., Sussex, 1971.

1661. FIELDING, R.F. An investigation into the subject vocabularies of native and immigrant pupils on leaving Junior School.
M.Ed., Leicester, 1972.

1662. FISHBURN, E. The portrayal of immigration in nineteenth century Argentine fiction (1845-1902).
Ph.D., London, University College, 1979.

1663. FORREST, C.R. Malnutrition in the Southern Rhodesian Bantu.
M.D., Glasgow, 1953.

1664. FRAGOMICHALOS, C. Plato's attitude to slavery.
Ph.D., London, King's College, 1979.

1665. FRASER, V. America and American Indians in the sixteenth and seventeenth century imagery.
M.Phil., Warburg Institute, London, 1975.

1666. FRYER, P. 'Standing at the crossroads': politics and the hero in black popular music.
Ph.D., Keele, 1980.

1667. GANNON, R.E. Deviant features of the English speech of selected speakers of Dominican Creole resident in London.
Ph.D., Essex, 1972.

1668. GIBBS, J.M. Nationalism and drama: an examination of the interaction of national mood and national traditions with the playwright in the early work of Henrik Ibsen, John M. Synge and Wole Soyinka.
M.Litt., Bristol, 1972.

1669. GLEES, P.A. The SPD, the Labour Party and the Foreign Office: a study of exile politics in London, 1939-45.
D.Phil., Oxford, 1979.

1670. GOODWIN-GILL, G.S. The entry, establishment and removal of aliens in national and international law.
D.Phil., Oxford, 1974.

1671. GOREN, R.C. Nationality and statelessness in international law.
M.A., Liverpool, 1966.

1672. GORODECKIS, M. Aspects of upbringing influencing assimilation among children of European immigrants in Great Britain.
Ph.D., Bedford College, London, 1968.

1673. GREEN, S.M. Language differences in West Indian and non-West Indian children.
M.Phil., London, Institute of Psychiatry, 1972.

1674. GRYGIER, T. Displaced persons: a study in social and criminal psychology.
Ph.D., London, School of Economics and Political Science, 1950.

1675. HAWKHEAD, K. Identification, preference and stereotyping behaviour of young children towards ethnic groups.
Ph.D., Bradford, 1979.

1676. JALAL, A. Jinnah, the Muslim League and the demand for Pakistan.
Ph.D., Cambridge, 1982.

1677. JORDAN, R.H. Studies in early Peloponnesian migrations.
M.A., Queen's Belfast, 1971.

1678. JULKA, P. Bilingualism: cultural context of thinking.
M.Phil., Nottingham, 1978.

1679. KANDIL, S.A.Y. An investigation of the adaptation to altered domestic conditions of immigrant families in the Tahrir province of the U.A.R.
M.Phil., London, Queen Elizabeth College, 1969.

1680. KAWWA, T. A study of the interaction between native and immigrant children in an English school, with special reference to ethnic prejudice.
Ph.D., London, Institute of Education, 1966.

1681. KHAIRALLAH, S.N. Arabic studies in England in the late seventeenth and early eighteenth centuries.
Ph.D., London, School of Oriental and African Studies, 1972.

1682. KIA, M. On cultural accent.
Ph.D., Institute of Education, London, 1980.

1683. KNOWLES, L.C. In search of a national voice: some similarities between Scottish and Canadian poetry, 1860-1930.
Ph.D., St. Andrews, 1981.

1684. LIM, D. The supply response of Asian and European miners in the tin industry in Malaya.
M.A., Sussex, 1968.

1685. MACRAE, J.T. A study in the application of an economic analysis to social issues: the Maori and the New Zealand economy.
Ph.D., London, External, 1976.

1686. McCREA, W.C. An exploratory study of the problem in the teaching of English to immigrant children.
M.Ed., Liverpool, 1969.

1687. MACDONALD, N. Migration and tuberculosis.
M.D., Edinburgh, 1962.

1688. MACKIE, M.L. Some aspects of foreign workers in Europe, with special reference to Western Germany.
M.A., Liverpool, 1973.

1689. MACLEOD, F. An experimental investigation into some problems of bilingualism.
Ph.D., Aberdeen, 1969.

1690. MAPURANGA, T.M.B. The emergence of 'Ekklesiyar Yan'uwa a Nigeria': an historical analysis, 1923-1977.
Ph.D., London, External, 1980.

1691. MWEGELERA, G.R.C. Mental illness in Africans and West Indians of African origin living in London.
M.Phil., London, Institute of Psychiatry, 1971.

1692. NAWAWI, R.B.H. The attitudes of Muslims towards Christians.
M.A., Birmingham, 1972.

1693. OKAFUR, S.O. The quest for authenticity in the Christianity of south eastern Nigeria.
M.Phil., Leicester, 1980.

1694. OWEN, R.A. A study of defective vision of indeterminate pathology in West Indian immigrants living in South London.
M.D., Cambridge, 1965.

1695. PAPAIOANNOU, A. The results of a standardisation of the WISC on Greek-Cypriot children.
M.A., London, External, 1968.

1696. POLUNIN, I.V. Studies on the diseases of the aborigines and other peoples of the Malaya Peninsula.
D.M., Oxford, 1952.

1697. RAJA INDRA, R. Sinhalese population growth in Ceylon between 1911 and 1946, with special reference to corrections for the under-registration of births and deaths etc.
M.Sc., London School of Economics, 1953.

1698. RIGO SUREDA, A. The evolution of the right of self-determination: a study of the United Nations practice.
Ph.D., Cambridge, 1972.

1699. ROBERTS, S.A. The growth of an integral legal system in Malawai: a study in racial distinctions in law.
Ph.D., London School of Economics, 1968.

1700. ROWLEY, K.G. An analysis of social relations between British and non-British children in primary and modern secondary schools in a midland town.
M.A., Keele, 1967.

1701. SANDERSON, P.J. Housing and community relations: a study of policy formation and execution in a voluntary organisation in Bradford.
M.Phil., York, 1981.
(Work of Bradford Shelter Housing and Renewal Experiment (SHARE) to improve 'community relations through housing' - influence of ideologically based policies in race relations)

1702. SCOTT, S.C.C. Development paediatrics: a survey of developmental similarities and differences concerning 50 white and 50 West Indian babies in Hackney, London, up to the age of 10 months.
M.D., London, Guy's Hospital Medical School, 1975.

1703. SMITH, J.H. The Congressional Black caucus: a study of black representatives' legislative behaviour in the United States Congress.
Ph.D., Kent, 1981.

1704. SOPIEE, M.N. Political unification in the Malaysian region, 1945-1965.
Ph.D., London School of Economics, 1972.

1705. SPERL, S.R. From Indians to Trinidadians: a study of the relationship between language behaviour, socio-economic and cultural factors in a Trinidad village.
M.Phil., York, 1981.
(East Indians in Trinidad, especially the move from Hindi speaking to English)

1706. UMOZURIKE, U.O. Self-determination in international law.
D.Phil., Oxford, 1969.

1707. VORHAUS, G. Linguistic and cultural affiliations of pupils of West Indian descent in English schools.
Ph.D., Brunel, 1981.

1708. WALLS, S. A la recherche du temps perdu et l'antisemitisme proustien.
M.A., Exeter, 1978.

1709. WARD, J.B. An observational approach to the study of classroom affiliations for the immigrant child.
Ph.D., London, Institute of Education, 1972.

1710. WELLS, J.C. Phonological adaptation in the speech of Jamaicans in the London area.
Ph.D., London, University College, 1971.

1711. WHITELEY, R.W. An examination of mental illness in migrants.
M.D., Queen's Belfast, 1960.

1712. WILLIAMS, D.O. Macaulay and the Commission of Tortola.
M.Sc., Bristol, 1978.
(Work of Thomas Babington Macaulay in the early abolitionist movement)

1713. WOOD, E.R. An investigation of some aspects of social class and ethnic group differentiation in a school based junior activities centre.
M.Ed., Newcastle Upon Tyne, 1973.

1714. WRIGHT, C.B. The physical working capacity of 12 year old Birmingham schoolboys of various ethnic origins.
M.Sc., Salford, 1978.

1715. YATES, P. Immigration and education: a study of an Asian community and a comprehensive school.
D.Phil., Sussex, 1981.

1716. YOUNG, T. The eugenics movement and the eugenic idea in Britain, 1900-14: a historical study.
Ph.D., London School of Economics and Political Science, 1980.

INDEXES

Reference is to item numbers

SUBJECT INDEX

ABALUYIA people: Anglican Church 449
ABBASIDS: slavery 1461
ABERDEEN: Chinese 1321
ABERDEENSHIRE: tinkers 1193
ABILITIES
    Asian & Scots children 1105
    Bangladeshi children 1107
    Immigrant children: Great Britain 1089
    Pakistani children 1135
    West Indian children 1147
ABOLITIONIST MOVEMENT 180
    Baptists 153,174
    European diplomacy 175
    Great Britain 147-50,152,154,156-61,
        163-4,166,168-70,174,
        179,181,183
    Ireland 172
    Scotland 151,173
    Unitarians 176
    U.S.A. 146,150,162,179,181
    Wales 167
(See also: EMANCIPATION OF SLAVES, SLAVERY,
    SLAVE-TRADE)
ABORIGINES' PROTECTION SOCIETY 1024
    South Africa 527,646
    West Africa 527
    Zimbabwe: 1899-1930 636
ACADIA: deportation 1549
ACHEBE, Chinua 265
ADOLESCENTS
    attitudes to ethnic minorities 1075
    Imperialism: Great Britain 1099
    self-concept minorities in Britain 1082
        : immigrants & British 1074
ADOLESCENTS, ASIAN
    in England: bilingualism 1113A
       Great Britain 1132,1251
       Manchester: expectations 1134
ADOLESCENTS, BLACK
    girls: group therapy 1290
    political socialisation 1158
    Ras Tafarians: London 1301
    Reggae music 1302
ADOLESCENTS, MUSLIM
    in Batley 1128
       Great Britain:
          mass media 1133
          social conditions 1122
ADOLESCENTS, WEST INDIAN
    in Great Britain: attitudes 1150
ADULT EDUCATION
    immigrants: Great Britain 1091
    Jewish immigrants: London East End 1136
ADVICE CENTRES
    : immigrants: Bradford 1043

AFGHANISTAN
    Hazara Mongols 702
    Pakhtuns 701
    Swat Pathans 700
AFRICA
    Christian churches & missions 392,406,
        467
    decolonisation: U.N.O. 518
    English literature: 1660-1807 269
    English novels: 1860-1939 258
    labour migration 519
    links with Glasgow 1314
    nationalism & religion 523
    nationalism & self-government 524A
    religion: Protestant attitudes 394
AFRICA, CENTRAL
    British racial attitudes: 1840-90 8
    Christian churches & missions 413,421
    migrant labour 609
    race & churches 413
AFRICA, EAST
    Chinese contacts 576
    Christian churches & missions 436,
        448-49
    Indians 521-22,577-78,580
    multi-racial societies:
       political representation 71-72
       settlers 579
       slavery: ending 158
          : Royal Navy 161
AFRICA, NORTH
    caste 528A
    Christian church 424,427,432
AFRICA, WEST
    Aborigines' Protection Society 527
    British attitudes: humanitarian
       pressure groups 533
    Christian churches & missions 450,460
    communalism 72
    slave trade 144
       : ending 160
AFRICA, WEST (FRENCH)
    nationalism 554
AFRICAN AFFAIRS: Zimbabwe
    1894-1914 634
    1923-1939: British opinion 620
    Aborigines' Protection Society 636
AFRICAN DRAMA 270-71
AFRICAN FICTION 240,243-44,248
    250,260,265-66
    268,278-79
    (French) 253
AFRICAN INLAND MISSION: Kenya 417A
AFRICAN LITERATURE 267-68
AFRICAN METHODIST EPISCOPAL CHURCH
    : South Africa 453

Subject Index

AFRICAN STUDENTS
  in Cambridge   1153
     London   1142
     Oxford   1153
AFRICAN WORKERS
  in South Africa
      class consciousness   660
      dockworkers   655A
      gold-mining   662
    Zaire: copper mines   608
    Zambia: copper mines   608
    Zimbabwe: mines: 1930-33   635
AFRICANS
  in English drama: 16th-17th c.   257
     Guyana   1438,1442-43,1447
     London: psychiatric illness   1300
(See also BLACKS)
AFRIKANERS
  in Botswana   679
    nationalism   671
AFRO-AMERICANS
  in Harlem: riot, 1935   1595
     New York City   1599
     Scotland: 19th century   1321
     Southern States   1600
     Watts   117
  'Black power'   1594,1603
  British opinion   1605
  Civil Rights   1596
  drama   242
  emancipation: Lincoln   1592
    : Courts, 1861-65   1590
  Father Divine Peace Mission   1591
  fiction   247,254
    : Faulkner   256,263
  history: 1900-1929
     cf. American suffragettes   1593
  immigration; U.S.A.   1601
  Martin Luther King   1606
  literary criticism   251
  literature   219,262,275
  race and housing   1602
  radical women   1608
  Reconstruction: Scottish attitudes 1597
  riots: Harlem   1595
  Union army   1598
  World War II   1607
    : soldiers in Britain   1614
AIRDRIE: Irish & labour movements 1204
AL-MAGHILI: Saharan Jews   197
AL-MAS'UDI   372
AL-MUSQTATAF   336
ALABAMA: Freedom movement   1594
ALCOHOLISM: ethnicity: Hawaii   877
ALGERIA
  André Gide   255
  nationalism: French rule   529

ALIENS
  in Commonwealth   88
    Egypt   530
    England: medieval   994-1004
    Great Britain   530,1010
  control   77
  law: English   1004A
  private property rights   90
ALIENS ACT, 1905   1010
ALL-INDIA CONGRESS SOCIALIST PARTY 730
ALL-INDIA MUSLIM LEAGUE   741
AMAMPONDO people:
  Wesleyan missionaries   418
AMBOYNESE REFUGEES: Netherlands 1384
AMERICAN FICTION: Jews   291,302,312-13
AMERICAN INDIANS
  in Andean Republics: literature 239
    Brazil   1434
     : slavery   1424
    Canada   1558-60,1562-63
    Colombia   1436
    Guyana   1441
    Mexico   1449-50
    North America
      Anglican Church: 18th c.   1541
      British   23,1609-10,1612-13
    Peru   1453,1457
    River Plate countries:
      literature   237
    United States
      James Fenimore Cooper's novels 238
      education   1611
      religion   1616
    Venezuela   1458
     : slavery   1424
AMERICAN TRAVELLERS: Japan   321
ANGLICAN CHURCH
  Abaluyia   449
  Chewa   464
  Huguenots   1182
  India   501
  Ireland   1344
  Jamaica   909
  North America: 18th c.   1541
  South Africa   410
ANGLO-BOER WAR, 1899-1902
  African participation   639
  African societies   694
  English poets   230
  race and civilisation   668
ANGLO-INDIANS: education   771
ANKOLE, Uganda:
  Christian churches & missions 462A,471
ANTHROPOLOGY
  education   92
  Great Britain: 1860s   26
  intelligence theories   31
  literature   218A
  racial theories   24

ANTI-SEMITISM
in Austria 931,973
Czechoslovakia 936
Europe: medieval 205
Germany 973-74
Great Britain 1214,1236
Marconi scandal 1227
Greco-Roman diaspora 196
London 1230
Vienna 931
(See also: JEWS)
ARAB CHRISTIANS: Palestine 1514
ARAB COUNTRIES
Palestinian Arab refugees 1490
ARAB LEAGUE: Palestine 1473
ARAB LITERATURE
English literature 357
nationalism 352
ARABIA
English literature 334
influences on:
Doughty 340
Meredith 342
Tennyson 342
Thomson 342
ARABIAN GULF
: Christian mission 476
ARABIAN THOUGHT
English influences: 19th c. 336
ARABS
in Bahrain 1462
Spain 1395,1399,1401,1403
Richard Burton 355
Chaucer: influences 370
English medieval literature 360
Jewish literature 331
Marxist theory 66
psychological differences
from English 1454A
(See also PALESTINIAN ARABS)
ARGENTINA
British 1426
Italians 1428
migration: economic development 1430
Welsh: Patagonia 1427,1429,1430A,1431
ARISTOPHANES: slavery 223
ARMENIANS
in Lebanon 1522
: refugees 1460
Syria 1530
: refugees 1460
Turkish Empire 1530-32
ASHER BEN JEHIEL, Rabbi. Responsa 1392
ASHRAMS: Christian church 510
ASIA
Christian church & missions 511
influence on French literature 324
Marxist thought 69
ASIA, SOUTH: minorities 70

ASIA, SOUTH-EASTERN
Chinese 718-19,723,725
: women 722
regionalism & nationalism 73
ASIAN ADOLESCENTS
in England: bilinguals 1113A
Great Britain 1251
Manchester: expectations 1134
ASIAN CHILDREN
in England
: secondary schools 1123
: socialisation 1118
Glasgow 1105
Great Britain
English language 1106
spoken English 1067
Hillingdon 1116
Wales: secondary schools 1068
ASIAN DOCTORS: England 1253
ASIAN STUDENTS: Nottingham 1124
ASIAN WOMEN
in Great Britain 1252
: pregnancy 1248
Newcastle 1254
West Yorkshire: home tuition 1259
ASIANS
in Camberwell: psychiatric illness 1257
England
: Midlands 1245A
: Potteries 1250
Glasgow 1324
Great Britain 1245A
: libraries 1246
: medicine 1241
: working-class 1243
Huddersfield
: information services 1125
Kenya 591
London 1258
Rochdale: housing 1055
concepts of self 6
housing 1055
information services 1125
libraries 1246
medicine 1241,1253
psychiatric illness 1257
(See also: BANGLADESHI, CHINESE, INDIANS, PAKISTANIS, SIKHS, UGANDAN ASIANS)
ASIATIC MODE OF PRODUCTION
Marxism 65
ASSIMILATION
African students 1153
immigrant children: Midlands 1101
immigrants 15
Canada 1543,1554
U.S.A. 1584
Jews: Bohemia 936
Sikh children: Leeds 1104A
West Indian students 1153
West Indians: England 1299
: Manchester 1288

Subject Index

AUSTRALIA
    colonisation   874
    immigration   865
        : British   860,862,864,866
            Scots   861
    Pacific Island labour   863,888
AUSTRALIANS
    in Papua & New Guinea   876
AUSTRIA
    anti-semitism   931,973
    Jews
        : return   930
        : socialism   983
    socialism: Jews   983
AUSTRO-HUNGARIAN EMPIRE
    Bosnia-Herzegovina   929
    Czechs   940
    dissolution: British opinion   928
BABYLON: Jews: business   199
BAHRAIN: Arabs   1462
BAKUNIN, Mikhail Aleksandrovich
    Italian Socialists   1379
BALUCHISTAN   1465
BANGLADESH   703-6
BANGLADESHI
    in Great Britain
        : entrepreneurship   1259A
BANGLADESHI CHILDREN
    : abilities   1107
BANTU
    : religion & Christian church   461
BANTU AND EUROPEANS   653,656-57
'BANTU' EDUCATION   649,697
BAPTISTS
    India   506
    Jamaica   904
        : emancipation   153
    slavery   174
    West African: West Indians   460
BARBADOS
    indentured & free labour   898
    politics & economic development   898A
BARDI family: Edward III   1001
BARUCH OF ROTHENBERG: See MEIER BEN BARUCH OF ROTHENBERG
BASEL MISSION:
    Ghana & Togoland   455A
BASQUES in France   952
BATLEY: Muslim adolescents   1128
BAVARIA: National Socialism   972
BECHUANALAND: See BOTSWANA
BELGIAN CONGO: See ZAIRE
BELGIUM:
    minorities & military service   64
BELIZE: race & class   1432
BELLOW, Saul   302-3
BENE ISRAEL IMMIGRATION SOCIETY
    settlement of Indian Jews in Israel   1517

BENGAL
    British community   764
    Christian churches & missions   477, 480-81,484,502,509
    Christian schools   761
    Muslims   772-73,779,782, 784-85,795,798
    nationalism   747
BENGALI MUSLIMS: Bradford   1260
BENGALI WORKERS: Great Britain   1261
BENJAMIN (Ze'eb) BEN MATISYAHU
    Responsa   202
BERGENGRUEN, Werner: critic of National Socialism   962
BERMUDA
    bi-racial schools   899
    British settlement   892
    slavery   141
BILINGUALISM
    Calca, Peru   1454
    Canada   1547
    Great Britain: Asian adolescents   1113A
    Guambia, Colombia   1437
    Hebrides   93
    Ireland: education   1353B
    Nigeria   93
    Nova Scotia   1546
    Pakistan   93
    Samoa: education   885
    Wales   1330-31,1334-35
(See also: LANGUAGE PROBLEMS & POLICIES; MULTILINGUALISM)
BIRMINGHAM
    British Union of Fascists   1016
    immigrants: industry   1048
    Irish   1199
    secondary schools: racial prejudice   1094
    slave trade   138
BLACK ADOLESCENTS
    in Great Britain
        group therapy: girls   1290
        political socialisation   1158
BLACK CHILDREN: self-esteem   100
BLACK CULTURE: education
    West Indians: London   98
BLACK NATIONALISM   115
BLACK PANTHERS: Israel   1475
'BLACK POWER'
    Great Britain: West Indians   1304
    U.S.A.   1594
BLACKS
    in Liverpool   1291
        London: docks   1281
        Manchester   1293
        : housing   1053
        Reading   1303
        Tyneside   1164
    British attitudes   4,170

Subject Index   109

BLACKS (contd.)
 English literature: 1765-1841 245
(See also: AFRICANS, WEST INDIANS)
BLANTYRE: Church of Scotland mission 458
BLUESHIRT MOVEMENT: Ireland 1361
BLYDEN, Edward Wilmot 115
BOHEMIA
 Czechs & Germans 938
 Jews: anti-semitism 936
BOLTON, Lancs.: Irish 1208
BOROCHIVISM 68
BOSNIA-HERZEGOVINA 929
BOSTON, Mass.
 Canadians 1626
 Irish 1628
BOTSWANA
 Christian churches & missions 427
 race relations 679
BRADFORD
 Bengali Muslims 1260
 Commonwealth Citizens' Advisory
  Panel 1043
 immigrants 1030
  : education 1079
 Pakistanis 1263,1269
BRAZIL
 colonisation: Mato Grosso 1434
 Hapda Maka Indians 1434A
 Japanese 1435
 religious pluralism 1433
 slave trade: abolition 149
 slavery: Indians 1424
BRAZILIAN LITERATURE: race 216
BREMEN MISSION: Ghana/Togoland 455A
BRISTOL
 Jews 1233
 Pakistanis 1265
 Sikhs 1277
 slave trade 136-37,139
 West Indians 1298
BRITISH
 in Argentina 1426
  Australia 860,862,864,866
  Caribbean 892
  India 760,764,766-70
  Israel 1510
  Malaysia 816
  North America 1535-6,1540,1542
  Virginia 1628
(See also ENGLISH, GREAT BRITAIN, IRISH,
 SCOTS, WELSH)
BRITISH COLUMBIA
 American Indians: education 1562
BRITISH GUIANA: See GUYANA
BRITISH HONDURAS: See BELIZE
BRITISH NORTH AMERICA ACT, 1867
 Canadian federalism 1551A
BRITISH TRAVELLERS
 in India 760
  Japan 321
  U.S.A.: racial minorities 1585

BRITISH UNION OF FASCISTS 1016
BRITTANY: regional policies 949
BRIXTON
 immigration & politics 1006
 mixed marriages 1029
 riots, 1981: newspapers 1026
BRUNEI
 Chinese 724
 Christian churches 508
BRUSSELS ANTI-SLAVE TRADE ACT, 1890 166
BUCHAN, John: imperialism 235
BUDDHISM & CHRISTIANITY 482
 Korea 494
BUDDHIST ASSOCIATIONS
 Great Britain 1244
 London 1161
BUGANDA
 community & state 605
 immigrants 600
 Roman Catholic Church 468
BURAKUMIN: Japan 810
BURMA
 Indians 707
 Shan 708
BURTON, Sir Richard
 Arabs & Islam 355
BUSINESS
 Bangladeshi: U.K. 1259A
 Chinese:
  Hong Kong 726
  Malaysia 725
  Singapore 725
 Japanese: Milan 1326
 Jews: Babylon 197
BUXTON, Sir Thomas Fowell:
 abolitionist movement 177
CALABAR: Roman Catholic Church 416
CALCA, Peru: bilingualism 1454
CALCUTTA: European community 767
CALIFORNIA: British immigrants 1617
CAMBERWELL:
 Asians: psychiatric illness 1257
CAMBODIA: Chinese 709
CAMEROONS: fiction 278
CANADA
 bilingualism 1546-47
 British 1548,1564-65
 cultural assimilation 1554
 deportation: Acadia 1549
 East Indians 1576
 education & minorities 95
 Eskimos 1556-57,1561
 federalism 1551
 French 1566-69
 John Galt 1533
 Wilmot Horton 1545
 immigrants 1543,1545,1550,
   1552-3,1555
 Indians 1558-60,1562-63
 Irish 1570

Subject Index

CANADA (contd.)
    Jews   1571-72
    migration to Boston   1626
    military service & minorities   64
    missionaries in Canada   498
    national identity & fiction   1544
    Scots   1317, 1573-75
CANADA COMPANY   1553
CANADIAN FICTION:
    national identity   1544
CANADIANS in Boston, Mass.   1626
CAPE BRETON, Nova Scotia
    Scottish Presbyterians   1317
CAPE COLONY
    Christian missions   409A
    railways   676
    slavery: 18th c.   698
    white & non-whites: politics   690
CAPE COLOUREDS
    in Woodstock   117
    Aborigines' Protection Society   646
    citizenship   682
    education   685
CAPITALISM: South Africa   640
CARDIFF
    Irish   1333
    race riots, 1919   1032
CAREERS ADVICE
    immigrant school-leavers   1072
CARIBBEAN
    Black education   897
    free-labour economy   896
    integrated education   899
    regional integration   895
    slave risings   186
    slave trade   126
    slave women   121
    slavery   125
        : abolition   183
        : economic aspects   184
CARIBBEAN FICTION   241, 246, 260
CARIBBEAN LITERATURE   252
CARIBS   894
CARPENTRAS, France: Jews   944
CASEMENT, Roger: ethnic minorities   1371
CASTE
    Christians & Hindus: India   765
    North-East Africa   528A
CASTELL, Edmund: Orientalism   383
CASTLEREAGH, Robert Stewart, Viscount
    ending of slave trade   164
CATALANS: nationalism   1393
CELSUS; Christians & Hinduism   479
CELTIC EDUCATION   1066
CELTIC SOCIETY:
    Northern Scotland   1310
CÉSAIRE, Aimé: colonialism   226
CEYLON See: SRI LANKA
C.E.Z.M.S.: Kashmir   475

CHAMBERLAIN, Joseph
    : South Africa   674
CHARYN, Jerome   312
CHAUCER, Geoffrey:
    Eastern influences   370
CHEROKEES: religion   1611
CHESTERTON, A.K.: Fascism   104
CHEWA people:
    Anglican church   464
CHICAGO: foreign language press   1502
CHILDREN
    attitudes to foreign teacher   1096
    cultural differences   94
    emigration from Britain   990
    ethnic identity: minorities   47
    racial attitudes   1062
CHILDREN'S LITERATURE
    Fascism: 1930-1976   229
    imperialism   228, 232A
CHILEANS in Sheffield
    : library services   1166
CHILEMBWE, John   185
CHINA
    Christian churches & missions   487, 490-91, 501, 505, 507, 515
    East Africa: contacts   576
    emigration   716-26
    English literature: 18th c.   326, 382
    ethnic minorities   714
    European children   712
    French literature: 18th c.   382
    Manchuria   711
    Muslim secessionist movements   710
    national integration   713
    Portuguese   715
    Ezra Pound   325
CHINA INLAND MISSION   501
CHINESE
    in Aberdeen   1321
    Brunei   724
    Cambodia   709
    Commonwealth   716
    East Indies   723
        : education   717
    Great Britain   1167
        : British working class   1170
        housing & education   1169
        seamen's strike, 1911   1170
    Hong Kong
        : cotton spinners   726
        education   717
    Indo-China   807
    Liverpool   1172
    London: restaurants   1171
    Malaysia   724, 832, 833A, 834
        : business   725
        : education   833
    Oceania   878
    Papua - New Guinea   882

Subject Index

CHINESE (contd.)
    Singapore   718,724,841,843-44
        : business   725
        : education   717
    South-East Asia   718-19,723,725
        : women   722
    Thailand: trading   858
    Transvaal: gold mines   678
    Yorkshire   1168
CHOTA-NAGPUR: Anglican Church   501
CHRIST APOSTOLIC CHURCH OF NIGERIA   450A
CHRISTIAN CHURCHES & MISSIONS
 <u>in</u> Africa   392,406,467
    : Central   413,421
    : East   436,448-49,466
    : North   424,427,432
    : South   411,415,417,420,425,
               445,453,457,461
    : West   450,460
    Arabian Gulf   476
    Asia   511
    Bengal   477,480-81,484,502,509
    Botswana   423
    Brunei   508
    Cape Colony   409A
    China   487,490-91,499,
               505,507,515
    Ethiopia   422,441
    Germany: Nazis   967
    Ghana   401,405,443
    Great Britain:
        West Indians   1285
    India   483,485,489,492-93,
           496-97,501,503-4,
           506,510,512-14
    Indonesia   495
    Ivory Coast   472
    Jamaica   396,908,912
    Japan   498
    Kashmir   475
    Kenya   411,417A,426,429
    Korea   463,469,494
    Leeward Islands   893
    Lesotho   409
    Madagascar   455
    Malawi   438,458,466A
    Malaysia   508
    Matabeleland   408
    Middle East   513
    New Zealand   873
    Nigeria   400,402-4,407,416,
            419,428,435,437,
            451-52,465,470
    Pacific Islands   883
    Palestine   500
    Rwanda   436B
    Senegambia   473
    Seychelles   511A
    Sierra Leone   430
    Singapore   498A

CHRISTIAN CHURCHES & MISSIONS (contd.)
 <u>in</u> Sri Lanka   482,485,488,516-17
    Syria   500
    Tanzania   442
    Uganda   436A,462A,468,471
    U.S.S.R.   1413
    Vietnam   478
    Zaire   462
    Zambia   426A,441,446A,459
    Zimbabwe 408,412,439,454,474,624
(See also: AFRICAN INLAND MISSION, AFRICAN METHODIST EPISCOPAL CHURCH, ANGLICAN CHURCH, BAPTISTS, BASEL MISSION, BREMEN MISSION, CHINA INLAND MISSION, CHURCH MISSIONARY SOCIETY, CHURCH OF SCOTLAND, CHURCH OF SOUTH INDIA, HUGUENOTS, IRISH CHRISTIAN BROTHERS, LONDON MISSIONARY SOCIETY, LOVEDALE INSTITUTE, MENNONITES, METHODISTS, MORAVIANS, MORMONS, PENTECOSTALISM, PLYMOUTH BRETHREN, PRESBYTERIANS, PROTESTANTISM, ROMAN CATHOLIC CHURCH, SOCIETY FOR AFRICAN MISSIONS IN IRELAND, SOCIETY OF FRIENDS, SOUTH AFRICAN GENERAL MISSION, UNITARIANS, UNIVERSITIES' MISSION TO CENTRAL AFRICA, VERONA FATHERS, WATCH TOWER MOVEMENT, WHITE FATHERS, WORLD COUNCIL OF CHURCHES)
CHRISTIAN MISSIONARIES:
    England: 19th c.   395,397,399
CHRISTIANITY & other religions   390,394
CHRISTIANS & HINDUS   479,481,765
    Jaffna   855
    Orissa   764A
CHRISTIANS & JEWS   190,193,198,205,208
CHUNG-YIN, Ma: Muslims in China   710
CHURCH MISSIONARY SOCIETY
 <u>in</u> Igboland   447
    Kashmir   475
    Kenya   411
    Nigeria   435,437,451
    West Africa   450
CHURCH OF SCOTLAND: Blantyre   458
CHURCH OF SOUTH INDIA   514
CIVIL RIGHTS MOVEMENT   1596
CLANRANALD   1313
CLARK, John Pepper   271
CLASS & RACE RELATIONS   828
CLASS CONFLICT: South Africa   659
CLASS CONSCIOUSNESS
    African workers: South Africa   660
    Indians: South Africa   652
    migrant dock workers: Durban   655A
CLASSICAL LITERATURE
    African races   220
    Jews   301
    slavery   221-24
COATBRIDGE: Irish & Labour movement   1204
COLCHESTER: Dutch & Flemish   1000
COLENSO, John William <u>bp. of Natal</u>   417
COLOGNE: emigrants to Canada   1550

Subject Index

COLOMBIA
    American Indians   1436
    bilingualism   1437
COLONISATION: English thought   14
COLOUR PREJUDICE   1
    Great Britain   1012
    teaching   1088
COMMONWEALTH
    aliens: legal position   88
    Chinese   716
    ethnic pluralism & public law   84
    federalism   76
    human rights   81A
    immigration & law   81
    nationality   82
    South African racial policy   692
COMMONWEALTH CITIZENS
    English law   1004A
COMMUNALISM
    Cyprus   332
    Fiji   74
    India   776
    Sri Lanka   74,75,845,851
    Trinidad   74
    West Africa   72
COMMUNIST PARTY
    France: Catholics   946
    South Africa   642,667
CONRAD, Joseph   359
    : imperialism   232,234-35
COOK ISLANDS: European view   889
COOPER, James Fenimore:
    novels & American Indians   238
CO-OPERATIVES: Israel   1474,1477,1510
COPTS, Egypt   533,536,537A
CORNWALL; Jews   1235
COVENTRY
    Punjab: children   1126
    silk workers to U.S.A.   1619
CREOLE ENGLISH: Nicaragua   1451
CREOLES
    : Jamaica   902A
    Sierra Leone   572
CRIME: race: Guyana   1446
CROWTHER, Samuel Ajayi   437
CROYDON: West Indians   1292
CUBA
    marriage, class & colour   900
    slave-trade   133
    : abolition   154
CULTURE CONFLICT:
    race conflict   25
CULTURES: East & West   29
CUNARD LINE: emigration   954
CYPRIOTS
    in Great Britain   1176
        Haringey   1173
        London   1174-75
        Manchester   1177
CYPRUS   932A
    communal conflict   932
    Greek-Cypriots   933

CZECHOSLOVAKIA
    Czech exiles: 30 Years War   939
    Czechs & Germans   938
    Czechs & Slovaks   937
    gypsies   935
    Jews: anti-semitism   936
    Slovaks   934
CZECHS
    Austro-Hungarian Empire   940
    exiles: 30 Years War   939
    independence: British opinion   928
DALLAS, Texas: Mexicans   1631
DALMATIA PROVINCE: immigration   114
DANMARKS NATIONAL SOCIALISTISKE
    ARBEDJER PARTI   941
DANZIG: German settlement   982
DAVIES, Dan Isaac:
    Welsh Language Society   1334
DE VALERA, Eamon
    Ulster question   1344A
DENMARK: National Socialists   941
DERBY: Punjabi children   1109
DERRY & ULSTER   1364
DESIRADÉ: race   901
DEVON: Jews   1235
DIAMOND-MINING
    South Africa: class & capitalism   691
DOMESTIC SERVANTS: Kampala   597A
DONOUGHMORE COMMISSION
    minorities in Sri Lanka   849
DOUGHTY, Charles Montagu
    Arabian influences   340
DRAVIDIANS   852
DREYFUS affaire   307-8
DRIEU LA ROCHELLE, Pierre   950
"DRUM" MAGAZINE   272
DRUZ in Lebanon   1522-23
DUBLIN: emigration to Canada   1550
DURBAN
    migrant dock workers   655A
    race relations   679
DURHAM Co.: Irish   1197
DUTCH
    in Colchester   1000
        England: 1570-1630   992
EAST ANGLIA
    emigration to New England   1623
EAST INDIA COMPANY
    religion   492
    slavery   729-30
EAST INDIES
    Chinese   723
    : education   717
EASTON: West Indians   1296
EBEID, Makram: Copts   533
EDGEWARE: Jews   1226
EDUCATION
    in Bengal   761
        Bermuda   899
        Bradford   1079

EDUCATION (contd.)
  in British Columbia
      : American Indians   1562
    Canada
      bilingualism   1547
      minorities   95
    Cape Colony
      Cape coloured; Indians   685
    Caribbean   897,899
    East Indies: Chinese   717
    Egypt   531
    Europe: Spanish Arabs   1403
        : Jews   194
    Germany:
      National Socialism   961,968,976
    Ghana   561
    Great Britain   1058-1104
      Asian   1105-35
      Black   1141-60
      Chinese   1169
      Irish   1205
      Jewish   1136-40
      minorities   95
      racial attitudes: changes 1069
      Roman Catholics   1071,1090
    India
      Anglo-Indians   771
      Churches   512,759,761-63,771,776
      'Untouchables'   803
    Ireland: bilingualism   1353
    Israel: Jews   211
    Kerala
      : missionary   512
        Syrian Christians   763
    Leeds   1120
    Libya   542-44
    Liverpool: Jews   1137
    London
      immigrants   1058,1060
      Jews   1136,1139,1213
      multi-racial schools   1065
      Pakistani girls   1268
      West Indian children   98
    Malaysia   823,830,833
    Mexico: Indians   1450
    Newcastle-upon-Tyne   1100,1113
    Nigeria   428,435
    Nova Scotia   1546
    Peru   1455
    Samoa: bilingualism   885
    Seychelles   571A
    Singapore   417,418A
    South Africa
      'Bantu'   649,697
      Cape Coloured   685
      Indians   685
    Sri Lanka
      cultural conflict   847
      language   858
      missionary   516

EDUCATION (contd.)
  in Tanzania: pluralism   596
    U.S.A.   897
      American Indians   1611
      immigrants   1580
      Jews   211
    Wales   1066,1068,1330,1334-35
    Zambia   446A
    Zimbabwe   412
    Black culture   98
    Celtic   1066
    Gaelic   1066,1310
    gypsies   1195,1371A
    Huguenots: England   1178
    multi-lingualism   99
    multi-racial societies   96,596
    race relations   1103
    social anthropology   92
(See also: ADULT EDUCATION, FURTHER
EDUCATION COLLEGES, SCHOOL TEXTBOOKS,
STUDENTS, TEACHERS, UNIVERSITIES)
EDWARDS, Mrs E.H.
  China missionary   515
EGYPT
  aliens: status   530
  Copts   533,536,537A
  education: nationalism   531
  Greeks   537
  non-Muslims   535
  race, culture & nationalism 534
  racial history   532
  slavery   104
EGYPTIANS in Uganda   598
ELIOT, George: Daniel Deronda 290,292,294
ELIOT, T.S.: Eastern influences 348
EMANCIPATION OF SLAVES
  in Caribbean   153,155
    Guyana   165
    Jamaica   153,155,910
    Trinidad   165
  Emancipated slaves
    British policies   147
    Lagos   568
    Sierra Leone   575
EMERSON, Ralph Waldo:
  Eastern influences   350
EMIGRATION
  Canada   1626
  Great Britain   984-91
  Greece   1339
  India   733-37
  Ireland   1356,1360,1362,1366,1370
  Malta   1381-82
  Scotland   1317-18
EMPIRE SETTLEMENT ACT, 1922   991
EMPLOYMENT
  Blacks: Great Britain   1049
  Blacks & whites: Great Britain 1077
  immigrants: Great Britain 1048-51

Subject Index

EMPLOYMENT (contd.)
  Indians
    : England   1044
    : Great Britain   1045-46
  racial discrimination   64
EMUNIN, Gush: West Bank   1501
ENGLAND
  aliens: medieval   994-1004
  French Protestants   1177A
  gypsies   1185, 1190
  Huguenots: education   1178
  Indian workers   1044
  Jews
    medieval   1216-18
    1730-1860   1231
    education   1137
    re-entry   1229
  Ras Tafarians   1283
(See also: GREAT BRITAIN)
ENGLAND: MIDLAND COUNTIES
  Asian immigrants   1245A
  immigrant children   1107
  immigrant workers   1051
  immigrants   1040
    : libraries   1064
  Indian workers   1045
  Muslims   1245A
  West Indian children   1157
ENGLAND: NORTHERN COUNTIES
  abolitionist movement   163
  Fascism   1020
  immigrant workers   1051
  Irish   1207
  mental illness: immigrants   1035
ENGLAND: POTTERIES
  Asians   1250
ENGLISH & ARABS
  psychological differences   1459A
ENGLISH DRAMA
  Africans: 16th-17th c.   257
  Eastern influences   366, 381
  Irish   280
  Jews   297-98
  Welsh   388
ENGLISH FICTION
  Africa   258
  Eastern influences   354, 356
  Jews   288-90, 292, 294, 297-98, 310
  race relations   218
  racism   217
  'underdeveloped countries'   216A
ENGLISH LANGUAGE
  Asian children   1106
  overseas students   1086
    barrier   1063
      Birmingham University   1077
      London   1083
  spoken English:
    immigrant & English children   1067

ENGLISH LITERATURE
  Africa: 1660-1807   269
  Arab influences
    : medieval   360
    19th c.   357
  Arabia   334
  Arabian Nights   316
  Blacks   245
  China: 18th c.   326, 352
  Eastern influences   315, 319, 353, 379
  imperialism   225, 227
  India   332, 364-65, 378
  Jews   306
  Near East   314, 378
  Persian influences   349, 375
  Saracens: medieval   993
  Scotland: 17th-18th c.   385
  Welsh   387, 389
  West Indians   274
ENGLISH POETRY
  Boer War   230
  Oriental influences   347
ESKIMOS: Canada   1556-57, 1561
ETHIOPIA
  Christian Church   422, 441
  despised occupational groups   538
  ethnic associations   539
  Falashas   541
  Italo-Ethiopian War   540
  Shoa Province:
    ethnic identity   526
ETHNIC GROUPS: mobility   51
ETHNIC MINORITIES See: MINORITIES
ETHNIC STEREOTYPES   45
ETHNICITY & LAW: Malaysia   826
ETHNOLOGY, BRITISH:
  A.H.L.F. Pitt-Rivers   10
EUGENICS: U.S. thought   7
EURIPIDES: slavery   223
EUROPE
  anti-semitism   205
  emigration: U.S.A.   1585
  Jewish stereotype   209
  nationalism & minorities   60
  slave trade: diplomacy, 1814-1818   175
EUROPE: CENTRAL
  ethnic minorities   927
  Jewish Rabbinate   213
  linguistic minorities   927
EUROPE: EASTERN
  ethnic minorities   927
  linguistic minorities   927
  Nazi occupation: S.S.   979A
EUROPE: SOUTHERN
  Jews: 15th-16th c.   202
EUROPE: WESTERN
  immigrant workers   924-26
    : class structure   924
    social security   926

EUROPEAN COMMUNITY	
migrant workers:	
social security	926
EUROPEAN CHILDREN: Shanghai	712
EUROPEAN WORKERS	
in South Africa	645
— Zambia	618
EUROPEANS	
in Calcutta	767
— Kenya	588,592
— Kisangasi:	
relations with Africans	612
— Natal: 1845-72	641
— South Kenya	663
— U.S.A.:	
immigration, 1870-1920	1584
EVOLUTION THEORIES: race	12
(See also: SOCIAL DARWINISM)	
EYSENCK, Hans Jürgen	
intelligence tests	32A
FALASHAS: Ethiopia	541
FARMER & GALTON	
(Birmingham): slave trade	138
FASCISM	
in Great Britain	1014-16,1019-20
— Ireland	1361
— Italy	1377-78,1380
children's literature: Britain	229
Marxist theories	9
(See also: NATIONAL SOCIALISM)	
FATHER DIVINE PEACE MISSION	1591
FAULKNER, William	
portrayal of Afro-Americans	256,263
FEDERALISM	
in Canada	1551
— Central Africa:	
African opposition	619
— Commonwealth	76
— Malaysia	829
— Nigeria	567
FICTION: imperialism	231
FIEDLER, Leslie	312
FIJI	
communal representation	74
demography	887
Indians	733,737,886
race relations	881
FINLAND	
gypsies	942
Lapps	943
FISHGUARD: bilingualism	1330
FLEMISH in Colchester	1000
FOOD HABITS	
Ugandan Asians: Great Britain	1249
West Indians: London	1287
FORMOSA: foreigners	727
FORSTER, E.M.	371
imperialism	232,236
Indian influences	329,344
FRANCE	
Algerian rule & nationalism	529
Basques	952
Communist Party: Catholics	946
history teaching: race &	
colonialism	93A
housing: immigrants	947A,954
immigrants: social mobility	947
Italians	945
Jews	944,948,953
North African immigration:	
housing	954
Protestantism	951
regionalism	949
Right-wing writers	949A,950,955
Tunisian nationalism:	
French policy	549A
FRASER, Donald	
Ngoni people, Malawi	466A
FREE COLOUREDS: Jamaica	903,905
FREE-LABOUR	
in Barbados	898
— Caribbean	896
— Jamaica	906
FRENCH	
in Canada	1567
— England: 1570-1630	992
17th c.	1177A
(See also: HUGUENOTS)	
— Montreal	1569
— Quebec	1566-68
— Senegal	570
FRENCH DRAMA: Jews	293
FRENCH LITERATURE	
Asian influences	324
China: 18th c.	382
FRENCH REFUGEES	
in Great Britain	1177A,1179,1181,1183
— Switzerland	1405
FULBE immigrants:	
Lunsar, Sierra Leone	573
FURNEAUX: intelligence tests	32A
FURNESS, Cumbria:	
emigration to Minnesota	1622
FURTHER EDUCATION COLLEGES	
immigrants	1085
overseas students: London	1083
GAELIC COMMUNITIES	1313
GAELIC EDUCATION	1066,1310
GAELIC FOLK-CULTURE	1306
GAELIC LANGUAGE	1316
GAELIC SOCIETY: Ireland	1351
GALT, John: Canadian immigrants	1553
GANDHI, Mohandas Karamchand	
India	742
South Africa	689
GARVEY, Marcus	116
GENEVA	
French & Italian refugees	1405
GENTILES & JEWS	215

116 Subject Index

GEOGRAPHY TEXTBOOKS:
   racial bias   93B
GEORGIA (U.S.A.): Scots   1633
GEORGIA (U.S.S.R.)
   National Communism   1415
GERMAN DRAMA
   Jews   297-98
   National Socialism   977
GERMAN FICTION: Jews   297-98
GERMAN LANGUAGE
   Eastern & Central Europe   927
GERMAN LITERATURE
   Jews   306
   National Socialism   975
GERMAN NATIONALITY
   Schleswig-Holstein   959
GERMAN REFUGEES:
   British government policies   1184
GERMANS
   in Bohemia: Czechs   938
      Palestine: National Socialism   1515
GERMANY
   anti-Semitism   973-74
   army: non-Germans   958
   Hitlerjugend movement   961
   National Socialism   956,965-66,970-72,
         974-75,977-78
      British opinion   964
      Christian sects   967
      education   961,968,976
      exiles   962
      German opinion   979
      working-class   969
      youth movements   961,981
   Nationality:
      Schleswig-Holstein   959
   neo-Nazism   960
   Pacific Islanders
      : employment   879
      : resistance to German rule   880
   racism   980
   socialism: Jews   983
   Zionism   963
GHANA
   adaptationist & assimilationist
     policies: Great Britain   524
   Basel & Bremen missions   455A
   Christian churches   401,443
   Denkyira   560
   Europeans: language & education   561
   Mossi immigrants   563
   Nationalism   559,562
   Newspapers: foreign owned   550
   Pentecostalism   405
   "stranger" communities   526,564
   Yoruba immigrants   558
GIBBS, Sir Hamilton   368
GIDE, André: Algeria   255

GLASGOW
   African links, 1870-1900   131⋅
   Asian & Scots children   110⋅
   Asians   132⋅
   Irish   162⋅
   race relations   131⋅
GOANS in Uganda   60⋅
GOLD COAST (18th century)
   slave trade   14⋅
(see also GHANA)
GOLD-MINING
   South Africa
      African labour   66⋅
      Chinese labour   67⋅
      labour   69⋅
      race relations   65⋅
GORDIMER, Nadine   249,27⋅
GOVERNMENT OF INDIA ACT, 1935   738,74⋅
GRACEHILL, Co. Antrim: Moravians   135⋅
GRAVESEND: immigrants: housing   105⋅
GREAT BRITAIN
   abolitionist movement   150,152,156-57
         163-64,166,168-70,177,179-8⋅
      Brazil   14⋅
      Caribbean   18⋅
      Cuba   15⋅
      East Africa   15⋅
         : Royal Navy   16⋅
      Sudan   15⋅
      Unitarians   17⋅
   'African affairs': Zimbabwe:
      British opinion   62⋅
   Afro-American soldiers:
      World War II   160⋅
   Afro-Americans: British opinion   160⋅
   alien bankers   100⋅
   alien merchants   996-9⋅
   aliens
      : medieval   994-95,999,1003-⋅
      16th century   100⋅
      control: 19th-20th c.   101⋅
      law   1004⋅
      status cf. Egypt   53⋅
   American Indians   1609-10,1612-1⋅
   anthropology: 1860s   2⋅
   anti-Semitism   1214,1227,123⋅
   Armenians   1531-3⋅
   Asian adolescents   125⋅
   Asian medicine   124⋅
   Asian women   1248,125⋅
   Asians
      : libraries   124⋅
      working-class   124⋅
   attitudes to Blacks: 17th-18th c.   ⋅
   Bangladeshi   1259⋅
   Bangladeshi children   110⋅
   Bengali workers   126⋅
   Black children:
      self-esteem   10⋅
   'Black power'   130⋅

GREAT BRITAIN (contd.)
- Buddhist organisations — 1244
- children's literature — 228-29,232A
- Chinese — 1167,1169
  - : British working class — 1170
- colonisation: 1766-1874 — 14
- colour prejudice — 1012
- Commonwealth citizens: law — 1004A
- education — 1058-1104
  - Asian — 1105-35
  - Black — 1141-60
  - Jewish — 1136-40
  - minorities — 95
- emigration — 984-90
  - to California — 1617
  - to North America — 1536,1540,1547
  - to South Africa — 647,688,696
  - to U.S.A. — 1617-25
  - juveniles — 990
  - trade unions — 986
- employment: immigrants — 1044-51
- Fascism — 1014-16,1019-20
- freed slaves — 147
- French refugees — 1179,1181,1183
- Garveyism — 116
- German refugees — 1184
- gypsies — 1185-95
- history teaching: race & colonisation — 93A
- housing — 1052-57
- immigrant school leavers — 1072,1076,1080
- immigration
  - control — 85
  - elections — 1009
  - employment — 1044-51
  - inner city planning — 1042
  - Parliament — 1013
  - politics — 86,1006-8
- imperialism
  - periodicals — 1027
  - Marxist views — 21
  - racial theories — 24
  - science: 1895-1940 — 32
  - South Africa — 674
  - youth — 1099
- India policies — 738,741,744,749,751
- Indian emigrant labour:
  - policies — 734
- Indians — 1044-46,1162-63
- Indology — 376
- industrial accidents: immigrants — 1043A
- Irish — 1191-1209
- Italians — 1163
- Jews — 195,1140,1211-37
- Marxists: imperialism — 22
- medical emigration — 101
- military service: minorities — 64
- Muslim India:
  - historical writing — 780,782,796
- National Front — 1017-18

GREAT BRITAIN (contd.)
- National Socialism: opinion — 964
- Near East: attitudes: 19th c. — 313A
- Nigerian students — 1294
- Oriental influences — 343
- Pacific Island labour policies — 888
- Pakistani students — 1264
- Pakistanis — 1162,1262,1267
- Palestinian policies — 1471,1489,1493-94, 1500,1506,1511-12, 1514,1516,1518
- Poles — 1240
- Powellism — 1021
- Protestant exiles from Europe — 992
- race relations — 1046
  - : law — 1005,1007,1012A
  - : news media — 1025
  - : Parliament — 1013
- racial attitudes
  - Central Africa: 1840-90 — 8
  - North America — 23
  - changes by education — 1069
- racial discrimination — 1022,1036
- racial riots — 1026,1032
- racial theories: imperialism — 24
- racism — 19
  - : periodicals — 1027
- racist language — 27
- reggae music — 1302
- religious sects — 1165
- secessionist movements
  - in Zaire & Nigeria — 520
- Sh'ia Imami Ismailia — 1247
- Sikhs — 1274-75,1278
- slave trade — 119,128,131,133
- Social Darwinism — 18
- South Africa: racial policies — 651,654
- Swaminarayan sect — 1242
- Turkish migrant workers — 1279
- Ugandan Asians — 1249
- Ukrainians — 1280
- West Africa: humanitarians — 553
- West Indians — 1282,1295,1299

GREECE: emigration — 1339
GREECE (ANCIENT)
- Jews — 207
- slavery — 107,223-24

GREEK-CYPRIOTS
- in Manchester — 1177
- Paphos, Cyprus — 933

GREEKS
- in Egypt — 537
- Turkey — 1527
- U.S.S.R. — 1411

GREY, Henry George, 3rd Earl Grey
- native policy in South Africa — 661

GUAMBIA, Colombia: — 37
- bilingualism — 14

GUJARATI-SPEAKING CHILDREN — 20
- in Leeds schools — 11

Subject Index

GUYANA
  Africans   1438,1442-43,1447
  Amerindians   1441
  East Indians   1438,1440,1442,1444,1446
  emancipation   165
  immigrants   918
  race & crime   1446
  race relations   1438,1448
  social conflict   1437
GYPSIES/TRAVELLERS
  in Aberdeenshire   1193
     Czechoslovakia   935
     England   1185,1190
     Finland   942
     Great Britain
       children   1186
       education   1195
       planning   1188,1191
       religion & magic   1194
       social mobility   1187
       social problems   1189
       social structure   1185
     Ireland   1350,1359,1371A
     Perthshire   1193
     Spain   1401
     U.S.A.   1627
     Wales   1185,1190
HAITI: British   902
HALMAHERN, Indonesia:
  Christian Church   495
HARDY, Robert Spence   482
HARLEM, New York
  Father Divine Peace Mission   1591
  riot, 1933   1595
HAWAII: alcoholism & ethnicity   877
HAZARA MONGOLS: Afghanistan   702
HEARNE, John   241
HEBRIDES, bilingualism   93
HERTFORDSHIRE: Indian children:
  intelligence   1130
HIGH COMMISSION TERRITORIES
  : race relations in South Africa   687
HINDU FAMILIES: East London   1256
HINDUISM
  English poetry: 19th century   380
  mysticism: influence on Europe
    12th-13th c.   337
HINDUISM & CHRISTIANITY   479,481,765
  Jaffna   855
  Orissa   764A
HIRSCH, Baron de   1572
HISTORY TEACHING
  race & imperialism:
  British & French schools   93A
HITLERJUGEND   961
HOLY GHOST FATHERS: East Africa   436
HOME TUITION: Asian women:
  West Yorkshire   1259

HONG KONG
  Chinese
    : cotton spinners   726
    education   717
HORTON, Wilmot   1545
HOUSING: immigrants & race
  in Gravesend   1052
    Great Britain   1169
    London   1054
    Lyon   947A
    Manchester   1053,1057
    Paris   954
    Rochdale   1055
    U.S.A.   1602
    Westminster   1056
HUDDERSFIELD: Asians:
  information services   1125
HUGUENOTS
  Anglican Church   1182
  artists: Great Britain & Ireland   1180
  education: England   1178
HUGHES, Langston   275
HUMAN RIGHTS
  international law   81A
  U.N.O.   80
HUNGARY
  Jews
    : Communist Party   1340
    : Liberalism   1341
IBN ADRET, SOLOMON BEN ABRAHAM.
  Responsa   1391
IBOS
  in Jos, N.Nigeria   566
    London   1286
IGBOLAND: Church Missionary Society   447
ILLINOIS: Mormons   1579
IMMIGRANT CHILDREN: Great Britain
  in Bradford: education   1079
    Midland counties   1101
    Newcastle-upon-Tyne   1100
  English language teaching: TV   1084
  infant schools   1082
  junior schools: English language   1095
  mental differences   1093
  religious beliefs & moral values   1087
  social acceptance:
    secondary schools   1081
  spatial ability   1089
  special education   1102
IMMIGRANTS/IMMIGRATION
  in Australia   865
    British   860,862,864,866
    Scots   861
    Birmingham   1048
    Bradford   1030,1043
    Canada   1544-45,1548,1551-55,
    England   1564-65,1570-76
    : Midland Counties   1040,1064
    France   946

IMMIGRANTS/IMMIGRATION (contd.)

Gravesend	1052
Great Britain	
adult education	1091
control	85
Further Education Colleges	1085
mental illness	1035
Parliamentary questions	1013
politics	86,1006-8
school leavers	1072,1076,1080
Israel/Palestine	1474,1477,1495-96, 1498-99
Kenya	85,597,599,600
Leeds	1031,1037
London	1033,1054
Lyon	947A
Manchester	1053,1057
Marseilles	947
New Zealand	860,867
Newcastle-upon-Tyne	1028
Nottingham	1038
Paris	954
Reading	1039
Sheffield	1098
South Africa: British	688,696
Sudan	546,549
Trinidad	911,918,920,922
U.S.A.	1578
assimilation	1584
education	1580
politics	86
trade unions	1589
Westminster	1056
Zimbabwe	
Africans: 1890-1970	628
Europeans	626

(See also under the various ethnic groups: INDIANS in, IRISH in ...)

IMPERIALISM

Aimé Césaire	226
children's literature	228,232A
fiction	231
English literature	225,227,232,234-36
Great Britain	
Marxist views	22
periodicals	1027
racial theories: 1894-1904	24
science: 1895-1940	32
youth teaching	1099
history teaching	93A

INCOME DIFFERENTIALS

white & non-whites: South Africa	684

INDIA

Anglo-Indians	
: education	771
Anglo-Indian fiction	322
Anglo-Indian poetry	367,377
army: Punjabi	800
British community	760,764,766,768-70
British government policies & relations	738,741, 744,749,751
caste	489,765
Chinese	833A
Christian Churches & missions	483,485, 489,492-93,496-97,501, 503-4,506,510,512-14
Christians & Hindus	480-81,764A,765
communal representation	776
education	759,761-62,771
elections, 1937	755
emigration	733-37
English literature	332,364-65,378
English poetry	380
Europeans	767
E.M. Forster	329-30
Gandhi	742
Government of India Act, 1935	738,744
Rudyard Kipling	345-46,373
language policies	91
Alun Lewis	330
minorities	70,728
: constitution	732
'Mlecchas'	804
Muslims	772-99
nationalism	739-40,742-43,745-49, 752-54,756,797
Nayars & Christians	762
Nehru	752
Portuguese	731,758
regionalism	739,747,754,757
slavery	729-30
Syrian Christians	762
'untouchables'	803-6

INDIAN ADOLESCENTS in Great Britain   1132
INDIAN ART: European attitudes   361

INDIAN CHILDREN

in Great Britain	
development	1070
educational progress	1117
maladjustment	1119
Hertfordshire: intelligence	1130
Newcastle-upon-Tyne	
: reading errors	1113

INDIAN JEWS   212,1517
INDIAN NATIONAL CONGRESS   742,745-46, 748,753,756
  : Muslims   781

INDIAN STUDENTS

in Great Britain	1131
London	1121

INDIANS

in Burma	707
Canada	1576
East Africa	521-22,577-78,580
England: workers	1044-45
Fiji	733,737,886

Subject Index

INDIANS (contd.)
   in Great Britain   1045-46
        leadership   1162-63
   Guyana   1438,1440,1442,
                                   1444,1446
   Kenya   587
   Malaysia   733,835-38
   Mauritius   737,840
   Newcastle-upon-Tyne   1254
   Singapore   835
   South Africa   521-22,652,
                                   672-73,689
      Cape Colony   685
      Natal   737
   Sri Lanka   733
   Trinidad   919-20
   Uganda   603
   Zanzibar   735
INDO-CHINA
   Chinese   807
   Laku   808
INDOLOGY: Great Britain   376
   : Sir William Jones   320,341
INDONESIA   495
   language problem   809
INDONESIANS in Malaysia   839
INDUSTRIAL ACCIDENTS: immigrants
   : Britain   1043A
INDUSTRIAL RELATIONS
   South Africa: race   644
INFORMATION SERVICES
   Asians: Huddersfield   1125
   immigrants: Sheffield   1095
INSTITUTE OF RACE RELATIONS   1023
INTELLIGENCE
   anthropology   31
   Indian children: Hertfordshire   1130
   Jewish children   1138
   race   33
   tests   32A,37
   theories   34-36
INTER-GROUP RELATIONS   38-42,48-52
INTERNATIONAL COUNCIL OF
   CHRISTIAN CHURCHES   398
INTERNATIONAL LAW
   : human rights   81A
INTERNATIONAL SOCIALIST LEAGUE:
   South Africa   667
IRAN
   Baluchistan   1465
   ethnic identity: Eastern Iran   1464
   Sir John Murray   351
   regional policy   1463
IRAQ
   Kurds   1469-70
   nationalism   1468
   Turks   1466
   'Yazidi'   1467
IRELAND
   Anglican Church   1344
   Blueshirts   1361

IRELAND (contd.)
   Church and state   1374,1374A
   culture and politics   1367
   education: bilingualism   1353
   emigration   1356,1360,1362,
                                   1366,1372
   exiles: 17th c.: writings   287
   Gaelic & Normans   1351
   gypsies   1350,1359,1371A
   Huguenots   1180
   Jews: re-entry   1229
   medical migration   101
   Moravians   1353
   nationalism   1354
     : literature   281-85
   police   1355
   Presbyterian Church   1342,1345,1370
   Protestants   1363
   Ulster Unionists   1353A
   U.S. slavery   129,172
IRISH
   in Airdrie   1204
   Birmingham   1199
   Bolton   1208
   Boston, Mass.   1628
   Canada   1570
   Cardiff   1333
   Coatbridge   1204
   Dundee   1320
   Durham Co.   1197
   England, North   1207
   Glasgow   1628
   Great Britain   1201,1208-9
     education   1205
   Lancashire   1198,1202
   Liverpool   1204A,1206
   London   1200,1203
   Luton   1208
   New York   1628
   Newcastle   1197
   North America   1534,1537-38
   Paisley   1320
   Scotland   1323
   York   1196
   English drama   280
   English stereotype   1011
   foreigners' attitudes   1366A
IRISH CHRISTIAN BROTHERS
   : Zambia   446A
IRISH LANGUAGE
   in education   1066
IROQUOIS: British relations   1610,1614
ISLAM
   Sir Richard Burton   355
   European attitudes   339
   Malaysia   819A,822
   medieval writers   328
   mysticism: influence on
      Europe: 12th-13th c.   337
   Nigeria   451,569

ISLAM (contd.)
(See also ARABS, DRUZ, ISMAILIS, MUSLIMS, SH'I'S, SUNNI)
ISLAM & CHRISTIANITY 451,513
ISMAIL, Khedive of Egypt
   slavery in Sudan 548
ISMAILIS
   London 1245
   Syria 1526
ISRAEL
   Arab-Israeli conflict 1509
   Arabs 1482
   army: national integration 1507
   Bene Israel Indian Jews 1517
   Black Panthers 1475
   British policies 1493-94
   co-operatives 1477,1499,1510
   elections: ethnicity 1483
   Hungarian Communist Party 1340
   immigrants 1474,1495,1498
     : wages 1505
   Jewish education 211
   Moroccan Jews 1499
   nationalism 1504
   Palestinian Arabs 1490,1502
   West Bank 1492,1501
   Yemenis 1481
(See also: JEWS, PALESTINE, ZIONISM)
ISSERLS, Moses: Jews in Poland 1387
ITALIAN REFUGEES
   in London 1210
     Switzerland 1405
ITALIANS
   in Argentina 1428
     France 945
     Great Britain 1163
     London 1209A
ITALY
   Fascism 1377-78,1380
   Japanese 1376
   regionalism 1375
   Socialists 1377
     : Bakunin 1379
IVORY COAST: Methodists 472
JACOB of Serug See: JAMES, Saint bp. of Bainan in Serugh
JACOBSON, Dan 249
JAFFNA: Roman Catholics & Hindus 855
JAMAICA
   Anglican Church 909
   Baptists 153,904
   Black children: self-esteem 100
   Creoles 902A
   emancipation of slaves 155,910
     : Baptists 153
   free coloureds 903,905
   missionaries 908,912
   race distinctions 907
   Ras Tafarians 911,1283
   slave & free labour 906

JAMAICA (contd.)
   slave-trade 122
   slavery 135
JAMAICAN STUDENTS
   in Great Britain: achievement 1159
JAMAICANS in London 1297
JAMES, Saint, bp. of Bainan in Serugh
   homilies against Jews 190
JAPAN
   American travellers: writings 321
   Burakumin minority 810
   Christian missionaries 498
   colonisation in Korea 312
   English travellers: writings 321
   Koreans 811
JAPANESE
   in Brazil 1435
     Milan: business 1326
JENSEN, Arthur Robert
   : intelligence theories 349,36
JEWISH BUND: Mensheviks 1420
JEWISH CHILDREN: intelligence 1138
JEWISH COLONIZATION ASSOCIATION 1572
JEWISH FICTION
   Eastern Europe 305
   Great Britain 311
   U.S.A. 291,302,312
JEWISH LITERATURE
   Arabs 331
   U.S.A. 219
JEWS
   in Austria 930,983
     Babylon: business 199
     Bristol 1223
     Canada 1571-72
     Carpentras, France 944
     Cornwall 1235
     Czechoslovakia 936
     Devon 1235
     Edgeware 1226
     England
       medieval 1216-18
       1730-1860 1231
       education 1137
       re-entry 1229
     Europe
       13th c. 189
       17th-18th c.: education 144
     Europe, Central 213
     Europe, Eastern 305
     Europe, Southern 202
     France 953
     Great Britain 1234
       education 1140
       emancipation 1232-33
       immigration 1221
       philo-semitism 1224
       social mobility 1222
     Hungary 1340-41
     Ireland: re-entry 1229

JEWS (contd.)
  in Isle-sur-Sorgue, France   948
    Leeds   1225,1228
    Liverpool: education   1137
    London   1215
      education   1139
      families   1219
    London: East End
      education   1136,1213
      newspapers   1212
      politics   1214
      psychiatric illness   1220
    Ottoman Empire   1528-29
    Palestine (Ancient)   1488
    Poland   1387
    Portugal   1394,1396-97
    Roman Empire   200,210,301
    Romania   1390
    Sahara   197
    U.S.A.   1629-30
    U.S.S.R.
      Jewish Bund & RS-DP   1420
      Musars   1416
      Socialism   1409
      Ukrainians   1410
    Vienna: anti-semitism   931
    Wilno   1422
    Yemen   1533
  American fiction   291
  business: Babylon   199
  diplomacy: Lucien Wolf   203
  education
    England   1137
    Europe   194
    Great Britain   1140
    Israel   211
    Liverpool   1137
    London   1136,1139,1212
    U.S.A.   211
  English drama   297-98
  English fiction   288-90,292,294, 297-98,310
  English literature   306
  family life   191,195,1219
  French drama   293
  German fiction & drama   297-98
  Kafka   304
  medical ethics   201
  nationalism   204
  popular literature   296
  Russian literature   309
  Scandinavian literature   295
  social stratification   187
  socialism: Germany & Austria   933
  stereotype: Europe   209
  Voltaire   299
(See also: ANTI-SEMITISM, ISRAEL, JUDAISM, PALESTINE, ZIONISM)
JEWS & CHRISTIANS   190,193,198,205,208
JEWS & GENTILES   215
JEWS & GREEKS   207
JEWS & MUSLIMS   192,197,206
JINJA, Uganda: race relations   604
JOHNSTON, Sir William, 1715-1734
  Superintendent of Indian affairs in North America: relations with Iroquois Indians   1610
JONES, Sir William, 1746-1794
  Indology   320,341,363
JORDAN: Palestinian refugees   1519
JORDON, Edward: free coloureds   903
JOS, N. Nigeria: Ibos   566
JOSEPH ibn Leb. Responsa   1528
JOSEPHUS: Jews & Greeks   207
JUDAISM
  Kafka   304
  Marx   188
JUDITH in German & English literature   306
JURA SEPARATISM: Berne   1404
JUSTICE, Administration of:
  South Africa: race   680
JUVENAL: race relations   108
JUVENILE DELINQUENCY
  West Indians: London   1141
KAFKA, Franz: Judaism   304
KAMPALA, Uganda
  domestic servants   597A
  Goans   602
KASHMIR: Christian Missions   475
KASIM: Akhmedjn: Turkestan   710
KASTNER, Erich: critic of National Socialism   962
KAYE, Sir John William   374
KEHILLATI, Yishu: West Bank   1501
KELANTAN, Malaysia
  Muslims   822
  Thais   839A
KENYA
  Asians   591
  Bariango Plains people   581
  Christian churches & missions   411, 417A,426,429,463,469
  colonial policy: critics   593
  communal representation   74
  immigration control   85
  Indians   587
  Kikuyu & British   588A
  labour force   582,594
  land policy   590
  racial co-operation   586
  settlers   525,583,585
  soldier settlers   583
  Somalis   584
  Swahili-speaking community   589
  whites   588,591
KERALA
  education
    : Christian missions   572
    : Syrian Christians   763

Subject Index 123

KHAN, Sir Syed Ahmad
   Muslim politics   788
KHARTOUM: immigrants   549
KHODJAS: London   1248
KIKUYU and BRITISH   588A
KIKUYU CENTRAL ASSOCIATION   426
KIMBERLEY
   diamond mines: class & capitalism   691
KING, Martin Luther   1606
KIPLING, Rudyard
   imperialism   234-36
   India   345-46,373
KISANGANSI, Zaire: race relations   612
KOREA
   Christians & Buddhists   494
   Japanese colonisation   812
   religious sects   1165
KOREANS in Japan   811
KRAEMER, Hendrik
   non-Christian religions   394
KRAUS, Karl: anti-semitism in Austria   931
KUMASI, Ghana
   Mossi immigrants   563
   "stranger" communities   526
KURDS in Iraq   1469-70
LABOUR
   Kenya   582,594
   Malawi   640
LABOUR MOVEMENTS
   Airdrie: Irish   1204
   Coatbridge: Irish   1204
   Great Britain: National Socialism   971A
   London: Irish   1207
LABOUR PARTY (GREAT BRITAIN)
   Jewish immigration: 1880-1910   1221
   Palestine: 1917-1949   1508
   South Africa   681
LAKU: Indo-China-Yunnan border   808
LAMARTINE DE PRAT, Marie Louis Alphonse de
   Eastern influences   338
LAMMING, George   241
LANCASHIRE: Irish   1198,1202
LAND: Malawi   610
LAND POLICIES
   Kenya   590
   Queensland   866A
   Zimbabwe: 1890-1945   632
LAND RIGHTS
   American Indians: Canada   1563
LANE, Edward William: Near East   313A
LANGUAGE PROBLEMS & POLICIES
   India   91
   Indonesia   809
   Sri Lanka   91,858
   Trinidad   923
(See also: BILINGUALISM, MULTI-LINGUALISM)
LAOS: ethnic minorities   813
LAPPS: Finland   943

LATIN AMERICA
   Spanish settlers   1425
LATIN AMERICAN LITERATURE
   Amerindians   237,239
LATVIAN NATIONALISM   1417
LEAGUE OF NATIONS: minorities   78
LEBANESE in West Africa   55
LEBANON
   Armenians   1460,1522
   Druz   1522-23
   Sh'ites   1520
   Sunnis   1521
LEEDS
   Gujarati-speaking children   1120
   immigrants   1031,1037
   Jews   1225,1228
   Pakistanis   1263
   Sikh children   1272
LEESE, Arnold: British Fascism   1019
LEEWARD ISLANDS
   Christian missions   893
   slavery   124
LESKOV, Nikolai Semenovich
   : Jews   309
LESOTHO
   Christian churches & missions   409
LESSING, Doris   277
LEWIS, Alun: Indian influences   330
LEYS, Norman
   : critic of Kenyan colonial policy   593
LIBERAL PARTY (Great Britain)
   Jewish immigration: 1880-1900   1221
LIBERALISM
   Rhodesian question   633
   South Africa   677
LIBERIA: integration   565A
LIBRARY SERVICES
   England: Midlands: immigrants   1064
   Great Britain: Asians   1246
   Sheffield
      Chileans   1166
      Pakistani adults   1111
      Pakistani children   1108
      West Indians   1149
(See also INFORMATION SERVICES)
LIBYA
   educational policy   542-44
   immigrants: 631-111B.C.   528
LIMA: migrants   1452
LINCOLN, Abraham
   : emancipation of slaves   1492
LINLITHGOW, Victor Alexander John Hope, 2nd Marquis of
   Vice-roy of India: 1936-43   751
LITERATURE & ANTHROPOLOGY   218A
LIVERPOOL, Robert Banks Jenkinson, 2nd Earl of
   emigration policies to S. Africa   647

Subject Index

LIVERPOOL
    Blacks   1291
    Chinese   1172
    emigrants   984
    Irish   1204A, 1206
    Jewish education   1137
    Muslims   1266
    race riots, 1919   1032
    slave trade   130
      : abolition   178
LIVINGSTONE, Charles
    Zambezi: expedition   414
LIVINGSTONIA MISSION   438
LOD, Israel: Bene Israel
    Indian Jews   1517
LONDON
    adolescent blacks & Ras Tafarians   1301
    Africans: psychiatric illness   1300
    alien merchants   998
    aliens: 1558-1640   1002
    Asians   1258
    Blacks: dockland areas   1281
    Buddhist associations   1161
    Chinese: restaurants   1171
    emigrants to Canada   1156
    Ibos   1286
    immigrants   1033
      : education   1058, 1060
    Indian students   1121
    Irish   1200, 1203
    Ismaeli Khojas   1245
    Italian Catholics   1209A
    Italian exiles   1210
    Jewish education   1139
    Jews   1215
      : family life   1219
    Maltese   1238-39
    mixed marriages   1029
    mugging   1041
    multi-racial schools
      : children's attitudes   1065
    Muslim associations   1161
    overseas students
      : English language   1083
    Pakistani girls: education   1268
    schools: immigrants   1060
    secondary schools: immigrants   1060
    slave trade   123
    West African students   1142
    West Africans
      : psychiatric illness   1300
    West Indian children
      : black culture   98
    West Indian students   1142
    West Indians   1289, 1297
      food habits   1287
      housing   1054
      prejudice against English   1284
      psychiatric illness   1300

LONDON: EAST END
    Hindu families   1255
    Jews
      adult education   1136
      education   1213
      newspaper opinion   1212
      politics   1214
      psychiatric illness   1220
LONDON BOROUGH OF HILLINGDON
    Asian children   1116
LONDON MISSIONARY SOCIETY   431
    South Africa   415
    Zambia   459
LONG, James: missionary in Bengal   502
LOVEDALE INSTITUTE   410A
LOZI people   616
LUNSAR, Sierra Leone
    Fulbe immigrants   573
LUTON, Irish   1208
LYON, France
    housing: immigrants   947A
LYSIAS: slavery   223
MACCLESFIELD
    silkworkers emigration to U.S.A.   1619
MADAGASCAR
    Malagasy-European relations:
      1861-95   699
    Quakers   455
MADRAS
    nationalism   754
    Roman Catholic education   759
MAIS, Roger   241
MALABAR: British community   770
MALACCA: race relations   825
MALAWI
    Chilenbwe rising   185
    Christian churches & missions   438, 458, 466A
    land & labour: 1891-1914   610
    migrant labour: Central Africa   609
    nationalist movement, 1891-1958   611
    settlers: African nationalism   607
MALAYS in Thailand   859
MALAYSIA   508
    British community   816
    Chinese   724-25, 832-34
    class & politics   828
    communalism   821
    decentralisation of power   819
    education
      Chinese & Malays   833
      unification   823, 830
    ethnicity & law   826
    federalism   829
    Indians   733, 835-38
    Indonesians   839
    Islam   819A, 822
    Malayans   831
      : Chinese   833
    Muslim law   814

MALAYSIA (contd.)
   national liberation Movement   824
   nationalism   820
   race relations   815,818,825,834
MALAYSIAN STUDENTS:
   racial attitudes   97
MALRAUX, André: Eastern influences   324
MALTA
   emigration   1381-82
   slavery   1383
MALTESE in London   1238-39
MANCHESTER
   Asian adolescents   1134
   Blacks   1053,1293
   housing   1053,1057
   Pakistanis   1271
   race relations   1057,1293
   West Indians:
      voluntary organisations   1288
MANCHURIA   711
   Christian churches & missions   491
MANGAN, James Clarence
   Irish nationalism   283
MAORIS   872A,B,873A,875
   effects of civilisation   869
   missionaries   873
   relations with British   868,871
MARCONI SCANDAL
   anti-semitism in Britain   1227
MARRIAGE
   Sikhs: Great Britain   1274
(See also MIXED MARRIAGES)
MARSEILLES: immigrants   947
MARX, Karl
   critique of Judaism   188
MARXISM
   Arabs   66
   Asiatic mode of production   65
   East   69
   Fascism   9
   imperialism: British   22
   'national question'   68
   psychology   9
MASHONALAND: Christian missions   439,454
MASS MEDIA
   Muslim & white adolescents   1133
(See also: NEWSPAPERS, PERIODICALS)
MATABELELAND: Christian missions   408
MATO GROSSO: Brazilian colonisation   1434
MAURITIUS
   Indians   737,840
   slave trade   127
MAURRAS, Charles   949A,955
MEDICAL ETHICS: Jews: 16th c.   201
MEDICAL MIGRATION   101
MEDICAL MISSIONARIES: East Africa   466
MEDICINE, ASIAN: Britain   1241
MEIER BEN BARUCH OF ROTHENBURG
<u>Responsa</u>
   Jews in 13th c. Europe   189

MENNONITES: Soviet Union   1421
MEREDITH, George
   Arabian influences   342
MESOPOTAMIA: slavery   111
METHODIST CHURCH & MISSIONS
   Amanpondo   418
   Cape Colony   434
   Ghana   412
   India   486
   Ireland   1349
   Ivory Coast   472
   Nigeria: education   435
   Sri Lanka   482,517
   Zimbabwe   412,474
MEXICANS in Dallas, Texas   1631
MEXICO
   Amerindians   1449
   : education   1450
MICHELET, Jules: nationalism   58
MIDDLE EAST
   British attitudes: 19th c.   313A
   British travellers: attitudes   327
   Christian churches & missions   513
   English literature   314,378
   imperialism & nationalism   1459
MIGRANT WORKERS
   Central Africa   609
   Durban: dock workers   655A
   Great Britain: Turks   1279
   Lyon, France   947A
   Pondoland: 1860-1930   637
   Sri Lanka   857
   Zimbabwe: 1890-1945   630
MIGRATION, INTERNATIONAL   102
   economics   103
   Sri Lanka   848,857
MILAN, Japanese businessmen   1376
MILITARY SERVICE: minorities   64
MILLIN, Sarah   277
MILNER, Alfred, Viscount: S. Africa   674
MINNESOTA: English: immigrants   1622
MINORITIES
   in Asia, South   70
     China   724
     Europe: nationalism   60
     Europe, Central & Eastern   927
     India   70,928
       : constitution   732
     Reading   1039
     Sri Lanka   849
     U.S.A.: British attitudes   1585
   children: ethnic identity   47
   education: Great Britain & Canada   95
   League of Nations   78
   legal protection   83
   military service   64
   nationalism: Europe   60
   political sociology   62
   self-concept   43

Subject Index

MINTO, Gilbert John Murray Kynoynmund Elliott, 4th Earl of
    Indian nationalism   797
MISSISSIPPI: Freedom movement   1594
MIXED MARRIAGES
    Brixton   1029
    New Zealand   872
'MLECCHAS': North India   804
MOFFAT, Robert   445
MOND, Sir Alfred   1211
MONTREAL   1569
MORAVIANS in Gracehill   1353
MORMONS
    emigration from Britain to U.S.A.   1621
    Illinois   1579
MOROCCEAN JEWS   1500,1505
    Israel   1499
MOSHVEI OLIM   1477
MOSLEY, Sir Oswald   1016
MOSSI migrants in Ghana   563
'MOZARAB'   1398
MUFTI OF JERUSALEM:
    Palestinian Arabs   1513
MUGGING: London   1041
MULTILINGUALISM
    in Senegambia   571
    Trinidad   917
    education   99
(See also: LANGUAGE PROBLEMS & POLICIES & BILINGUALISM)
MULTI-RACIAL SOCIETIES
    class   44
    education   96
    political representation
        Africa, East   71-72
        Africa, West   72
        Asia, South   70
        Commonwealth   76
        Fiji   74
        India   70
        Kenya   74
        Sri Lanka   74-75
        Trinidad   75
    political theory   54
MURRAY, John
    Persian correspondence   351
MUSARS   1416
MUSLIM LAW: Malaysia   824
MUSLIM LEAGUE   745
MUSLIM POLITICAL PHILOSOPHY: India   783
MUSLIMS
    in Batley: adolescents   1128
        Bengal   772-73,779,782,784-85, 787,798
        Bradford   1260
        China   710
        England: Midlands   1245A
        Great Britain
            adolescents
                mass media   1131

MUSLIMS in Great Britain (contd.)
        social conditions   1112
    in Liverpool   1266
        London   1161
        Punjab   774A,795
        Spain   1399,1401-3
        Tyneside   1164
        Uttar Pradesh   793
MUSLIMS & JEWS   192,197,206
NAIPAUL, Vidiahar Surajprasad   241,246
NAMIBIA: parties & interest-groups   670
NATAL
    Christian churches & missions   417
    Grey's 'native' policy   661
    Indians   737
    race riots, 1906-1908   664
    Zulus   675
NATIONAL COMMUNISM: Georgia   1415
NATIONAL FRONT   1017-18
NATIONAL LIBERATION MOVEMENTS
    Burma & Malaya   824
NATIONAL SOCIALISM
    in Bavaria   972
    Denmark   941
    Germany   956,966,978
        anti-semitism   974
        British Labour Movement   971A
        British opinion   964
        Christian sects   967
        education   968,976
        German drama   977
        German literature   975
        German public opinion   979
        ideology: Rosenberg   965
        working-class   969
        youth movements   961,981
    Norway: Quisling   1385
    Saxony   971
    Westphalia   970
    German Christians in Palestine   1515
    German exiled writers   962
    psychology   3
(See also: FASCISM, NATIONAL FRONT & NEO-NAZISM)
NATIONALISM   53,55,57,58,63
    Africa   524A
    Africa, West (Francophone)   554
    Afrikaner   671
    Bangladesh   706
    Catalan   1393
    Europe: minorities   60
    French Canadians   1567-68
    Germany: Schleswig-Holstein   959
    Ghana   559,562
    Great Britain: liberalism   56
    India   739-40,742-43,745-50, 752-54,756
    Iraq   1468
    Ireland   1354
    Irish: Canada   1570

NATIONALISM (contd.)
  Israel 1504
  Jews: U.S.A. 1630
  Latvia 1417
  Malawi 611
  Malaysia 820
  Palestinian Arabs 1502
  Scotland 1305,1308-9,1315
  Sri Lanka 851
  Sudan 545
  Tunisia 549A
  Wales 1327,1329,1332,1336-37
NATIONALISM & IMPERIALISM
  in Middle East 1459
NATIONALITY: Commonwealth 82
NAVY: suppression of slave trade
  in East Africa 161
NEHRU, Jawarharlal 752
NEO-NAZISM: West Germany 960
NETHERLANDS: Amboynese refugees 1384
NEW ENGLAND
  immigrants from East Anglia 1623
  immigrants from Taunton 1623
NEW GUINEA
  resistance to German rule 880
NEW HEBRIDES 884,891
NEW ORLEANS: immigration port 1578
NEW YORK
  attitudes to Afro-Americans 1599
  Irish 1628
  Puerto Ricans 1632
NEW ZEALAND
  colonisation 874
  immigration 860,867
  Maoris 872A,B,873A,875
    : effect of civilisation 869
    : relations with British 868,871
  missionaries 873
  native affairs 870
  race relations 875
NEW ZEALAND COMPANY 874
NEWCASTLE-UPON-TYNE 1028
  Asian women 1254
  immigrant children 1100
  Indian children: reading errors 1113
  Irish 1197
  Pakistani children: reading errors 1113
NEWFOUNDLAND: English settlers 1564-65
NEWS MEDIA: race relations 1025
NEWSPAPERS & PERIODICALS
  Brixton riots, 1981 1026
  Chicago: foreign language 1582
  Jews: London East End 1212
  racialism & imperialism 1027
  West Africa: foreign control 550
(See also: MASS MEDIA, NEWS MEDIA)
NGUGI WA THIONG'O 267
NICARAGUA: Creole English 1451
NIGER MISSION 404,437

NIGERIA
  bilingualism 93
  Christ Apostolic Church 450A
  Christian churches & missions 400,
    402-4,407,416,419,428,
    437,452,450A,465,470
    : education 435
  Christians & Muslims 451
  federalism 567
  freed-slaves: Lagos 568
  Ibos in Jos 566
  Islam 569
  newspapers: foreign owned 550
  secessionist movements:
    British attitudes 520
NIGERIAN CHILDREN
  in Great Britain 1144
NIGERIAN DRAMA 270
NIGERIAN FICTION 260,265,278
NIGERIAN STUDENTS
  in Great Britain: career hopes 1294
NON-VIOLENT RESISTANCE
  Africans: South Africa 643
  Afro-Americans 1596
NORMANDY: Protestantism 951
NORTH AMERICA
  Anglican missionaries 1541
  British immigration 1535-36,1540,1542
  British racial attitudes 22
  Irish immigration 1534,1537-38
  Jewish family life 195
  Scots immigration 1539
(See also: CANADA, U.S.A.)
NORTHERN IRELAND
  De Valera's attitudes 1344A
  divisions 1368
  international law: minorities 1373
  I.R.A. & Republicans 1343
  Loyalists 1365
  Methodism 1349
  minorities 1358,1373
  Orangemen 1348,1369
  Presbyterian Church 1345
  religion 1352
  Republicans
    I.R.A. 1343
    Orangemen 1348
  Roman Catholic Church 1346
NORTHERN IRELAND SOCIAL DEMOCRATIC
& LABOUR PARTY 1357
NORTHERN NIGERIA MISSION 404
NORTHERN RHODESIA See: ZAMBIA
NORWAY: National Socialists: Quisling 1385
NOTTINGHAM
  Asian students 1124
  Punjabi children 1109
  race relations 1038
  Sikhs 1276
NYASALAND See: MALAWI
OCEANIA: Chinese 878

OJIBWA INDIANS	1558
OKOT P'BITEK	267
ORANGEMEN MOVEMENT	1348,1369
ORIENTAL JEWS: Israel	1507
ORIENTALISM	
Great Britain: 17th c.	383
ORIGEN	
Hinduism	479
Jews & Christians	193
ORISSA	757
Christians & Hindus	764A
ORWELL, George: imperialism	232,236
OVERSEAS STUDENTS	
in Birmingham: University	1077
Great Britain	
English language	1063,1086
needs	1104
problems	1078
London: English language	1083
Wolverhampton	1073
PACIFIC ISLANDERS	
British government recruitment of workers	888
German employment of workers	879
missionaries	883
Queensland sugar industry	863,888
rsistance to German rule	880
PAISLEY, Irish	1318
PAKHTUNS: Afghanistan	701
PAKISTAN	840A-B
bilingualism	93
(See also: MUSLIMS in India)	
PAKISTANI ADOLESCENTS	
in Great Britain	1132
PAKISTANI CHILDREN	
in Great Britain: ability	1135
Newcastle: reading errors	1113
Sheffield: libraries	1108
PAKISTANI GIRLS	
in London:	
socialisation & education	1268
PAKISTANI STUDENTS in Great Britain	1264
PAKISTANIS	
in Bradford	1263,1269
Bristol	1265
Great Britain	
leadership	1162
respiratory diseases	1267
venereal disease	1262
Leeds	1263
Manchester	1271
Newcastle-upon-Tyne	1254
Sheffield: library services	1111
PALESTINE (Ancient & Medieval)	
Arabs	1472
Jews	1488
monasteries & nunneries	500

PALESTINE (Modern including Mandate period)	
Arab Christians	1514
Arab General Strike, 1936	1484
Arab League	1473
Arab politics: Mufti of Jerusalem	1513
Arabs: Zionism	1491
British policies	1511,1516,1518
: 1945-	1489
: Arab revolt	1471
: Arabs & Zionists	1480
: economic policy	1512
: immigration policy	1500
geography of problem	1485
German Christians: Nazism	1515
immigration policy	1500
insurgency	1479
Jews	
: 1800-1882	1503
: 1882-1914	1496
Labour Party (Great Britain)	1508
Palestine Communist Party	1478
United Nations policies	1497
United States policies	1489,1629
(See also: ISRAEL)	
PALESTINE COMMUNIST PARTY	1478
PALESTINIAN ARABS	1471-73,1480,1482,1484,1516
Arab host-states	1490
Jewish immigration	1496,1500
Jordan: refugees	1519
Mufti of Jerusalem	1513
nationalism: identity	1502
Palestine Communist Party	1478
West Bank	1501
Zionism	1491
PANARE: relations with Venezuelan State	1458
PAPHOS, Cyprus	933
PAPUA - NEW GUINEA	
Australians	876
Chinese	882
PARENTAL ATTITUDES: multi-racial schools	1061
PARIS: North African immigrants	954
PATAGONIA: Welsh	1427,1429,1430A,1431
PATON, Alan	249
PATON, N.J.: English silkworkers	1619
PENTECOSTALISM: Ghana	405
PERSIAN LITERATURE	
English literature 15th-16th c.	375
19th c.	349
PERSIAN POETRY: English	318
PERTHSHIRE: tinkers	1193
PERU	
Amerindians	1453,1457
bilingualism	1454
education: racial integration	1455
migrant associations	1452

PERU (contd.)
   Spanish colonial policy:
      Amerindians   1453
PERUZZI family: Edward III   1001
PITT-RIVERS, Augustus Henry Lane-Fox   10
PLAID GENEDLAETHOL CYMRU   1336
PLANTATIONS: white indentured labour   120
PLAUTUS, Titus Maccius: slavery   222,224
PLINIUS SECONDUS, Caius:
   race relations   108
PLYMOUTH BRETHREN: Zambia   459
POLAND
   Jews   1387
   religion and state   1388
   Warsaw Rising, 1944   1386
POLES in Great Britain   1240
POLICE
   Great Britain: race relations   87
   Ireland   1355
   U.S.A.: race relations   87
POLITICAL SOCIALISATION:
   black adolescents in Great Britain 1158
   English & Asian children:
      English secondary schools   1118
PONAPE: resistance to German rule   880
PONDOLAND: migrant labour   637
PORT OF SPAIN, Trinidad: race   915
PORTUGAL
   black slaves & freedmen   1389
   Jews   1396
PORTUGUESE
   China   715
   India   731,758
POTOK, Chaim   312
POUND, Ezra
   Chinese influences   325
   Fascism   233
POWELL, Enoch   1021
PRAIRIE PROVINCES, Canada
   assimilation of immigrants   1543,1554
PREJUDICE   1-3,21
PREJUDICE, COLOUR & RACIAL
   in Birmingham: secondary schools   1094
      Great Britain   1012
         teaching   1088
      London: West Indians against
         English   1284
PRESBYTERIAN CHURCHES & MISSIONS
   in India   493
      Ireland   1342,1345
      New Hebrides: cargo cult   891
      Scotland: emigration to
         Cape Breton   1317
      U.S.A.: slavery   118
   missionaries, 1873-1929   391
PRESSURE GROUPS
   British policy to West Africa   553
   campaign against racial
      discrimination   1022
   Zimbabwe: 1898-1923   625

PRIMITIVE METHODIST MISSIONARY
   SOCIETY: Zambia   426A,459
PRIMITIVE SOCIETY
   English attitudes: 16th century   23
   Scottish attitudes: 18th century   11
PROTESTANTISM/PROTESTANTS
   African religion   394
   exiles in England   992,1177A
   Normandy   951
   U.S.A.: race relations & theology 1587
PSYCHIATRIC ILLNESS
   Africans: London   1300
   Asians: Camberwell   1257
   immigrants: North of England   1035
   Jews: London East End   1220
   West Indian children   1154
   West Indians: London   1300
PUERTO RICANS in New York   1632
PUNJAB
   Indian Army   800
   Muslims   774A,795
   Sikhs   802
PUNJABI CHILDREN
   in Coventry   1126
      Derby   1109
      Great Britain
         child rearing   1110
         thought processes   1115
      Nottingham   1109
      Smethwick   1129
PUNJABI TEACHERS
   British schools: speech   1127
PUNJABIS in Wolverhampton   1273
QUAKERS: See SOCIETY OF FRIENDS
QUEBEC: French   1566-68
QUECHUA   1457
QUEENSLAND
   land policy & settlement   866A
   Pacific Island workers:
      sugar industry   863,888
QUISLING, Vidkun:
   National Socialism: Norway   1385
RACE and CLASS: Belize   1432
RACE and IMMIGRATION in politics:
   Great Britain & U.S.A.   86
RACE in literature: Brazil   216
RACE RELATIONS   28,30
   in Botswana   279
      Desiradé   901
      Durban   279
      Fiji   881
      Glasgow   1317
      Great Britain
         law   1005,1007,1612A
         news media   1025
         Parliament   1013
         police   87
      Guyana   1438,1448
      Kenya   586
      Leicester: University   1034

Subject Index

RACE RELATIONS (contd.)
  in Malaysia   815,818,825,834
     Manchester   1057,1293
     New Zealand   868,871,875
     Nottingham   1038
     Roman Empire   108
     South Africa   279,658,687
     U.S.A.: police   87
     Zambia   613-14
  educational theory   1103
  English fiction   218
  law: Britain   1005,1007,1012A
  news media   1025
  police   87
RACE RELATIONS ACT, 1976   1012A
RACE RIOTS
  in Brixton, 1981   1026
     Cardiff, 1919   1032
     Harlem, 1935   1595
     Liverpool, 1919   1032
     Natal, 1906-8   664
RACIAL ATTITUDES
  British
    : America   23
    : Blacks   4,170
    : Central Africa, 1840-90   8
  English students   97
  Malayan students   97
  Scots: 18th century   11
RACIAL BIAS: text books   93A
RACIAL CONFLICTS: culture conflict   25
RACIAL DISCRIMINATION
  campaign against: Great Britain   1022
  in employment   6A
  : Zimbabwe   621
RACIAL DISTINCTIONS: Jamaica   907
RACIAL LANGUAGE
  British government & politics   27
RACIAL POLICIES: South Africa
  British opinion   651
  Commonwealth attitudes   692
RACIAL PREJUDICE
  Birmingham: secondary schools   1094
RACIAL THEORIES   13,28A
  anthropology   20
  British imperialism, 1894-1904   24
RACIALISM/RACISM   13,16
  in Great Britain   19
     : periodicals   1027
     South Africa   655
     U.S.A.   1583
  English fiction   217
  history textbooks   93A
  ideology   5
  World Council of Churches
    campaign against   980
RAILWAY BUILDING: Cape Colony   676
RAINIS, Janis   1417

RAS TAFARIANS
  in England   1283
     Jamaica   911,1283
     Kingston, Jamaica   911
     London: speech   1301
RASHID ALI, al-Gailani:
  Iranian nationalism   1468
READING, Berks.
  Blacks   1303
  minorities   1039
READING (EDUCATION)
  Indian & Pakistani children   1113
  West Indian children   1141A
REFUGEES/EXILES
  Amboynese in Netherlands   1384
  Czechs   939
  English Catholics in Spain   1398
  French in Britain   1179,1181,1183
     Switzerland   1405
  Germans in Britain   1184
  international law   79
  Italians in London   1210
     Switzerland   1405
  Palestinian Arabs in Jordan   1519
  Silesians: West Germany   957
  Sudanese   546-47
REGGAE MUSIC
  black adolescents: Great Britain   1302
REGIONALISM
  France: Brittany   949
  India   739,747,754,757
  Yugoslavia   1423
RELIGION: gypsies: Great Britain   1194
RELIGIOUS PLURALISM: Brazil   1433
REPUBLICANS: Ireland   1343
RESPIRATORY DISEASES
  Pakistanis in Great Britain   1267
RESTAURANTS: Chinese   1167,1171
RHODESIA/SOUTHERN RHODESIA
  See ZIMBABWE
RHODESIAN FRONT: African affairs   623A
ROCHDALE: Asians: housing   1055
ROMAN BRITAIN; ethnicity   110
ROMAN CATHOLIC CHURCH & MISSIONS
  in Africa   467
     Brunei   508
     Buganda   468
     Calabar   416
     Great Britain: education   1071,1090
     Ireland   1370,1374,1374A
     Ivory Coast   472
     Jaffna: Hinduism   855
     Lesotho   409
     Madras: education   759
     Malaysia   508
     Nigeria   482
     : education   435
     Northern Ireland   1346
     South Africa   425
     Sri Lanka   855-56

ROMAN CATHOLIC CHURCH & MISSIONS (contd.)
  in Vietnam   478
  Emilian community in London   1209A
  English exiles in Spain   1398
ROMAN EMPIRE
  freedmen   106,109,113
  immigration   114
  Jews   200,210,301
  race relations   108
  slavery   105,112-13
ROME (Ancient): Jews   200
ROSENBERG, Alfred:
  National Socialist ideology   965
ROSS, W. McGregor: critic of
  Kenyan colonial policy   593
ROTIMI, Ola   271
RUMANIA: Jews   1390
RUSSIAN SOCIAL-DEMOCRATIC PARTY
  (Mensheviks): Jewish Bund   1420
RWANDA: White Fathers   436B
SAHARA: Jews   197
SAINT-ENGRÂCE, Soule: Basques   952
SAMOA
  bilingualism: education   885
  resistance to German rule   880
SAMUEL, Sir Herbert
  Palestine immigration policies   1500
SANDWELL: Asian doctors   1253
SARACENS: English attitudes   993
SASKATCHEWAN: Indians   1559
SAXONY: National Socialists   971
SCANDINAVIAN LITERATURE: Jews   295
SCHOOL-LEAVERS:
  West Indians: London   1146
SCHOOL TEXTBOOKS
  racial bias: geography   93B
  racialism: history   93A
SCHREINER, Olive   277
SCIENCE: British imperialism   32
SCOTLAND
  abolitionist movements   151,173
  African links   1314
  Afro-Americans   1321
  Asians   1324
  Celtic community   1310
  Chinese   1320
  emigration   1317-18
  English literature   385
  Gaelic community   1313
  Gaelic culture   1306,1316
  Gaelic education   1311
  Irish   1320,1323
  nationalism   1305,1308-9,1315
  racial attitudes: 18th century   11
  religion   1312
  Scottish fiction   384
  James Thomson   386
  U.S.A.: reconstruction   1597

SCOTS
  in Australia   861
    Canada   1573-75
    North America   2539
    U.S.A.   1633-36
      War of American
      Independence   1636
  English stereotype   1011
SCOTT, Sir Walter   218A
SCOTTISH HIGHLANDS
  emigration to Australia   861
  emigration to Canada   1317,1575
SCOTTISH ISLES
  emigration to Australia   861
  emigration to North America   1539
SCOTTISH MISSIONARIES: India   503
SCOTTISH NATIONAL PARTY   1305,1309
SEAMEN'S STRIKE, 1911   1170
SEGREGATION: Zimbabwe   627
SENEGAL: French   570
SENEGAMBIA
  Christian churches & missions   473
  multilingualism   571
SERGIUS the Stylite:
  Christians & Jews   198
SETTLERS
  East Africa   579
  Kenya   525,583-84
  Tanzania   595
  Zimbabwe   525,628
SEVETTIJÄRVI, Finland: Skolts   943
SEYCHELLES: education   511A
SHAN: Burma   708
SHANGHAI: European children   712
SHEEHAN, Patrick Augustine, 1852-1913
  Irish nationalism   1354
SHEFFIELD
  information services: immigrants   1098
  library services
    Chileans   1166
    Pakistani adults   1111
    Pakistani children   1108
    West Indians   1149
SHELLEY, Percy Byssh:
  Eastern influences   369
SHEPSTONE, Sir Theophilus   653
SH'IA IMĀMĪ ISMAILIAS: Great Britain   1247
SHI'IS: Lebanon   1520
SIERRA LEONE
  Christian churches & missions   430
  Creoles   572
  domestic slavery   574
  freed-slaves   575
  Fulbe immigrants   573
  newspapers: foreign owned   550
SIKH CHILDREN: Leeds   1272
SIKH WOMEN: Great Britain   1275
SIKHS
  in Bristol   1277
    Canada   1576

Subject Index

SIKHS (contd.)
  in Great Britain
      : generation differences   1278
      : marriage   1274
    Nottingham   1276
    Punjab   802
SILESIAN REFUGEES: West Germany   957
SILK-WORKERS
  emigration from England to U.S.A.   1619
SINGAPORE
  Chinese   718,724
    business   725
    education   717
    marriage   843
    Pang   841
    women   844
  Christian missions: education   498A
  Indians   835
  Malays   842
SINHALESE   850
  and Tamils   854
SKOLTS in Sevettijärvi   943
SLATER, Thomas Ebenezer
  work in India   496
SLAVE COAST (18th century)
  slave trade   144
SLAVE COMPENSATION   182
SLAVE CULTURE
  U.S.A.: 18th century   132
SLAVE RISINGS   185-86
SLAVE-TRADE
  Anglo-U.S. relations   131
  Birmingham   138
  Bristol   136-37,139
  Caribbean   126
  Cuba   133
  English   119,128,144-45
  English poetry   264
  Jamaica   122
  Liverpool   130
  London   123
  Mauritius   127
  U.S.A.: Southern States   143
  Virginia   145
SLAVE WOMEN: Caribbean   121
SLAVERY/SLAVES   142
  in Bermuda   141
    Brazil: Amerindians   1424
    Cape Colony: 18th c.   698
    Egypt (ancient)   104
    Greece (ancient)   107
    India   729-30
    Jamaica   135,906
    Malta   1383
    Mesopotamia   111
    Portugal   1389
    Roman Empire   105
    Sierra Leone   574
    South Africa:
      colonial policy, 1806-26   648

SLAVERY/SLAVES (contd.)
  in Sudan   548
    U.S.A.: Southern States
      Irish views   129
      Presbyterians   118
    Venezuela: Amerindians   1424
    Yorubaland   134
  English poetry   264
(See also: ABOLITIONISTS, EMANCIPATION)
SLOVAKS
  Czechoslovakia   934
  Czechs   937
  independence: British opinion   928
SMETHWICK: Punjabi children   1129
SMITH, William, 1756-1835
  abolitionist & reformer   148
SOCIAL DARWINISM
  Great Britain, 1860-1914   18
  U.S.A.   7
SOCIAL MOBILITY
  immigrants in Marseilles   947
SOCIAL SECURITY
  migrant workers: European Community   926
SOCIALISATION
  Pakistani girls: London   1268
SOCIALISM
  Jews
    Austria   983
    Germany   983
    U.S.S.R.   1409
SOCIETY FOR AFRICAN MISSIONS
  IN IRELAND   433
SOCIETY FOR THE SUPPORT OF
  GAELIC SCHOOLS   1311
SOCIETY OF FRIENDS:
  Madagascar   455
SOLDIER SETTLERS: Kenya   583
SOLOMON BEN ADRETH
  See IBN ADRET, SOLOMON BEN ABRAHAM
SOMALIS in Kenya   584
SOUTH AFRICA
  Aborigines' Protection Society   527,646
  African fiction   248
  African National Congress   693
  African periodicals   272
  African reservations   676
  African working class: resistance   660
  Afrikaner nationalism   671
  Anglican clergy: politics   410
  'Bantu' education   649,697
  Bantus & Europeans   653,656-67
  Boer War, 1899-1902
    Africans   639,694
    race & civilisation   668
  British immigrants   647,688,696
  British Labour movement   681
  Cape Coloureds
    citizenship   682
    education   685
    status   686

SOUTH AFRICA (contd.)

capitalism	640
Chinese labour	678
Christian churches & missions	410A,411, 415,417,420,425,434, 445,453,457,461
black & white women	650
class conflict & state	659
Communist Party of South Africa	642,667
diamond mining	691
dock workers: Durban	655A
education	
'Bantu'	649,697
Cape Coloured	685
Indian	685
fiction	249,259,277
Gandhi	689
gold mining	658,695
'home lands'	638
imperialism	674
income differences:	
whites & non-whites	684
Indians	521-22,652,672-73
education	685
industrial relations & race	644
justice & administration	680
labour	
Chinese	678
gold mines	662,695
railway building	676
Tswana	683
white	645
liberalism	677
Namibia: plural society	669
native policy: Earl Grey	661
non-violent opposition: Africans	643
race & racism	655
race relations	687
Botswana & Durban	679
gold mining	658
racial policy	
British opinion	651,654
Commonwealth	692
racial riots: Natal	664
railway building	676
slavery	
Cape Colony, 18th c.	698
colonial policy, 1806-26	648
Swazis	665
theatre	261
Tswana	683
whites	
Cape	690
labour	645
population	663
Natal	641
writers in exile	252
Zulus	675
British images	665
SOUTH AFRICAN GENERAL MISSION: Zambia	459
SOUTH CAROLINA	1581
SOUTH MANCHESTER, Conn.:	
English silk worker immigrants	1629
SOUTHALL: immigration & politics	1006
SOUTHERN CHRISTIAN LEADERSHIP CONFERENCE	1596
SOUTHERN RHODESIA See: ZIMBABWE	
SOYINKA, Wole	218A,271
SPAIN	
Catalan nationalism	1393
colonial policy: Peruvian Indians	1453
English Catholic exiles	1398
gypsies	1401
Jews	1391-92,1394,1396-97
'Mozarab'	1395
Muslims	1399,1401,1403
settlers in Latin America	1425
slave trade: Cuba	133
SPANIARDS	
in Latin America	1425
Trinidad	921
SPANISH LANGUAGE: Trinidad	917
SPORT: integration of West Indian children	1152
SRI LANKA	
Christian churches & missions	482,485, 488,516-17
communal conflict	845,851
communal representation	74,75
Dravidians	852
education	
cultural conflict	847
language	858
immigrant labour	857
Indians	733
labour migration	848
language	
education	858
policies	91
minorities	849
nationalism	850
Roman Catholics	856
& Hindus	855
Sinhalese	850
& Tamils	854
Tamils	846,854
STEPHENS, James	286
STEPNEY: immigration & politics	1006
STEREOTYPES	
ethnic	45
Irish: by English	1011
Jewish	209
Scots: by English	1011
Welsh: by English	1011
STEWART, James: Lovedale	410A
STRATHNAVER: Celtic society	1310
SUDAN	
immigrants	546,549
nationalism	545
refugees	546-47

Subject Index

SUDAN (contd.)
    slavery   548
        : ending   159
S'ŪDRAS: India   803,806
SUNNIS: Lebanon   1521
SUTHERLAND, Efua   27
SWAHILI speaking communities: Kenya   589
SWAMINARAYAN sect: Great Britain   1242
SWARAJYA PARTY   745
SWAT PATHANS: Afghanistan   700
SWAZILAND   666
SWITZERLAND
    French & Italian refugees   1405
    Jura separatism   1404
SYRIA
    Armenians   1460
    Christians   1525
    Ismailis   1526
    monasteries & nunneries   500
SYRIAN CHRISTIANS
    in Kerala: education   763
SYRUS, Ephraem
    hymns against Jews   208
TAITA people: Kenya: CMS   411
TAMALE, Ghana: Yoruba migrants   558
TAMILNAD, India: nationalism   739
TAMILS   846
    & Dravidians   740
    & Sinhalese   854
TANNA, New Hebrides
    Presbyterians & cargo cult   891
TANZANIA
    adaptationist & assimilationist policies   524
    Christian churches & missions   442
    education: plural society   596
    settlers: agriculture   595
TAUNTON
    emigration to New England   1625
TEACHERS
    attitudes   1059
        to West Indian children   1148
TENNYSON, Alfred 1st Baron
    Arabian influences   342
TERENCE: slavery   222,224
THACKERAY, William Makepeace
    Eastern influences   343
THAILAND
    Chinese   858
    Malays   859
THAIS in Kelantan   839A
THEODOSIUS. Sphaerica
    Arab translation   358
THIRTY YEARS' WAR
    Czech exiles   939
THOMSON, James
    Arabian influences   342
    Scotland   386
TOGOLAND: Bremen missions   455A

TRADE UNIONS
    in Great Britain: emigration   986
        U.S.A.: immigration   1589
TRANSVAAL
    Chinese   678
    Indians   673
TRAVANCORE
    Christians, Hindus & caste   765
    Nayars & Christians   762
TRINIDAD
    communal representation   74
    disease & race: women   913
    East Indians   919-20
    emancipation   165
    immigration   915-16,920,922
    land & labour   916
    language   923
    race   915
    Spanish language   917
    youth   914
TRINIDADIAN FICTION   260
TRINIDADIANS in London   1297
TROELTSCH, Ernest:
    non-Christian religions   394
TSWANA: land & labour   683
TUNISIA:
    French policy:
        Tunisian nationalism   549A
TURKESTAN: Muslims   710
TURKEY/OTTOMAN EMPIRE
    Armenians   1530-32
    Greeks   1527
    Jews   1528-29
    migrant workers: Great Britain   1229
    Western Europe   525
TURKISH-CYPRIOTS
    in Haringey   1173
        London   1174
TURKMEN in Russian Empire   1418
TURKS
    in Great Britain: migrant workers   1229
        Iraq   1466
TURNER, Nat: slave rising   185
TUSCANY: Fascism   1380
TYNESIDE: Muslims & Blacks   1164
UGANDA
    Christian churches & missions   436A,468,471
    Egyptians, 1870-1889   598
    ethnic groups: politics   601
    Goans   602
    immigration   597,599,600
    Indians   603
    race relations   604
    Verona Fathers   424A
UGANDAN ASIANS
    in Great Britain: food habits   1249
UKRAINE
    Jews, 1917-1918   1410

UKRAINE (contd.)	
nationalism	
1775-1835	1419
20th century	1412
1920-1939	1414
1939-1945	1407
UKRAINIANS in Great Britain	1280
ULSTER UNIONIST PARTY	1353A
UNDERDEVELOPED COUNTRIES	
Christian churches	398
English fiction	216A
U.S.S.R./RUSSIA	
Church and State	1413
foreign settlement	1406
Greeks	1411
Jews	1416
Jewish Bund & Mensheviks	1420
socialism	1409
Ukrainians	1410
Wilno	1422
Latvian nationalism	1417
Mennonites	1421
National Communism: Georgia	1415
national stratification	1413A
Pan-Slav movement	1408
Turkmen	1418
Ukrainian nationalism	1407,1412, 1414,1419
UNITARIANS: Great Britain:	
U.S. slavery	176
UNITED MINEWORKERS OF AMERICA:	
immigration	1589
UNITED NATIONS	
decolonisation in Africa	518
human rights	80
Palestinian problem	1497
Rhodesian independence	631
UNITED STATES	
abolitionist movements	146,150,162, 179,181
Afro-Americans	117,1590-1608
children: self-esteem	100
literature	219,242,247, 254,262,275
American Indians	1609-11
British	1617-25
Canadians	1626
China & 'open door' policy	890
education	211,897,1580
foreign language press	1582
gypsies	1627
immigration	1578
assimilation	1584
education	1580
race & politics	86
trade unions	1589
integrated education	897
Irish	1628

Subject Index 135

UNITED STATES (contd.)	
Jews	1629-30
education	211
writers	219
Mexicans	1631
minorities	
british attitudes	1585
military service	64
North-South relations	1577
Pacific area policy	890
Palestine policy	1489,1629
police & race relations	87
Puerto Ricans	1632
race relations	87,1587-88
racialism	1583
Reconstruction	1597
Scots	1633-36
slave trade: Anglo-U.S. relations	131
slavery	132
Irish attitudes	129,172
Scottish attitudes	173
Unitarians	176
Social Darwinism	7
Welsh	1637
UNITED STATES: MIDDLE WEST	
British	1630
Scots	1634
UNITED STATES: SOUTHERN STATES	140
Afro-Americans	1594,1596,1600,1603
'Black power'	1594
'Martial South'	1577
race relations	1586
slave trade	143
slavery	140
: Presbyterians	118
South Carolina: politics	1581
UNIVERSITIES MISSION TO CENTRAL	
AFRICA: Zambia	459
UNIVERSITIES	
Birmingham	
overseas students & English language	1077
Cambridge	
West Indian & West African students	1153
Leicester: race relations	1034
Oxford	
West Indian & West African students	1153
UNTOUCHABLES: India	803,805-6
UNYAMWEZI, Tanzania: Christian church	444
UTTAR PRADESH: Muslims	793
UWANDA, Tanzania: Church & State	442
VENEREAL DISEASE	
Pakistanis in Great Britain	1262
VENEZUELA	
Amerindians	1458
: slavery	1424
VERONA FATHERS: Uganda	424A
VIENNA: antisemitism	931

Subject Index

VIETNAM: Christian church — 478
VILNA: Jews — 1422
VIRGINIA
  British immigrants — 1628
  slave trade — 145
VIVEKANANDA: Hinduism — 479
VOLTAIRE: Jews — 299
VOLUNTARY ORGANISATIONS
  West Indians: Manchester — 1288
WAKEFIELD, Gibbon: colonisation — 874
WALES
  abolitionists — 167
  colonisation — 1338
  education
    immigrants — 1068
    Welsh language — 1066,1330,1334-35
  gypsies — 1185,1190
  Irish — 1333
  language — 1066,1326,1330-31,1334-35,1337
  nationalism — 1327,1329,1332,1336-37
  racial characteristics — 1325
WALLENT, Edward — 312
WALLOONS in England, 1570-1630 — 992
WARBURTON, Bartholomew Elliott
  George. The Crescent and the Cross — 314
WARSAW RISING, 1944 — 1386
WARTHELAND: German settlement — 982
WATCH TOWER MOVEMENT: Central Africa — 421
WATTS: Afro-Americans — 117
WELSH
  in Patagonia — 1427,1429,1430A,1431
    U.S.A. — 1637
  English drama — 388
  English literature — 387,389
  English stereotype — 1011
WELSH LANGUAGE SOCIETY — 1334
WELSH NATIONAL PARTY — 1329
WEST BANK (Israel) — 1492,1501
WEST INDIAN ADOLESCENTS
  in Great Britain: attitudes — 1150
WEST INDIAN CHILDREN
  in Great Britain — 1151,1157
    abilities — 1147
    attainments — 1147
    attitudes to school — 1156
    development — 1070
    language — 1143,1145,1155,1160
    psychiatric illness — 1154
    reading — 1141A
    spoken English — 1067
    sport: integration — 1152
    teachers' attitudes — 1148
  London
    black culture: self-concept — 98
    delinquency: remand homes — 1141
    school leavers — 1146
  Wales: performance level — 1068
WEST INDIAN STUDENTS — 1142,1153

WEST INDIANS
  in Bristol — 1298
    Croydon — 1292
    Easton — 1296
    Great Britain — 1282,1295,1299
      'black power' — 1304
      Christian Church — 1285
      leadership — 1162
    London — 1289
      food habits — 1287
      housing — 1054
      prejudice against English — 1284
      psychiatric illness — 1300
    Manchester — 1288
    Sheffield — 1149
  English literature — 274
(See also: BLACKS)
WEST NILE, Uganda: ethnic groups — 601
WESTERN CULTURE: Eastern culture — 29
WESTMINSTER: immigrants: housing — 1056
WESTPHALIA: National Socialists — 970
WHITE FATHERS: Rwanda — 436B
WIECHERT, Emil: critic of
  National Socialism — 962
WILLIAMS (Engineer): Patagonia — 1429
WILLIAMS, Dennis — 241
WITWATERSRAND: black & white
  women in Churches — 650
WOLF, Lucien: Jewish diplomacy — 203
WOLVERHAMPTON
  overseas students — 1073
  Punjabis — 1273
WOMEN
  Afro-American: radicalism — 1608
  Asian
    Great Britain — 1252
      : pregnancy — 1248
    Yorkshire: home tuition — 1259
  Chinese
    Singapore — 844
    South-East Asia — 722
  Sikh: Great Britain — 1275
  Trinidad: disease & race — 913
  West Indian slaves — 121
  Witwatersrand: Church & race — 650
WOODSTOCK, Cape Town:
  Cape Coloured — 117
WORKING CLASS
  British
    antisemitism: London — 1230
    Chinese — 1170
  German: National Socialism — 969
WORLD COUNCIL OF CHURCHES
  campaign against racism: Germany — 980
  underdeveloped areas — 398
WORLD WAR, 1914-1918
  German missions in Ghana/Togoland — 455A
WORLD WAR, 1939-1945
  Afro-Americans — 1607
    : service in Britain — 1604

WORLD WAR, 1939-1945 (contd.)	
children's literature: Britain	229
WRIGHT, Richard	247
WYOMING: Scots	1634
YAZIDI; Iraq	1467
YEATS, W.B.	
anthropology	218A
Eastern influences	333,335
Irish nationalism	281,283-84
YEMEN: Jews	1533
YEMENIS in Israel	1481
YORK: Irish	1196
YORKSHIRE	
Asian women: home tuition	1259
emigration to North America	1535
Hong Kong Chinese	1168
YORUBA MISSION	403
YORUBAS	
Christian churches & missions	400,470
African churches	470
migrants: Ghana	558
slavery	134
YUGOSLAVIA: regionalism	1423
ZAIRE	
African workers: copper mines	608
Christian churches & missions	462
race relations	612
secessionist movements:	
British attitudes	520
ZAMBIA	
African opposition to Federation	619
African resistance to European rule	615
African workers: copper mines	608
Christian churches & missions	426A, 441,459
education	446A
ethnicity in towns	617
European workers	618
Lozi people	616
race relations	606,613-14
settlers: African nationalism	607
ZANGWILL, Israel	311
ZANZIBAR: Indians	735
ZIMBABWE	
Aborigines' Protection Society	636
'African affairs'	
British opinion, 1923-39	620
Rhodesian Front	623A
African immigrants	629
African migrants	630
African policy: missionaries	624
African workers: mines	635
Christian churches & missions	408,412, 439,454,474
coercion	622
discrimination: African workers	621
European immigrants	626
European liberals	633
land policy	632

ZIMBABWE (contd.)	
Native Department, 1894-1914	634
pressure groups	625
race relations	606
repression & resistance, 1945-1964	623
segregation	627
settlers	
African nationalism	607
agriculture	628
United Nations	631
ZIONISM	214
Arabs	1491
: 1936-39	1476
British	1487
: Palestine	1480,1493-94,1506,1512
Germany, 1897-1917	963
Hungary	1340
ZOLA, Emile: Dreyfus affaire	308
ZULUS	
British images	665
Natal	675

AUTHOR INDEX

ABDEL AZIZ AHMED, L.N.	313A	ANIKPO, M.O.C.	566
ABDEL-HAMID, M.S.	314-15	ANISULOWO, S.A.	1043A
ABDEL RAHMAN, A.W.A.	1471	ANKRAH-DOVE, L.	1058
ABDUAL RAZAK, A.	814	APPLEBY, B.L.	934
ABDULAI, O.N.	518	APPLEGATE, J.M.	956
ABDULLAH, A.M.C.	316	APPLETON, L.	543
ABOAGYE-DA COSTA, A.A.	77	AR-RASHEED, M.H.	244
ABRAHAM, C.E.R.	815	ARAB, S.A.	243
ACTON, T.A.	1185	ARESTY, A.E.	289
ADAMS, M.C.C.	1577	ARIYARATNE, R.A.	845
ADAMS, R.A.	1520	ARIZPE-SCHLOSSER, L.	1449
ADEGBOLA, E.A.A.	400	ARNOLD, D.J.	739
ADINARAYANSIH, S.P.	1	AROONAN, K. NAMBI	740
AGBETI, J.K.	401	ARUMUGAM, V.	91
AGNIHOTRI, R.K.	1272	ASAD, T.	774A
AGOVI, J.K.E.	240	ASHBY, B.E.	1105
AHLIJAH, W.O.C.K.	1141	ASHDOWN, P.D.	1432
AHMAD, L.I.	1466	ASHTON, C.P.M.	876
AHMAD, M.	317	ASIEGBU, J.U.J.	147
AHMAD, M.J.	318	ASLAM, M. Ph.D.,London, 1960	320
AHMAD, N.	241	Ph.D., Nottingham, 1979	1241
AHMAD, W.	738	ASPINWALL, B.	148
AHMED, L.N. Abdel Aziz		ASSIMENG, J.M.	406
See: ABDEL AZIZ AHMED, L.N.		ASTLEY, F.J.D.	220
AHMED, R.	772	ATIYAH, N.W.	1521
AHMED, S.	773	ATKINSON, A.M.	1028
AHMED, S.H.	1259A	ATKINSON, D.	1106
AHMED SHAH, S.Z.	475	ATKINSON, M.	119
AILES, J.A.	992	AURORA, G.S.	1044
AJAYI, J.F.A.	402	AWAD, M.	1459
AJAYI, W.O.	403-4	AWAR, K.	809
AKERS, J.N.	118	AYANDELE, E.A.	407
AKUFFO, F.W.B.	405	AZIZ, K.K.	775
AL-JABIRI, K.F.F.	1467	AZIZ AHMED, L.N. Abdel	
AL-JAMIL, K.	1468	See: ABDEL AZIZ AHMED, L.N.	
AL-KHFAJI, T.M.H.	1472		
AL-MAHJUBI, G.	542	BADRI, S. el-	
AL-RAHEB, H.	288	See: EL-BADRI, S.	
AL-TAMEENI, A.M.K.	476	BADRUD-DIN, A.A.	1473
ALEEM, M.A.	774	BAGLEY, C.R.	2
ALEXANDRIS, A.	1527	BAHADOORSINGH, I.J.	776
ALI, J.S.	1525	BAHCHELI, T.S.	932
ALI, M.	840A	BAHRIN, T.S.	839
ALI, M.M.	477	BAILES, E.S.	1633
ALIER, V. Martinez-		BAILEY, A.M.	65
See: MARTINEZ-ALIER, V.		BAILEY, J.P.	1426
ALJUBOURI, D.A.H.	993	BAIN, D.	1305
ALLAN, P.M.L.	1590	BAKER, D.L.	1014
ALLEN, G.	146	BAKER, W.	290
ALLEN, T.N.	892	BAKHIET, G.M.A.	545
ALTAMIRANO RUA, T.	1452	BAKIR, A.M.	104
AMBASTHA, K.P.	319	BALFOUR, R.A.C.S.	861
AMPALAVANAR, R.	835	BALLENTYNE, A.W.G.	994
ANDERSON, D.M.	581	BANKS, M.Y.	846
ANDERSON, E.	1141A	BANTON, M.P.	1281
ANDREWS, H.P.	1571	BARAKAT, E.E.	530
ANDREWS, W.D.E.	242	BARBER, M.J.	1543

BARBER, P.	78	BICKERTON, Y.J.	877
BARBOUR, W.M.	1342	BILLIG, M.G.	38
BARBU, Z.	3	BILLINGHAM, A.L.	957
BARER, R.G.	1474	BILLINGTON, L.	150
BARI, A.F.M.A.	1107	BINGHAM, R.L.	151
BARKER, A.J.	4	BINNS, D.	1186
BARNES, D.F.L.	384	BIRAM, F.	1213
BARNES, R.P.	1591	BIRBALSINGH, F.M.	1544
BAROT, R.	1242	BIRD, J.R.	6A
BARR, P.M.	321	BIRKS, D.M.	1030
BARROW, R.H.	105	BIRTWHISTLE, T.M.	152
BARTH, T.F.W.	700	BLACK, I.M.	1476
BARTLETT, R.P.	1406	BLACK, P.A.	638
BARTON, S.W.	1260	BLANCHET, W.L.	478
BASHEAR, S.	66	BLANCHET-COHEN, T.	409
BASHIR, A.Al-R.A. el-		BLAXTER, L.	1163
See: EL-BASHIR, A.Al-R.A.		BLUME, H.S.B.	1214
BASTIN, R.	984	BLUNDEN, M.A.	410
BATE, W.	1059	BLUNT, M.E.	71
BATH, K.S.	1273	BOCKSTOCE, J.R.	1556
BATRAWI, A.M. el-		BOJCUN, J.M.	1407
See: EL-BATRAWI, A.M.		BOKHARI, Z.A.	322
BAY-PETERSEN, O.	225	BOLTON, J.L.	997
BAYLISS, G.M.	1211	BOND, J.A.	777
BEACH, S.A.	1325	BONNER, P.	639
BEAGLEHOLE, J.H.	70	BOOTH, J.R.	606
BEARDSMORE, V.	1592	BOURHIS, R.Y.	1326
BEARDWOOD, A.	995-96	BOWEN, C.	226
BECKLES, G.L.A.	913	BOWEN, K.D.	1344
BECKLES, H.M.	120	BOWMAN, J.F.V.	1344A
BECKLES, McD.	898	BOWRING, W.J.W.	595
BEDOYAN, H.	1522	BOZZOLI, B.	640
BEECHEY, F.E.	1196	BRADLEY, W.C.A.A.	1167
BEECHEY, V.	5	BRAITHWAITE, R.H.E.	245
BEESE, F.K.	221	BRATCHEL, M.E.	998
BEINART, W.J.	637	BRATHWAITE, E.	902A
BELLE, G.A.V.	898A	BRAZIL, D.E.	1061
BELLENGER, D.T.J.	1177A	BREAKWELL, G.M.	39
BENEDICT, B.	1161	BREWER, J.D.	1016
BENEWICK, R.J.	1015	BRIEF, D.	800
BENNETT, J.J.	1212	BROCK, S.M.	410A
BENNIE, M.J.	572	BROMILEY, W.P.	641
BENSKI, T.	1319	BROOKES, A.A.	1626
BENSON, S.W.	1029	BROOKS, A.K.	642
BENTLEY, S.	1162	BROOKS, P.M.	1187
BERESFORD, P.C.F.M.	1343	BROOKSHAW, D.R.	216
BERGER, M.	32A	BROTZ, H.M.	187
BERGSTROM, G.W.	741	BROUGHTON, E.S.	323
BERK, F.	1173	BROUGHTON, G.	246
BERNSTEIN, D.	1475	BROWN, D.W.	1477
BERROW, J.H.	280	BROWN, J.	1345
BEST, N.J.	703	BROWN, J.M.	742
BETHELL, L.M.	149	BROWN, L.B.	867
BETTS, G.S.	1243	BROWN, R.M.C.S.	281
BHACHA, P.K.	1274	BROWNE, S.A.	1004A
BHATNAGAR, J.K.	1060	BRYSON, D.B.	411
BHATT, R.S.	728	BUCKLEY, E.M.	412
BHATTI, F.M.	1576	BUCKMAN, J.	1031
BHEBE, M.B.	408	BUDEIRI, M.K.	1478
BHOWNAGARY, A.	6	BUNKER, S.K.	413

BURCHELL, R.A.	1617	CHAPLEN, E.F.	1063
BURNS, J.R.	1593	CHAPMAN, B.	1375
BURTON, F.P.	1346	CHAPMAN, M.K.	1306
BUSH, B.M.	121	CHAPMAN, W.R.	10
BUSH, J.A.	1618	CHARSLEY, S.R.	597
BUSH, J.F.	1214	CHARTERS, D.A.	1479
BUSS, P.H.	958	CHATTOPADHAYAY, A.K.	729
BUTCHER, D.A.P.	573	CHAU, H.J.S.Y.	325
BUTCHER, J.G.	816	CHAUDHRI, J.J.M.	801
BUTLER, A.F.	7	CHAUDHURI, T.	480
BUTLER, B.B. Jensen- See: JENSEN-BUTLER, B.B.		CHEAL, D.J.	41
		CHENG, L-K.	841
BUTT, A.J.	1557	CHENG, T.C.	717
BUTT PHILIP, A.A.S.	1327	CHERTKOW, P.S.	1348
BUTTERWORTH, A.E.	1282	CHEUNG, C.H.W.	1168
BYRON, M.T.	899	CHIASSON, R.J.	1546
		CHICK, J.D.	550
CADDICK, B.F.	40	CHIDOLUE, A.B.	567
CADFAN, N.H.	1427	CH'IEN, C.S.	326
CADWALLER, B.	324	CHIN, E.Y.Y.	576
CAIRNS, H.A.C.	8	CHOONG, C.P.	481
CALLAWAY, H.L.	92	CHUGTAI, M.	777
CALLOWAY, C.G.	1609	CIECHANOWSKI, J.M.	1386
CALMAN, D.A.	836	CLACK, G.	644
CALMANN, M.J.	944	CLARE, D.W.	1064
CAMERON, H.M.W.	1545	CLARK, R.I.	960
CAMERON, J.M.	1573	CLARK, T.D.	247
CAMPBELL, M.C.	903	CLARKE, D.G.	621
CAMPBELL, P.C.	716	CLARKE, P.B.	1245
CAMPISAND, M.S.	1347	CLAYTON, A.H.L.Q.	582
CANDAMITTO, V.	1244	CLEAVES, P.J.	868
CAPLAN, L.	519	CLEMENTS, R.V.	986
CAREY, A.T.	1142	CLENDENNEN, G.W.	414
CARLEBACH, J.	188	CLINTON, D.K.	415
CARNIE, J.W.	1062	CLOW, D.	1108
CARR, W.	959	COCKRAM, G-M.G.E.	81
CARRIER, J.W.	1215	COHEN, D.	189
CARRINGTON, G.W.	727	COHEN, M.Y.	1480
CARROTHERS, W.A.	985	COHEN, P.S.	1481
CARSON, J.	1005	COHEN, R.L.	1136
CARTER, D.J.	643	COHEN, S.	1216
CARTER, R.S.	9	COHEN, T. Blanchet- See: BLANCHET-COHEN, T.	
CARTER, S.P.A.	914		
CASEY, T.	33	COLACO, L.	733
CASHMORE, E.E.H.	1283	COLLETT, P.R.	1459A
CASPER, E.R.	79	COLLINS, B.E.A.	1320
CASSIA, P. Sant See: SANT CASSIA, P.		COLLINS, S.F.	1164
		CONDRY, E.F.	1307
CASTLES, G.	924	CONNELLY, R.K.	1188
CASTLES, S.	924	CONWAY, A.A.	1578
CATER, J.J.	53	CONWAY, I.C.	961
CATHERALL, G.A.	153,904	CONYBEARE, C.	227
CAWTE, L.H.	154	COOKE, C.M.	416
CELL, G.M.	1564	COOKE, J.H.	1349
CHADUKA, N.L.	620	COOPER, A.J.	417
CHAKRAVARTI, N.R.	707	COOPER, B.L.	248
CHAKRAVARTI, R.	80	COOPER, H.	1528
CHANDRAN, J.R.	479	COOTER, R.J.	1197
CHANDY, V.	93	COPE, T.H.	417A
CHANRAWI, A.S.W. el- See: EL-CHANRAWI, A.S.W.		COPLANS, B.A.R.	482

CORLETT, J.A.	538	DENNINGTON, G.L.	1438
COSGRAVE, I.K.	190	DESAI, R.H.	1045-46
COSTA, A.A. Aboagye da		DESHAIES-LA FONTAINE, D.	1566
See: ABOAGYE-DA COSTA, A.A.		DESHEN, S.A.	1483
COULTHARD, G.R.	237	DEVILLY, P.B.	282
COURIE, J.A.	869	DEWICK, E.C.	390
COUSINS, W.M.	155	DEX, J.	1047
COZIN, M.L.	1165	DHANDA, P.	840
CRAGG, D.G.L.	418	DICKEY, A.F.	1007
CRAMPTON, E.P.T.	419	DICKINS, E.P.	962
CRANDALL, G.F.	1594	DICKSON, R.J.	1534
CREHAN, C.A.F.	420	DIKIGOROPOULOS, A.I.	932A
CROFTS, D.	1143	DIMMOCK, G.W.	1032
CROMER, G.N.	191	DIN, A.A. Badrud	
CROSS, J.S.W.	421	See: BADRUD-DIN, A.A.	
CROWLEY, F.K.	862	DIXON, E.A.A.	1321
CROWTHER, K.J.	758	DIXON, J.T.	1535
CRUMMEY, D.E.	422	DIXON, P.F.	156
CUMPSTON, I.M.	734	DJAMOUR, J.	842
CURRAN, H.V.	1144	DJURSAA, M.	941
CUSHING, P.H.	291	DOBBY, E.H.C.	817
CUSHION, K.G.	222	DOHERTY, J.M.	1033
		DOMB, R.	331
DA COSTA, A.A. Aboagye-		DONALDSON, A.R.	283
See: ABOAGYE-DA COSTA, A.A.		DOSANJH, J.S.	1109-10
DACHS, A.J.	423	DOUGLAS, J.M.	597A
DAHYA, B.U.-D.	1245A	DOVE, L. Ankrah-	
DAJANI, A.M.	192	See: ANKRAH-DOVE, L.	
DAKIN, E.	1217	DOW, D.A.	391
DALTON, B.J.	870	DOWNING, J.D.H.	1025
DALY, C.B.	424	DOYLE, F.J.	425
DAMIANI, H.E.E.	327	DREW, N.J.	332
DANCEY, R.M.	122	DREXLER, M.J.	1308
DANIEL, J.E.	1328	DRURY, C.M.	487
DANIEL, N.A.	328	D'SOUZA, M.B.	1065
DAS, G.K.	329	DUDER, C.J.D.	583
DAUGHTREY, J.	1482	DUDLEY, M.P.	1111
DAVID, R.	249	DUFF, A.M.	106
DAVIDI, A.	718	DUNAE, P.A.	228
DAVIDSON, A.K.	483	DUNCAN, B.C. Kirk-	
DAVIES, D.H.	1329	See: KIRK-DUNCAN, B.C.	
DAVIES, J.A., M.A., Wales, 1970	330	DUNCAN, N.C.	1008
M.A., London, 1958	1330	DUNCKER, S.J.	905
DAVIES, R.H.	645	DUNLOP, D.M.	1529
DAVIS, G.E.	813	DUNN, R.	1009
DAVIS, N. Yuval-		DUNNE, M.A.	759
See: YUVAL-DAVIS, N.		DUNNING, R.W.	1558
DAVIS, W.B.S.	484	DURANT, J.R.	12
DE LANGE, N.R.M.	193	DURING, S.C.	292
DE SILVA, I.W.	847	DURKACZ, V.E.	1066
DE SILVA, K.M.	485	DUROJAIJYE, S.M.	1067
DE SILVA, P.W.	486	DUTTA, A.	848
DE SLIBE, M.A. Jiminez		DYCK, N.E.	1559
See: JIMINEZ DE SLIBE, M.A.		DYSON, K.K.	760
DE SOUZA, F.R.C.	577		
DEAKIN, N.	1006	EADE, P.J.K.	779
DEARBORN, N.W.	11	EADES, J.S.	558
DELIA, E.P.	1381	EASTON, E.G.	1322
DELLAQIACOMA, R.	424A	EBEID, A.A.	531
DENICH, G.E.	1238	EDELSTEIN, C.S.	293
		EDGAR, J.R.	1246

Author Index

EDGECOMBE, D.R.	646	FISCIAN, C.E.	1284
EDMONDS, M.J.	832	FISHER, M.J.	338
EDNEY, S.R.	1610	FISHMAN, I.	194
EDWARDS, I.E.	647-48	FITTER, R.S.	1113
EDWARDS, P.M.	1634	FITZHENRY, R.	623
EDWARDS, V.K.	1145	FLANAGAN, M.T.	1351
EGGER, V.T.C.E.F.	67	FLEISS, A.	1052
EISENBERG, P.S.	649	FLETT, H.	1053
EL-BADRI, S.	544	FONTAINE, D. Deshaies-La	
EL-BASHIR, A.Al-R.A.	546	See: DESHAIES-LA FONTAINE, D.	
EL-BATRAWI, A.M.	532	FORBES, A.D.W.	710
EL-CHANRAWI, A.S.W.	333	FORDOM, M.J.	229
EL-FEKI, M.M.M.	533	FORRESTER, D.B.	489
EL-MOWAFY, M.I.	334	FORSYTH, W.D.	860
EL-SAFI, M.A.G.H.	584	FORTH, C.E.	195
EL-SHEIKH, M.A.R.	598	FORTT, J.M.	600
ELDER, J.M.	1309	FOSSICK, S.	1048
ELDRIDGE, J.E.T.	1034	FOSTER, J.	490
ELLISS, J.D.	878	FOX, P.C.	185
ELLMAN, L.J.	1112	FRANCIS, I.K.	238
ELMAN, P.	1218	FRANKEL, J., Ph.D., L.S.E., 1951	719
ELZUBEIR, M.A.	1068	Ph.D., Cambridge, 1961	1409
EMMOTT, D.H.	761	FREEBERNE, J.D.M.	1169
ENGHOLM, S.F.	599	FREEDMAN, H.	1392
EPSTEIN, I.	1391	FREEDMAN, M.	720,818
ERGUN, T.	925	FREEMAN, P.G.	1484
ESPINOSA, M.T. San Roman		FREESTON, D.G.	1189
See: SAN ROMAN ESPINOSA, M.T.		FRENCH, C.J.	123
EVANS, D.	1595	FREND, W.H.C.	427
EVANS, E.	1331	FRIEDMAN, I.	963
EVANS-VON KRBEK, J.H.P.	701	FRISCHWASSER, H.F.	1488
EZEJIOFOR, G.O.	81A	FROST, R.A.	586
		FULLER, C.J.	762
FACHLER, M.	1219	FULTON, A.	491
FADNER, F.L.	1408		
FAFOWORA, O.O.	520	GABRIEL, J.G.	13
FAIRCLOUGH, A.	1596	GADAMU, F.	539
FARAG, F.F.	335	GAINER, B.	1010
FARAG, N.R.	336	GAITSKELL, D.L.	650
FARINPOUR, A.A.	1463	GAKWANDI, A.	250
FARQUHAR, D.	893	GALLOWAY, J.	385
FEAKES, B.A.	1069	GALWAY, R.N.	1352
FEAR, J.M.	1611	GANGULY, S.R.	1113A
FEARER, J.	1436	GANN, L.H.	613-14
FEKI, M.M.M. el-		GARAI, G.	1340
See: EL-FEKI, M.M.M.		GARCIA, D.	1547
FELDMAN, D.M.	426	GARRARD, J.A.	1221
FELTOE, G.	622	GARTON, I.M.	157
FENELEY, J.E.	337	GASH, I.J.	492
FERNANDO, C.N.V.	488	GASKELL, A.	711
FERNANDO, Q.G.	849	GASSER, B.F.	230
FERNANDO, S.J.M.	1220	GASSICK, T.J. Le	
FERRY, E.B.M.	1350	See: LE GASSICK, T.J.	
FIELDING, I.J.	585	GATES, H.L.	251
FIELDING, N.G.	1017	GEGGUS, D.P.	902
FIELDING, R.J.	426A	GEHANI, T.G.	493
FIGUERUA, P.E.	1146	GELDENHUYS, D.J.	651
FINER, A.R.	1070	GEORGE, G.	763
FINNIE, H.M.	1597	GEORGE, J.G.	426
FIRTH, S.G.	879	GEY VAN PITTINS, E.F.W.	82

GHIKA, P.D.	1114	GULLICK, C.J.M.R.	894
GHOSH, K.K.	819	GUNDARA, J.S.	735
GHOSH, R.N.	14	GUNN, H.D.	1631
GHOSH, S., Ph.D., London, 1954	743	GUPTA, L. Sen-	
Ph.D., London, 1966	764	See: SEN-GUPTA, L.	
GHUMAN, A.S.	1115	GUTWIRTH, E.	1394
GILMAN, R. Kornfield-		GUY, D.E.	935
See: KORNFIELD-GILMAN, R.		GWARZO, H.I.	197
GINWALA, F.N.	652	GWYNN, R.D.	1177B
GIRDHAR, D.S.	1275		
GISH, O.	101	HADDEN, M.A.	712
GITHIGE, R.M.	429	HAINES, J.T.	43
GITTINS, A.J.	430	HAINSWORTH, P.A.	946
GLENDENNING, F.J.	93A	HAIRE, J.M.	495
GLOVER, D.	1071	HALL, D.G.H.	906
GLYN-JONES, E.M.	158	HALL, J.	1149
GOLD, D.J.	1453	HALLAM, R.N.M.	1247
GOLD, P.J.	239	HALLAS, D.	1332
GOLDMAN, S.M.	54	HALSALL, P.	1116
GOLDRING, P.	1548	HAMDY MAHMOUD, A.el H.	339
GOODALL, N.	431	HAMEED, A.	340
GOODENOUGH, S.S.	915	HAMID, M.S. Abdel-	
GOODFELLOW, D.M.	653	See: ABDEL-HAMID, M.S.	
GOODLOE, R.W.	392	HAMMOND, H.K.	1073
GOODMAN, M.H.	1598	HAMPSHIRE, A.P.	1579
GOODRIDGE, C.A.	916	HAMZAH, A.B.	819A
GOODSON, D.C.	1486	HANAK, H.H.	928
GOONERATNE, D.D.M.	850	HANDCOCK, W.G.	1565
GOONETILLEKE, D.C.R.A.	216A	HANDLEY, J.E.	1323
GORDON, A.D.	744	HANNA, M.I.	551
GORDON, R.A.	745	HANNA, S.G.	1353
GOTLIEB, H.B.	964	HARBINSON, J.F.	1353A
GOTTLIEB, P.	1222	HARCUS, A.R.	432
GOVEIA, E.V.	124	HARDING, A.W.	1311
GOWARD, N.J.	1393	HARDSTONE, P.C.N.	820
GRACE, A.M.	1147	HARGEY, T.M.	159
GRACE, J.J.	574	HARRÉ, J.N.	872
GRANATH, A.	1198	HARRIS, H.	107
GRANEEK, J.J.	196	HARRIS, J.	108
GRANT, J.W.	252	HARRIS, M.	864
GRATIER, M.M.	253	HARRIS, S.	1223
GRAUMAN, R.A.	15	HART, D.R.	1580
GRAVES, A.A.	863	HARTLEY, H.P.	1074
GRAYSON, J.H.	494	HARTLEY, S.E.	496
GREEN, P.A.	1148	HASAN, M., PhD., Cambridge, 1967	840B
GREENSHIELDS, T.H.	1460	Ph.D., Cambridge, 1977	781
GREENSTREET, D.K.	851	HASLOP, G.S.B.	1612
GREENWOOD, P.N.	1011	HASSAN, A.M.	534
GREER, C.S.	1599	HASSAN, R.	341
GREVILLE, S.E.	871	HATTON, J.D.	655
GREWAL, J.S.	780	HAWARI, R.	342-43
GRIFFIN, C.C.M.	945	HAYES, J.C.	1353B
GRIFFIN, C.E.	42	HAYES, P.M.	1385
GRIFFITHS, H.	654	HAYES, R.C.	565
GRIFFITHS, M.	1433	HAYMAN, A.P.	198
GRIFFITHS, N.E.S.	1549	HAYNES, J.M.	1117
GRIMBLE, I.A.	1310	HEARN, S.A.	344
GRÖNFURS, M.J.	942	HEINEMAN, B.W.	1022
GRUBB, M.	1072	HEISLER, H.	44
GRYSKIEWICZ, N.	1279	HEMPENSTALL, P.J.	880

Author Index

HEMSON, D.	655A	HUSSAIN, M.D.	782
HENKO, J.P.	1410	HUTCHINSON, B.A.	657
HENLEY, P.S.	1458	HUTCHINSON, G.P.	965
HENRIQUES, I. Ramacharan-		HYNES, M.P.	1199
See: RAMACHARAN-HENRIQUES, I.			
HENRIQUES, L.F.	907	IDIZKOWSKI, H.A.	1355
HERRINGTON, E.I.	160	IDRUS, F.	1078
HERRMAN, I.M.	1487	IFTIKHAR, A.	1264
HERSHON, C.J.	1137	INDRAPALA, K.	852
HERSKOVITS, J.F.	568	INENEJI, N.B.C.	83
HICKEY, J.V.	1333	INGHAM, K.	497
HICKS, D.W.	93B	INGLIS, C.B.	882
HIGMAN, B.W.C.	125	INGOLD, T.	943
HILL, C.S.H.	1285	INUMARU, K.F.	1376
HILL, D.	1075	INYANG, P.E.B.	435
HILL, D.M.	1150	ION, A.H.	498
HILTON, J.	1076	IQBAL, S.H.	783
HINDBALRAJ, Singh		ISAAC, S.B.	536
See: SINGH HINDBALRAJ		ISHAK, F.M.	348
HISCOCK, P.R.	109	ISLAM, M.M.	1261
HITCH, P.J.	1035	ISSALYS, P.F.	84
HITCHCOCK, R.	1395		
HJEJLE, B.	730	JABBI, B.B.	294
HOBBS, M.E.J.	596	JABIRI, K.F.F. al-	
HOBBS, P.	126	See: AL-JABIRI, K.F.F.	
HOGAN, E.M.	433	JACKSON, J.A.	1200
HOGG, E.J.L.	254	JACKSON, P.A.	1632
HOGGARTH, P.F.	1454	JACKSON, R.	1118
HOLES, C.D.	1077,1462	JACOB, J.G.	1396
HOLM, J.A.	1451	JACOBS, L.	199
HOLMAN, N.M.S.	623A	JACOBS, S.	17
HOLT, A.E.	535	JACOMBS, M.E.	200
HOMANS, H.Y.	1248	JAFAREY, S.	1250
HOPA, N.K.	872A,B	JAKOBOVITS, I.	201
HOSKIN, A.J.	16	JAMES, L.	521
HOSSAIN, A.S.M.T.	1262	JAMIL, K. al-	
HOUGHTON, V.P.	94,1151	See: AL-JAMIL, K.	
HOWELL, R.C.	161	JARRETT, M.E.	231
HOY, C.H.	95	JASSAT, E.M.	522
HUANG, S.K.S.	843	JAVADI-TABRIZI, H.	349
HUANG, T.	721	JAWAD, S.N.	1469
HUGHES, A.G.	1138	JAYASURIYA, T.D.	853
HUGHES, C.A.A.	881	JAYAWARDENA, C.	1439
HUGHES, J.E.	1334	JEFFCOATE, R.L.	96
HUGHES, W.J.	387	JEFFERY, P.M.	1265
HUMM, P.	162	JENKINS, J.R.G.	1404
HUMPHREY, J.C.	529	JENKINS, M.E.	256
HUMPHREYS, V.E.	926	JENNINGS, P.M.	223
HUMPHRIES, M.O.W.	255	JENSEN-BUTLER, B.B.	966
HUNT, E.M.	163	JERROME, D.M.	1286
HUNT, G.P.	552	JEYARATNAM, K.	821
HUNT, S.P.	1249	JIMINEZ DE SLIBE, M.A.	1424
HUNTER, M.M.	656	JOHANPUR, F.	350
HUNTER, P.A.	722	JOHNSON, A.W.	1036
HURLEY, J.	1354	JOHNSON, S.C.	1536
HURT, N.K.	434	JOHNSTON, H.J.M.	987
HUSAIN, S.S.	345	JOHNSTONE, F.A.	658
HUSAIN, S.S.A.	346	JONES, A.M.	947
HUSSAIN, A.B.Md.A.	1263	JONES, B. Pierce	
HUSSAIN, I.	347	See: PIERCE JONES, B.	

Author Index

JONES, C.J.	1287	KIERAN, J.A.P.	436
JONES, D.L.	1635	KILLAM, G.D.	258
JONES, E.D.	257	KILLEEN, J.E.M.	296
JONES, E.M. Glyn-		KILPATRICK, J.W.	908
See: GLYN-JONES, E.M.		KIM, O.P.M.	810
JONES, G.J.	18	KIMBLE, D.B.	559
JONES, G.L.	1488	KINDER, C.R.	1288
JONES, H.K.	1079	KING, A.G.	601
JONES, H.S.	1455	KING, C.E.	967
JONES, I.M.	746	KING, J.R.	1037
JONES, M.A.	988	KING, L.V.	1450
JONES, M.D.	1489	KIRK-DUNCAN, B.A.C.	909
JONES, M.K.	127	KITROEFF, A.	537
JONES, P.C.	947A	KITZINGER, S.E.H.	1153
JONES, P.J.T.	1152	KLEIN, L.C.	297-98
JONES, S.	702	KLINE, C.G.	436A
JOSEPH, B., Ph.D., London, 1928	55	KLUG, A.L.	1492
Ph.D., London, 1942	202	KNIGHT, M.J.	999
JOSHI, M.	1251	KNOWLES, S.E.	927
		KOHNSTAMM, J.	948
KALLARACKAL, A.M.	1119	KORNFIELD-GILMAN, R.	612
KALOTA, R.S.	803	KOUTAISSOFF, E.	299
KAMHAWI, L.W.	1490	KRAUSZ, E.	1225-26
KANDELA, R.E.	1080	KRAWCHENKO, B.A.	1412
KANGA, A.S.	1120	KRECH, S.	523
KANGWANA, J.B.B.	85	KRIKORIAN, M.K.	1530
KANITKAR, H.A.	1121	KRISHNA, G.	748
KANJAMALA, A.	764A	KRISHNAMURTHY, B.S.	610
KANNANGARA, A.P.	747	KU, D.Y.	812
KAPLAN, D.E.	659	KUPER, J.S.	602
KAPLANOFF, M.D.	1581	KUPPERMAN, K.O.	1613
KAPUR, R.A.	802	KUWINPANT, P.	858B
KARADAWI, A.A.	547	KWAPONG, A.O.A.	528
KARIDIS, B.	1411	KWIDINI, D.J.	624
KARIM, A.K.N.	784		
KATZ, D.S.	1224	LA FONTAINE, D. Deshais-	
KATZNELSON, I.	86	See: DESHAIES-LA FONTAINE, D.	
KAUFMAN, S.D.	72	LADBURY, S.A.	1174
KAUFMANN, S.B.	765	LAISHLEY, J.	45
KAYYALI, A.W.S.	1491	LAMB, D.P.	128
KEEP, G.R.C.	1537	LAMBERT, R.V.	660
KEITH, R.C.	713	LANE, C.O.	1413
KEMPER, K.D.	87	LANGE, N.R.M. de	
KENNEDY, P.D.	1574	See: DE LANGE, N.R.M.	
KENNETT, W.A.	56	LANGTON, P.J.	854
KENNY, M.	1425	LASS, R.H.	284
KENRICK, D.S.	295	LAU WAI, H.	97
KERR, B.M.	1201	LAURENCE, K.M.	917
KERSHAW, R.G.	839	LAURENCE, K.O.	918
KESBY, J.D.	883	LAW, D.T.S.	1356
KESSLER, C.S.	822	LAWLESS, D.J.	1550
KHAN, A.R.	704-5	LAWRENCE, D.	1038
KHAN, I.M.	351	LAWRENCE, E.M.	34
KHAN, M.A.	1266	LE GASSICK, T.J.	352
KHAN, R.A.	731	LEBZELTER, G.C. Volz-	
KHAN, V.J.M. Saifullah-		See: VOLZ-LEBZELTER, G.C.	
See: SAIFULLAH-KHAN, V.J.M.		LEDERMAN, S.	1081
KHATOON, L.	785	LEE, M.E.	625
KHEDERI, H.	1629	LEE, P.	661
KHESHAK, S.H.	1470	LEE, T.R.	1054

LEE W.S.	549A	MACDONALD, B.F.	260
LEE SOW LING	823	MACDONALD, M.I.	1083
LEIFER, M.	1493	McDOWALL, D.B.	1523
LENNON, J.F.	1582	McEWEN, P.J.M.	626
LEVENE, M.	203	McGHIE, D.	1423
LEVY, A.	1397	McGOVERN, P.G.	34A
LEVY, N.	662	McGREGOR, R.	607
LEW, M.S.	1387	MACHINGAIDZE, V.E.M.	628
LEWIS, A.D.	353	McINTOSH, W.L.	1601
LEWIS, G.E.D.	833	McINTYRE, S.S.	21
LINCOLN, I.S.	73	McKAY, D.H.	1602
LINDAU, B.	569	McKAY, M.J.	499
LINDEN, I.	436B	MACKELVIE, M.J.	1026
LINDORES, E.A.	354	MACKENZIE, A.J.	22
LINDSTROM, V.R.	1289	MACKENZIE, J.A.	1551
LING, Lee Sow		MACKENZIE, K.	164
See: LEE SOW LING		MACKINTOSH, J.D.	1539
LINGARD, A.W.	110	McLANE, J.R.	749
LINTHWAITE, J.M.	1494	McLAREN, R.M.	261
LITTLE, K.L.	1012	McLEAN, A.C.	1084
LLOYD, D.C.	285	MacLEAN, J.R.	165
LOBEL, R.F.	259	McLEAN, M.	524
LOCKHART, A.	1538	McLEAN, M.L.	1575
LOIELLO, J.P.	437	McLELLAN, J.M.	510
LONG, A.V.	910	MacLENNAN, B.W.	1290
LONG, V.	1437	MacLEOD, D.J.	1583
LOOMIE, A.J.	1398	MACMILLAN, M.O.	766
LORD, A.H.	1055	MADDEN, A.F.	873
LORD, M.B.	1428	MADGWICK, R.B.	865
LOUDEN, D.M.	1082	MAGÓ, M.S.	58
LOUIS, A.S.	1627	MAHER, J.	129
LOURIE, E.R.	1399	MAHER, J.E.	1413A
LOURIE, J.I.	1495	MAHJUBI, G. al-	
LOVECY, J.	949	See: AL-MAHJUBI, G.	
LOWE, W.J.	1202	MAHMOUD, A. el H. Hamdy	
LOWENKOPF, M.	565A	See: HAMDY MAHMOUD, A. el H.	
LUCAS, F.E.	1082A	MAHMOUD, F.M.	356
LUCE, H.F.	1377	MAHMOUD, Z.N.	59
LUGET, P.J.F.	1178	MAHMUD, S.	1252
LUIS, G.T.	732	MA'IAI, F.	885
LUNN, K.J.	1227	MAINI, P.L.	587
LYNCH, H.R.	115	MAINWARING, D.J.	60
LYON, M.H.	19	MAKAMBE, E.P.	629
LYONS, A.P.	20	MALIK, M.A.	1267
		MALIK, Y.K.	919
MA'AT, Y.S.	355	MANDAZA, I.M.D.J.	607
McALLISTER, I.	1357	MANDEL, N.J.	1496
McANALLEN, M.C.	1358	MANGAT, J.S.	578
MACARTNEY, W.J.A.	57	MANGRU, B.	1440
McCALLUM, D.P.F.	1600	MANLEY, D.R.	1291
McCARTHY, M.	498A	MANNERS, J.	1497
McCARTHY, P.J.	1359	MANNING, M.A.	1361
McCEARNEY, J.	949A	MANYONI, J.R.	1039
MacCLANCY, J.V.	884	MANZALOUI, M.A.	357
McCRACKEN, E.M.	663	MARA, P.	968
McCRACKEN, K.J.	438	MARETT, V.P.	1085
MACDERMID, G.E.	1317	MARGOT, A.G.	807
McDERMOTT, M.	1203	MARGRAVE, R.D.	1619
McDONAGH, A.M.	1204	MARKS, S.E.	664
McDONAGH, O.O.G.M.	1360	MARSDEN, R.M.	1341

MARSH, Q.R.H.	1018	MOHAN, M.	887
MARSH, T.N.	23	MOHAN, P.R.L.	1253
MARSHMENT, M.A.	217	MOLLOY, S.D.	262
MARSTERS, T.L.	1086	MONAGHAN, D.M.	263
MARTELL, B.	1123	MONTGOMERY, D.P.	1191
MARTIN, D.	1362	MOORE, R.J.	1442
MARTIN, S.J.R.	665	MOORES, K.	1089
MARTIN, T.J.	358	MOREHOUSE, F.M.I.	1540
MARTINEZ, P.K.	1179	MORGAN, P.D.	132
MARTINEZ-ALIER, V.	900	MORGAN, P.J.	1378
MARVELL, J.	1087	MORRELL, J.E.	1019
MASANI, Z.M.	750	MORRIS, H.S.	603
MASHASHA, F.J.	666	MOSELEY, G.V.H.	714
MASHINGAIDZE, E.K.	439,630	MOSLEY, P.	525
MASON, D.J.	667	MOSS, B.G.	1636
MASON, M.	1434	MOSSEK, M.	1500
MASON, T.W.	969	MOWAFY, M.I. el-	
MASSOUD-MOGHADDAM, F.	46	See: EL-MOWAFY, M.I.	
MATHER, B.H.	501	MSGENA, B.V.	1049
MATTAR, O.M.S.	359	MTUBANI, V.C.D.	464
MAUND, J.C.	232	MUBITANA, K.	441,617
MAWI, N.El-H.,H.M.A.,El-A.	1533	MÜHLBERGER, D.W.	970
MAY, J.	1170	MUKHERJEE, S.	363
MAYALL, D.	1190	MUKHERJI, B.	1124
MAYER, A.C.	886	MULLARD, C.P.	1023
MAZRUI, A.A.'A.	524A	MULLEN, J.	442
MEEBELO, H.S.	615	MUNN, G.H.	24
MEGAHEY, A.J.	1363	MUNSLOW, A.	1584
MELOT, S.M.	950	MURDOCH, T.V.	1180
MENEZES, M.N.	1441	MURPHY, M.J.	1585
MERRITT, J.E.	130	MURPHY, T.	265
METCALFE, R.D.	1567	MURPHY, T.D.	1364
METGE, A.J.	873A	MURRAY, D.R.	133
METLITZKY, D.	360	MURRELL, P.S.J.	232A
MEYERS, S.R.	204	MUTIBWA, P.M.	699
MICHAEL, J.H.	301	MYKULA, W.	1414
MIERS, S.	166		
MIKRE-SELLASSIE, G.A.	440	NAHAR, S.	787
MILDON, I.W.	1292	NAISH, J.M.	901
MILES, G.J.	723	NAJENSON, J.L.	68
MILES, M.G.	1603	NAMBI, Aroonan K.	
MILIMO, M.C.	616	See: AROONAN K. NAMBI	
MILLER, D.	1498	NASSIBIAN, A.	1531
MILLER, H.J.	1088	NASSON, W.R.	668
MILLER, M.J.	302	NATH, J.	1254
MILLER, P.D.	116	NAYLER, H.	1125
MILLOY, J.S.	1560	NAZ, S.	788
MILNE, A.T.	131	NDEM, E.B.	1293
MILNER, D.L.	47	NDYABAHIKA, J.	393
MINKOVITZ, M.	1499	NEARCHOU, V.	1175
MIRZA, N.A.	1576	NELSON, S.	1365
MISRA, B.	88	NEMENZO, F.	824
MITCHELL, M.J.	1568	NESBITT, E.J.	1276
MITRA, M.	786	NEWELL, W.H.	833A
MITTER, P.	361	NEWMAN, D.	1501
MOGG, B.D. Tempest-		NEWMAN, J.A.	303
See: TEMPEST-MOGG, B.D.		NEWSON, L.A.	921
MOGHADDAM, F. Massoud-		NG, K.C.	1171
See: MASSOUD-MOGHADDAM, F.		NGAVIRUE, Z.	669
MOHAMMED, N.	920	NICHOLLS, A.W.	1181

NICHOLLS, D.J.	951	OWUSU, M.O.	271
NICHOLSON, J.R.	1027	OZIGBOH, R.A.	452
NICHOLSON, M.R.	1614		
NICOL, A.R.	1154	PACKER, E.B.	1620
NIEUWENHUYSEN, J.P.	670	PAGDEN, A.R.D.	1615
NIEW SHENG TENG	724	PAGE, C.A.	453
NIVEN, A.N.R.	266	PAGE, D.J.H.	790
NJOROGE, S.N.	267	PAGE, N.M.G.	989
NKALA, J.C.	631	PAHAD, E.	672
NKETSIA, K.	443	PAIGE, J.P.	1126
NOAKES, J.D.	971	PAPWORTH, J.D.	1206
NOLAN, F.B.	444	PARASHER, A.	804
NOLAN, N.G.	1366	PARFITT, T.V.	1503
NOORUZZAMAN, A.H.M.	789	PARKES, J.W.	205
NORRIS, J.A.	394	PARNABY, O.W.	888
NORRIS, R.A.	1155	PAROLIN, G.	1209A
NORTHCOTT, W.C.	445	PARRY, B.	364
NOTTINGHAM, J.M.	1502	PATTERSON, D.	305
NWOGA, D.I.	268	PATTERSON, H.O.L.	135
NWORAH, K.K.D.	553	PATTERSON, S.	1050
		PATTISON, S.D.	233
OAKLEY, R.E.	1176	PAYNE, A.J.	895
O'BRIEN, M.C.	1366A	PAYNE, J.F.	1157
O'BRIEN, R.	1228	PEACH, G.C.K.	1295
O'BRIEN, R.R.C.	570	PEADEN, W.R.	454
O'CONNELL, B.	1204A	PEARSON, D.G.	1296
O'CONNELL, V.E.	1443	PEARSON, R.	767
ODAMTTEN, S.K.	446	PEETZ, E.A.	455
ODDIE, G.A.	502	PENNY, H.H.	35
O'DONOGHUE, R.	446A	PERLMAN, M.	206
OGDEN, D.G.	1415	PERRINGS, C.A.	608
OGODE, E.S.	269	PETERSEN, O. Bay-	
OKADA, K.	971A	See: BAY-PETERSEN, O.	
O'KEEFE, B.M.	1256	PETRYSHYN, W.R.	1280
OKEKE, D.C.	447	PETTERSON, D.R.	579
OKELY, J.M.	1192	PHILIP, A.A.S. Butt	
OKEY, R.F.C.	929	See: BUTT PHILIP, A.A.S.	
OKLADEK, F.	930	PHILLIPS, E.R.	1090
OKO, A.	270	PHILO, N.J.	48
OKPARA, E.	1294	PHIZACKLEA, A-M.	1158
OLIVER, R.A.	448	PICKARD, O.G.	1040
OLOMOLATYE, F.'O.O.	1156	PIERCE JONES, B.	388
O'MEARA, D.	671	PIGGIN, F.S.	504
OMULOKOLI, W.A.O.	449	PIGGOTT, C.A.	1312
O'NEILL, J.A.	1172	PILGRIM, E.I.	168
O'NEILL, S.G.	1367	PILLAY, P.D.	673
ONSELOW, C. van		PINTER, F.M.	1368
See: VAN ONSELOW, C.		PINTO, R.T.	1257
ONYEIDU, S.O.	450	PITMAN, R.	365
OPPENHEIMER, A.	304	PITT-RIVERS, G.L.F.	25
O'REILLY, G.W.	1205	PITTINS, F.E.W. Gey van	
OROGE, E.A.	134	See: GEY VAN PITTINS, F.E.W.	
ORR, J.M.	503	PLASCOV, A.O.	1519
OSHUN, C.O.	450A	PLENDER, R.O.	102
OSMAN, S.	825	PLOWRIGHT, P.S.	366
O'TOOLE, J.J.	117	POCOCK, D.F.	580
OTT, S.J.	952	POLLARD, P.H.	1297
OWEN, G.E.	167	POOL, O.	1091
OWEN, M.H.	1335	PORTER, A.N.	674
OWOH, A.C.	451	PORTER, R.S.	505

PORTUGALI, J.	1504	REID, J.M.	170
POTTER, S.C.	395	REIS, J.B.G.	171
POTTS, E.D.	506	RENEHAM, M.A.	560
POULTER, C.E.	26	RENFORD, R.K.	768
PRATT, J.H.	507	REYNOLDS, K.M.	457
PRATT, M.J.	1041	RIACH, D.C.	172
PREMPEH, S.	455A	RICE, C.D.	173
PRESEDO, V. Vázquez–		RICH, P.	677
See: VÁZQUEZ-PRESEDO, V.		RICHARDS, A.M.	137
PRICE, C.A.	1382	RICHARDS, D.	218A
PRIDHAM, G.F.M.	972	RICHARDS, W.A.	138
PRINGLE, A.D.	675	RICHARDSON, A.	866
PRYCE, K.N.	1298	RICHARDSON, P.D.	139
PSARIAS, V.	1177	RICHARDSON, P.G.L.	678
PULZER, P.G.J.	973	RICHES, D.J.	1561
PURDIE, E.	306	RICHMOND, A.H.	1299, 1552
PURKIS, A.J.	676	RIDLEY, H.M.	975
PYLE, H.A.	286	RIEMER, S.	1505
		RIFF, M.A.	936
QUINN, P.L.S.	1139, 1229	RINN, J.	1318
		RITTER, S.A.H.	275
RABINOWITZ, L.I.	953	RIVERS, G.L.F. Pitt–	
RABKIN, D.	272	See: PITT-RIVERS, G.L.F.	
RABY, AL.	1092	RIVIERE, P.G.	1445
RAHEB, H. al–		RIVIERE, W.E.	896
See: AL-RAHEB, L.		RIZVI, J.M.	792
RAHMAN, A.W.A. Abdel		RIZVI, S.A.G.	751
See: ABDEL RAHMAN, A.W.A.		ROBB, J.H.	1230
RAHMAN, K.	218	ROBERTS, D.A.	1369
RAHMAN, M., Ph.D., London, 1976	706	ROBERTS, E.K.R.R.	1637
Ph.D., London, 1968	791	ROBERTS, H.W.	1586
RAJAK, T.	207	ROBERTS, J.K.	389
RAMACHARAN-HENRIQUES, I.	273	ROBERTS, M.J.	276
RAMNARINE, T.	1444	ROBINSON, F.C.R.	793
RAMSARAN, J.A.	274	ROBSON, P.C.	208
RAMSELL, P.J.	911	RODGERS, R.J.	1370
RANGACHAR, C.	1093	ROGERS, B.	1094
RAPAPORT, I.	111	ROGERS, P.H.	588A
RASHEED, M.H. ar–		ROKER, L.F.	1000
See: AR-RASHEED, M.H.		ROLLO, D.A.T.	1628
RASHEED, N.S.	1461	ROMAIN, R.I.	897
RASHID, A.K.M.H.	1127	ROMAIN SRZEDNICKI, M.J.I.	1388
RASHID, S.	1268	ROMAN ESPINOSA, M.T. San	
RASKI, J.S.	234	See: SAN ROMAN ESPINOSA, M.T.	
RAVINDRANATHAN, T.R.	1379	ROONEY, J.	508
RAWNSLEY, S.J.	1020	ROSAK, E.	937
RAY, S.	367	ROSBERG, C.G.	74
RAYNER, W.R.	736	ROSE, N.A.	1506
RAZAK, A. Abdual		ROSEL, A.	307
See: ABDUAL RAZAK, A.		ROSEN, K.	1416
REA, W.F.	456	ROSENTHAL, P.S.	368
RECKORD, M.	912	ROSS, A.C.	458
REDLEY, M.G.	588	ROSS, G.F.	49
REED, P.A.	1128	ROSS, P.	308
REES, A.M.	169	ROSTOWSKI, R.	103
REES, D.G.	136	ROTBERG, R.I.	459
REEVES, F.W.	27	ROUMANI, M.M.	1507
REHFISCH, F.	1193	RUA, T. Altamirano	
REICHMANN, E.G.	974	See: ALTAMIRANO RUA, T.	
REID, H.A.	1434A	RUBENS, M.L.	540

RUBESS, B.N.	1417	SCOTT, M.J.	386
RUDD, E.M.	1095	SCOULOUDI, I.	1002
RUMYANECK, J.	1231	SCRATON, P.	1371A
RUSSELL, E.	1001	SCRUTON, A.M.	1562
RUSSELL, H.O.	460	SEAL, A.	753
RUSSELL, J. de B.	1587	SEIKALY, S.M.	537A
RUSSELL, M.	679	SELLASSIE, G.A. Mikre-	
RWEGELERA, G.G.C.	1300	See: MIKRE-SELLASSIEK, G.A.	
RYALL, D.A.	396	SELVARATNAM, V.	838
RYAN, S.	1301	SEN-GUPTA, L.	805
		SENGUPTA, K.	509
SACHS, A.	680	SEYMOUR, O.C.	1616
SACKEY, J.A.	561	SHABOUL, A.M.H.	372
SADATY, F. Zahir Al		SHACHAR, I.	209
See: ZAHIR AL SADATY, F.		SHAH, S.	1258
SAFI, M.A.G.H. el-		SHAH, S.A.	236
See: EL-SAFI, M.A.G.H.		SHAH, S.Z. Ahmed	
SAHAJPAL, T.R.	369	See: AHMED SHAH, S.Z.	
SAID, A.R.	826	SHALLCROSS, H.M.	1510
SAIFULLAH-KHAN, V.J.M.	1269	SHANG, A.E.L.	828
SAIGH, J.S.	370	SHAPIRA, J.	1233
SAIHOO, P.	708,859	SHARMA, R.	1130
SAINT, C.K.	1129	SHARMA, R.S.	806
ST RIMAIN, C.	1100	SHAROT, S.A.	1234
SALBSTEIN, M.C.N.	1232	SHARP, J.S.	682
SALEH, T.A.	571	SHAW, G.	510
SALIM, A.I.	589	SHEARD, E.R.	1098
SALOLE, G.M.	526	SHEFFER, G.	1511
SAN ROMAN ESPINOSA, M.T.	1400	SHEIKH, M.A.R. el-	
SANCHEZ, R.	1456	See: EL-SHEIKH, M.A.R.	
SANCTON, A.B.	1569	SHENG TENG, Niew	
SANDERS, I.L.	752	See: NIEW SHENG TENG	
SANDERSON, F.E.	601	SHEPPARD, C.A.	889
SANDHU, K.S.	837	SHERMAN, A.J.	1184
SANDISON, A.G.	235	SHIELS, R.	922
SANSOM, C.J.	681	SHILLINGTON, K.T.J.	683
SANT CASSIA, P.	933	SHORT, A.W.	564
SARAY, M.	1418	SHORT, K.R.M.	174
SARDAR, Z.M.	1096	SHOULDICE, F.J.	1372
SARFO, K.	562	SHROPSHIRE, D.W.T.	461
SARGENT, A.J.	1508	SHUKMAN, H.	1420
SARRAFF, R.G.	1042	SHUKRY, M.F.	548
SARVAN, C.P.	277	SIBANDA, C.J.	632
SAUNDERS, A.C. de C.M.	1389	SIEBERT, W.S.	684
SAUNDERS, D.	61	SILVA, I.W. De	
SAUNDERS, D.B.	1419	See: DE SILVA, I.W.	
SAVERIMUTTU, N.M.	855	SILVA, J.W.	511
SAW, S.H.	827	SILVA, K.M. De	
SAWYER, R.M.	1371	See: DE SILVA, K.M.	
SCAZZOCCHIO, F.	1457	SILVA, P.W. De	
SCHILDKROUT, E.	563	See: DE SILVA, P.W.	
SCHLOSSER, L. Arizpe-		SILVERSTEEN, R.A.	1012A
See: ARIZPE-SCHLOSSER, L.		SIMANJUNTAK, B.	829
SCHNEIDER, J.E.	1390	SINGER, A.F.V.	1464
SCHOEN, D.E.	1021	SINGH, A.I.	794
SCHOENBERGER, M.A.	541	SINGH, A.K.	1131
SCHOLES, A.G.	990	SINGH, K.K.	373
SCHONTHAL, D.J.J.	1509	SINGH, N.N.P.	374
SCOTT, B.	1097	SINGH, R.N.	685
SCOTT, D.W.	62	SINGH, T.	1446

Author Index 151

SINGH HINDBALRAJ	1277	STONE, I.R.	511A
SIRCAR, K.	737	STONE, J.	688
SKELTON-SMITH, I.	528A	STONE, M.A.	98
SKILLING, H.G.	938	STOTT, G. St J.	310
SKINNER, K.E.M.	1429	STRIZOWER, S.	212
SKINNER, M.R.	50	STROTHARD, J.A.	1553
SLADE, R.M.	462	STUART, F.C.	177
SLATTERY, B.	1563	STUART, R.G.	464
SLIBE, M.A. Jiminez de		STUBBS, G.M.	1554
See: JIMINEZ DE SLIBE, M.A.		SUKDEO, I.D.	1448
SLOAN, K.	976	SULLY, G.H.	1182
SMALLPAGE, E.	175	SUNTHARALINGAM, R.	754
SMALLWOOD, E.M.	210	SURATGAR, K.	375
SMART, D.J. Treais-		SUSSER, B.	1235
See: TREAIS-SMART, D.J.		SWAI, B.	770
SMITH, A.D.S.	63	SWAISLAND, H.C.	527
SMITH, B.J.	1512	SWANSON, K.B.	376
SMITH, C.A.	140	SWITZER, K.B.	1572
SMITH, F.	309	SYDER, S.N.	178
SMITH, G.A.	1604	SYKES, M. St C.D.	51
SMITH, I. Skelton-		SYNOTT, A.J.	186
See: SKELTON-SMITH, I.			
SMITH, J.E.	141	TABRIZI, H. Javadi-	
SMITH, R.T.	1447	See: JAVADI-TABRIZI, H.	
SNOWDON, F.M.	1380	TADMAN, M.	143
SOFER, C.	604,686	TAGGAR, Y.	1513
SORRENSON, M.P.K.	590	TAHA, A.D.	1401
SOUTHWOLD, M.	605	TALA, K.I.	279
SOUZA, F.R.C. de		TALBOT, I.A.	795
See: DE SOUZA, F.R.C.		TALOOKDAR, B.K.	377
SOUZA, G.B.	715	TAMEENI, A.M.K. al-	
SOUZA, M.B. D'		See: AL-TAMEENI, A.M.K.	
See: D'SOUZA, M.B.		TANGRI, R.K.	591,611
SPACKMAN, A.	75	TASEER, M.D.	378
SPEAR, T.G.	769	TASIE, G.O.	465
SPIEGLER, J.S.	554	TAYAL, M.K.	689
SPIER, A.B.	1132	TAYLOR, D.D.	755
SPOONER, B.J.	1465	TAYLOR, G.C.	179
SPRINGHALL, J.O.	1099	TAYLOR, G.P.	866A
SPURLING, D.J.	278	TAYLOR, J.A.	977
SRIVASTAVA, S.R.	1324	TAYLOR, J.J.	634
SRZEDNICKI, M.J.I. Romain		TAYLOR, P.A.M.	1621
See: ROMAIN SRZEDNICKI, M.J.I.		TAYLOR, S.	978
STAFFORD, F.A.	1056	TEMPEST-MOGG, B.D.	398
STANGE, D.C.	176	TENG, Niew Sheng	
STANIFORD, P.	1435	See: NIEW SHENG TENG	
STANLEY, B.	397	TENKORANG, S.	144
STANLEY, N.S.	28	THAIKOODAN, J.	572
STANWORTH, H.	1101	THEOBALD, J.R.P.	931
STEBBING, J.R.	687	THOMAS, E.M.	112
STEELE, M.C.	633	THOMAS, J.A.	1541
STEGMANN, G.M.	618	THOMAS, J.Y.	466
STEINBERG, M.B.B.	211,1140	THOMPSON, M.A.	1278
STEINER, F.B.	142	THOMPSON, T.J.	466A
STEPHEN, D.A.V.	575	THOMPSON, W.	1314
STEPHENSON, P.E.	1336	THORNBERRY, P.	1373
STEVEN, F.M.I.	462A	THORNTON, M.	467
STEWART, J.A.	1313	TIDRICK, K.	1159
STIBBS, T.P.C.	463	TING, C.P.	834
STIRRAT, R.L.	856	TIWARI, R.	771

Author Index

TOBIAS, A.	213	WALSHE, A.P.	693
TOMLINSON, B.R.	756	WALTER, B.M.	1208
TOMLINSON, S.	1102	WAN, A.H. bin O.	831
TONER, P.M.	1570	WARD, K.	469
TOPLEY, M.D.	844	WARD, R.H.	1057
TOYE, E.C.	180	WARLICK, J.R.	69
TRAPIDO, S.	690	WARWICK, P.	694
TREAIS-SMART, D.J.	890	WASSERSTEIN, B.M.J.	1516
TREBLE, J.H.	1207	WASSERSTEIN, D.J.	1402
TREFFGARNE, C.B.W.	571	WASTELL, R.E.P.	182
TRESCATHERIC, B.	1622	WASTI, S.R.	797
TREVAIL, J.J.	1605	WATSON, E.M.	1135
TRIGG, E.B.	1194	WATSON, G.	1304
TROUST, J.C.	1405	WATTS, R.L.	76
TROYNA, B.	1302	WEAVER, P.R.C.	113
TSIMHONI, D.	1514	WEBB, K.	1315
TURLEY, D.M.	181	WEBSTER, J.B.	470
TURNBULL, M.R.M.	874	WEBSTER, Y.O.	30
TURNER, D.M.	1259	WEEKES, D.J.	471
TURNER, J.C.	52	WEEKS, D.C.	1532
TURNER, W.	36	WEIL, S.	1517
TURRELL, R.V.	691	WEINER, M.A.	811
TYACK, N.C.P.	1623	WEINTRAUB, F.J.	955
		WEIR, K.	1160
ULLAH, F.S.K.	379	WEIS, P.	89
URRY, J.	1421	WEISBROD, L.	214
USSISHKIN, A.N.	1515	WELCH, A.W.	472
		WELLS, A.R.	979
VAIDYA, Y.C.	29	WENKERT, R.	1588
VALIANT, G.L.	1133	WERBNER, P.	1271
VAN DER WERFF, L.L.		WERFF, L.L. van der	513
See: WERFF, L.L. van der		WERTIMER, S.	991
VAN ONSELOW, C.	635	WESUMPERUMA, D.	857
VAN ZWANENBERG, R.M.A.		WETTINGER, G.	1383
See: ZWANENBERG, R.M.A. van		WEYMONT, M.E.	514
VARMA, S.P.	380	WHALLEY, W.	183
VAUGHAN, J.	1303	WHEELER, L.M.	979A
VÁZQUEZ-PRESEDO, V.	1430	WHITE, A.W.J.	954
VGENOPOULOS, C.G.	1339	WHITEHEAD, R.M.	636
VILDOMEC, V.	99	WHITNEY, J.C.	215
VILLIERS, C.S.	830	WHYTE, J.H.	1374
VOLZ-LEBZELTER, G.C.	1236	WICKENDEN, H.J.	1625
VON KRBEK, J.H.P. Evans-		WICKS, M.C.W.	1210
See: EVANS-VON KRBEK, J.H.P.		WILKINSON, E.M.	1183
		WILKINSON, J.F.	891
WADDINGTON, C.S.	219	WILLIAMS, C.	1337
WAGENBERG, R.H.	692	WILLIAMS, C.P.	399
WAHI, T.	796	WILLIAMS, E.E.	184
WAI, H. Lau		WILLIAMS, E.R.	1338
See: LAU WAI, H.		WILLIAMS, G.	1430A
WAINWRIGHT, M.D.	1624	WILLIAMS, L.H.	1003
WAITE, P.	145	WILLIAMS, R.B.	1431
WALDENBURG, L.M.	1237	WILLIAMS, S.	1103
WALIGGO, J.M.	468	WILLIAMS, W.G.	224
WALKER, A.R.	808	WILLIAMSON, H.R.	515
WALKER, I.	1013	WILLIAMSON, R.J.	980
WALKER, S.K.	1134	WILLMINGTON, S.	1024
WALL, T.	287	WILLMOTT, W.E.	709
WALLACE, L.V.	939	WILMER, S.E.	619
WALPOLE, K.A.	1555	WILMOT, L.H.	981

WILSON, A.J.N.	114	WORBOYS, M.	32
WILSON, D.K.	516-17	WORDEN, N.A.	698
WILSON, E.L.	1606	WORRALL, R.V.	1195
WILSON, F.A.H.	695	WRIGHT, P.L.	1051
WILSON, F.L.	1209	WYATT, T.G.	1004
WILSON, J.A., M.Ed., Leeds, 1923	37	WYLIE, D.S.	593
Ph.D., Queen's Univ.		WYNN, D.R.	1589
Belfast, 1965	1542	WYNN, N.A.	1607
WILSON, J.C.	756A		
WILSON, J.P.	1166	YAGHMOOR, F.H.	381
WILSON, P.	473	YAMASEE, A.K.	1403
WILSON, S.J.	858	YATES, J.S.	90
WINAWER, H.M.	1422	YOUNG, L.Y.	100
WINEHOUSE, B.I.	311	YOUNG, W.L.	64
WINFORD, D.	923	YU, S-P.	382
WINIATA, W.	875	YUVAL-DAVIS, N.	1630
WISELEY, W.C.	982		
WISTRICH, R.S.	983	ZAHIR AL SADATY, F.	549
WITCOMB, J.D.	696	ZAIDI, S.Z.H.	798
WITHERS, C.W.J.	1316	ZAKARIA, R.A.	799
WITHRINGTON, M.P.	1104	ZAMICK, M.	383
WITTERMANS, T.	1384	ZAMIR, M.	1524
WOLF, T.W.	757	ZAMMIT, E.L.	1239
WOLFSON, J.E.E.	697	ZAROD, H.	1608
WONG, S-L.	725-26	ZEMAN, Z.A.B.	940
WOOD, G.A.	31	ZUBRZYCKI, J.	1240
WOOD, G.J.	1043	ZUCKER, D.J.	313
WOODCOCK, A.C.	592	ZVOGBO, C.J.E.	474
WOODS, C.J.	1374A	ZWANENBERG, R.M.A. Van	594
WOOLF, M.P.	312	ZWEIG, R.W.	1518